MISSY'S TWITCH

Jon Pepper

NORTH COVE PRESS
New York

Missy's Twitch

Cover design by Diane Pepper

More information is available at www.jonpepperbooks.com.

Printed in United States of America

ISBN: 979-8-9862629-4-9

Published by North Cove Press
New York, NY
www.northcovepress.com

"The flapping wings of a butterfly can be felt on the other side of the world."

—Chinese proverb

PART ONE

Twitchy Woman

1. PATIENTS ARE A VIRTUE

It took only a moment for the psychologist known as Dr. Iz to diagnose the patient entering her office on New York City's Upper West Side on a hot summer morning: Missy Mayburn Crowe had "opportunity" written all over her.

With a mess of brown tresses and a multitude of body piercings, the wealthy heiress to an oil and gas fortune wore her emotional distress on her sleeveless arms, one of which was covered with dull blots of incomprehensible ink. Were they statements of rebellion? Expressions of alienation? Cat pictures? Soon enough, Dr. Iz would find out all that had gotten under, into, and on top of Missy's skin.

"Apologies for the heat in here," Dr. Iz said, fanning herself with a spiral notebook. "The rolling brownout hit our neighborhood this morning, making our air conditioning useless. Best I could do was open the windows."

"I'm totally cool with that," Missy said, before checking herself. "Well, actually not *cool*, cool. I mean, I'm kinda sweaty, to tell the truth."

Dr. Iz offered a bemused smile and directed Missy to an oversized easy chair covered in worn blue-and-white linen. "Please, Missy. Make yourself comfortable. Would you like some water? Organic coffee or tea?"

"Tea sounds good," said Missy, flopping heavily into the chair, as if felled by the enormous emotional burdens she carried. "What do you have?"

"Well, let's see," Dr. Iz said, moving to a small pantry and scanning the shelves. "I have everything from Earl Grey to green tea to Poo Poo Pu-Erh."

The exotic sound of that last offering caught Missy's ear. As an enlightened graduate fresh from an ivy-covered American citadel of higher education, Missy didn't go for just any old colonialist brew. "Poo Poo... what?" she called.

"Pu-Erh," Dr. Iz replied. "Would you like to try it?"

Missy scrunched her nose. "What is it?"

"It's made from the droppings of insects that feed on tea leaves," Dr. Iz explained. "I understand farmers in Taiwan use magnifying glasses and tweezers to harvest the teeny-tiny doo-doos. The tea is quite rare and very expensive. But it was a gift from a longtime patient, and I'm happy to share it with you."

"Are you having some?"

"I just might," Dr. Iz replied.

Missy gulped. Pot, peyote, and psilocybin mushrooms hadn't helped Missy's gnawing anxiety, nor had they relieved the odd twitch in her arms that caused them to suddenly fly away from her body. To decline this poop juice would clearly make her sound like some dopey philistine from… wherever philistines come from. "Okay. I'll give it a try," Missy said.

The door to the microwave banged shut as Dr. Iz prepared the tea. Missy looked around the office, with its open casement windows overlooking the park, a large vase of sagging blue hydrangeas and white lilies, a few gnats swirling around a bowl of sweet cherries on the coffee table, and bookcases lined with dusty volumes on psychology, which prominently featured Dr. Iz's best-sellers from her heyday. There was *Get a Grip, Honey,* her number one *New York Times* bestseller from twenty years earlier, offering blunt, common-sense advice to distressed women. That was followed by *Got a Grip*, then *Lost the Grip*, and, finally, *Get Another Grip* before she ran dry of gripping titles, fresh advice, and readers. The office had the feel of faded elegance, which made sense since it had been many years since Dr. Iz had been a boldface media star, ubiquitous with her books and her looks: oversized black horn-rimmed glasses and blunt-cut platinum gray hair. Once a fixture on bus placards, billboards, and taxi signs, Dr. Iz had largely disappeared from public view, but Missy remembered her seminal exhortation. *Get a grip, honey.* That's exactly what Missy wanted to do.

Missy called out. "This is not a cultural appropriation, is it?"

Dr. Iz responded without looking back. "What isn't, dear?"

"Me having this tea? It's, like, Chinese, right?"

"From that neighborhood, yes."

"I'm not Chinese."

"You may have noticed," Dr. Iz replied. "Neither am I." She turned away from the pantry carrying a tray with two teacups and approached Missy. "What if we just keep this our little secret?"

Missy lifted the delicate porcelain cup and inhaled deeply, then recoiled with a shudder. She held the cup and cocked her head, studying the tea. She couldn't *see* any insect droppings, but then again, if they were in there… so what? Wasn't that, like, totally natural? Everything in nature was good and benevolent, except for volcanic eruptions, earthquakes, category five hurricanes, arsenic, sharknados, and stuff like that. She held her breath and sipped carefully, then pulled back in dismay. *Eww…*

"Too hot?" Dr. Iz asked.

Hot? Too hot? Oh no! Suddenly, triggered by the strange gremlin that had recently taken hold of her psyche, Missy's arm twitched involuntarily and swung out swiftly, sending her teacup flying out of her hand, sailing through the air, and out the open window. A clatter could be heard below as the cup smashed on the sidewalk, and a man's voice called up, "*Hey!* Whattaya doin' up there?"

"Oh my God!" Missy exclaimed. She leapt from her chair and ran to the window.

Dr. Iz trailed close behind. "Apparently that was not your cup of tea."

"Sadly, it was," Missy said.

Down below, a uniformed doorman glared up at Missy and Dr. Iz with his hands on hips. "Sorry!" Dr. Iz called. The man waved her off with two hands and a look of disgust, and Missy returned to her seat.

"I am *sooo* sorry," Missy said, putting both hands to her face. "I don't know what to say. It wasn't the tea at all. I mean, that was totally fine. Weird, yeah, but fine. I just never know when this bizarre twitch is going to hit me. It comes out of nowhere."

Dr. Iz nodded, then put a hand gently on Missy's back to guide her to the seating area. "It comes from somewhere, Missy. Let's find out where exactly." Dr. Iz perched herself on a large white leather chair opposite Missy and picked up her notebook and pen. She cocked her head and regarded the most promising paddler to come rolling down her income stream in some time.

Dr. Iz's practice had suffered for decades since she had slapped a whining guest on her TV show and told her to "suck it up, buttercup." Unfortunately, the poor woman did suck it up—hoovering forty sleeping pills, which ended her anxiety once and for all. The public uproar, followed by lawsuits from the dead victim's family, lost media contracts, and a sudden exclusion from polite company, nearly put her out of business, but she hung on to her shingle by softening her tough-love approach and catering to an affluent clientele with garden-variety rich people problems. Feelings of inadequacy. Too much booze. Too little sex. It was as predictable as a movie on the Hallmark Channel, but it paid the ever-increasing rent. Missy, however, presented the possibility of an entirely new line of business: A patient with a famous name and a bizarre affliction. Who knows where this could go? "Why don't we start with what just happened," Dr. Iz said, her voice dropping to a suitably grave octave. "How long have you had this twitch?"

Missy rubbed her forehead. "Oh, God. I don't know. Early June, I guess. It started right after I began my new job and the weather started getting really warm."

"I see," Dr. Iz said. "Did your PCP help?"

Missy dismissed the question with a wave of her hand. "I stopped doing that my junior year. Once I found out it was a horse tranquilizer, I was done-zo."

"I mean your primary care physician," Dr. Iz persisted. "Did you see a medical doctor?"

"Oh, right," Missy said, with a blush. "He sent me to a clinic on the Upper East Side. They hooked me up to all kinds of wires and electrodes. Stuck me with needles. Banged my knees and elbows with this weird little hammer. They said there was, like, nothing physically wrong with me—no epilepsy, or Parkinson's or anything like that—but maybe I should see a shrink." Then, afraid she'd used offensive slang, said, "Sorry."

"It's okay," Dr. Iz assured her. "Why did you select me?"

"My father suggested it. I guess, maybe, he used to see you on TV, or something? Of course, I already knew who you were. Your books were in our home when I was growing up. I remember *Get a Grip, Honey*. That was the big one, right?"

"Indeed. That kicked off the whole *Gripping* series," Dr. Iz said with a sigh. "Those books were quite popular. Glad to know someone in your home found them useful."

Missy sighed. "Well... I don't know if my mother actually *read* them," she said. "I think she used *Get a Grip, Honey* as a coaster."

"That wasn't exactly my intent."

"It was Mother's. She used to throw back a lot of white wine in the morning when she watched TV," Missy said. "I remember sitting with her when you were on *Oprah* and thinking, 'Dang! That Dr. Iz is, like, so freaking smart.' You knew the answer to everything."

Dr. Iz shifted uneasily in her chair. "Let's try to get some answers for you."

Missy took a deep breath and braced herself for uncomfortable questioning.

"Have you been feeling any extra anxiety lately?" Dr. Iz asked.

Missy chuckled mirthlessly. "That's all I feel. Anxiety. It's, like, totally overwhelming." Her right arm twitched again, but less violently, and Missy reflexively reached over with her left hand to hold her right shoulder.

Dr. Iz idly doodled spirals on her pad. "What worries you most?"

"It's everything coming at me all at once," Missy said. "It's kind of this... giant blob."

Dr. Iz nodded. "Let's identify one issue. What comes to mind first?"

"Well," Missy said, glancing at the ceiling, "mostly I'm obsessing over the fact that our planet is dying."

"Is it?"

Missy shrugged. "Well, yeah. Everyone knows that. It's all you hear. We've got, what, five years—maybe seven years, tops—before we hit this point of no return? Then it's—" she made a downward spiral motion with her hand. "I mean, that's terrible for everybody, but it's even worse for me."

"How so?"

Missy paused for effect. "Because it's my fault."

"My goodness," Dr. Iz exclaimed, as she jotted *narcissistic tendencies*. "What exactly did you do?"

"My name is Crowe, right?" Missy said it in a tone that sounded both haughty and apologetic at the same time. "And you may know that my great-great-great grandfather was Homer Crowe, who started my family's energy business, the Crowe Power Company? I'm sure you've heard of it."

"Oh yes," Dr. Iz said. "I write to them once a month."

"Why?"

"I pay my electricity bill."

"Ah, right," Missy said, sounding puzzled. *Why wouldn't she just Venmo it?* "Well, anyway… Homer Crowe was, like, one of the original gangstas on climate change. He built his whole business around energy from fossil fuels. And for the past century, all my family business has done is make the problem worse, spewing out more and more gigatons of carbon dioxide, choking the planet. Look at us now. The planet is gonna die." Her arm twitched. "And I'll be held responsible."

"Not if everyone's dead, dear," Dr. Iz said before taking a dainty sip of her tea.

Missy's brow furrowed.

"Sorry," Dr. Iz said, squelching her impulse to be even more blunt. "Tell me how all this makes you feel. A bit hopeless, perhaps?"

"Yes. Exactly," Missy said. "Hopeless."

Dr. Iz nodded empathetically. "That's understandable. We all feel that way from time to time when events seem beyond our control. But it's important to realize that we're never helpless. You can do something about your situation."

"I do some things," Missy said, defensively. "I mean, I sign petitions to boycott this company or that company." She paused, thinking. "I go to marches to protest what these big corporations are doing to screw our planet. I even picketed outside Crowe Power headquarters last year." She looked at Dr. Iz, waiting for an approving look. Finding no response, Missy searched her memory files for some other noble posture she had taken. *Nah. Nothing…*

"It's good you're taking actions to address your anxiety, Missy," Dr. Iz offered. "Even the smallest steps can help the cause."

Smallest steps? Missy scrunched her face. *She was a freaking climate warrior! A leader of her generation!* Why didn't Dr. Iz recognize that? "I do what I can," Missy said with a sniff.

Dr. Iz considered feel-good measures Missy might take. What had she just read the other day from a magazine in her waiting room? "Climate change isn't my area of expertise; I'm not that kind of scientist," she explained. "But I understand there are steps each of us can take to lessen our impact. For instance, you could use cold water when you wash your clothes."

Missy nodded sullenly. "That's an idea. I could probably have them to do that."

"Who?"

"Whoever does my laundry."

"Who is that?" Dr. Iz asked.

Missy's expression went blank. "I don't know."

"You don't?"

"Well, no," Missy replied, annoyed. "Do you know who does your laundry?"

"Yes. As a matter of fact, I do," Dr. Iz said. "Her name is Dr. Iz."

Missy blinked hard. *Whoa. That's weird.* "Yeah. Okay. I've heard some people do it themselves. All I know is that in my case, it gets done. Haven't given a lot of thought about who or where." She shrugged and cocked her head. *Why was this even important?*

Dr. Iz struggled to maintain a sympathetic posture. "Here's another idea," she said. "You could take public transit. The bus. The subway…"

Missy flashed impatience. "Yeah, yeah, yeah. I did that."

"You mean… once?"

"Believe me. It was enough," Missy said. "It's really sick down there. There are these gross puddles of… whatever on the floor. Crazy people talking gibberish. You wait around forever—like, five, ten minutes—for a train." Sensing Dr. Iz's disapproval, she said, "I mean, I'd love to do it all the time. But I have this driver? Harvey? Last thing I want to do is put him out of work, especially in an economy like this. He might have a family."

"You don't know?"

"I don't know what?"

"Whether he has a family?" Dr. Iz asked.

"Well, no," Missy replied. She squinted. "Is that bizarre?"

"How long has he worked for you?" Dr. Iz pressed.

"Off and on," Missy said, thinking, "I guess about four years. He was my aunt's driver before she died."

"You've shared a car with Harvey for four years, but you don't know if he has a wife, a partner, a kid, a hamster?"

"Dr. Iz, when I'm in the car, I'm on the phone or texting. I don't want to give him the third degree."

Dr. Iz leaned back in her chair and crossed one leg over another. "Missy, asking someone whether they have a family is not generally considered an affront, nor an interrogation. It's just part of normal human intercourse. People do it every day."

Missy shrugged. "I guess for some people, yeah. I could see that." But, Missy thought, I'm not just some people. *I'm a Crowe. We don't get involved in the personal lives of the help.*

Dr. Iz bit lightly on the end of her pen. She could go on with more suggestions, but what was the point? Missy lived in a bubble that floated high above, in the stratosphere accessible only to Chinese spy balloons and Sidewinder missiles. At Missy's altitude, doing something about climate change required no personal sacrifices other than dutifully sending money to support the right causes, attending rallies and conferences, and heckling other people for failing to get with the program. But why did she bother, Dr. Iz wondered. Perhaps it was penance for her vast wealth and her family history. "Tell me about your job," Dr. Iz said. "Your card says you're an executive at Crowe Power."

"I am. But definitely *not* the part that uses fossil fuels. I won't work in that part—ever," Missy declared. "I have certain principles, you know."

"Understood," Dr. Iz sighed.

Missy continued proudly, "I'm at the green subsidiary, CroFusion."

"What a great starting point. Didn't your company do a demonstration of fusion last year at the Statue of Liberty?"

"We did. My mother lit the torch with this little blip of electricity from fusion."

"That's wonderful," Dr. Iz said. "It sounds like you're in a position to make real change."

Missy shrugged. "Maybe."

"What's your job?"

"I'm vice-president of strategy? I'm supposed to help us take fusion to the next step. It's, like, the hottest area in green energy right now. The holy grail, they say."

"Very impressive," Dr. Iz said.

"I guess," Missy said sullenly. "I haven't been going to work. I mean, I went one day, and I got this ID badge to get into the building. And I attended a management meeting and met a bunch of people, which was a very weird experience. As the daughter of the company chairperson, everyone looks at you like you're some kind of freaky totem, or a business genius. Anyway… I haven't been back since that first day."

"You don't go to the office at all?"

"Well, no," Missy said. "Not with this—" she jerked her arm, "twitchy thing. How can I?"

"I see."

"I mean, I could go knocking into people. Send papers flying off the desk. Break lamps. Who knows? It's totally embarrassing. That's why I need your help. I've got to get this fixed so I can go to work."

Dr. Iz tapped her pen against her chin, thinking. "What triggers this twitch, do you think? Are there images you see, or words that are said, that make your arm fly up like that?"

Missy narrowed her eyes. "I think maybe it's words. I mean, a little while ago, you asked if the tea was too hot. It wasn't, as it turned out. It just kinda smelled bad." She paused and squinted at Dr. Iz, who was sipping her tea. "Do you like it?"

"I'm drinking Earl Grey," Dr. Iz said with a shrug.

"Not Poo Poo Pu-Erh?"

Dr. Iz chuckled. *I don't drink that shit.* "My tastes are not as refined as yours."

Missy acknowledged her comment with an affirming nod. *Whose are?*

Dr. Iz gathered herself and said, "Please go on. You were talking about triggers."

Missy continued with a sigh, "Well, yeah. So, even hearing the word 'hot' makes me think of climate change and global warming and melting ice caps and rising seas and dying species and—oh, just the whole terrible thing. It comes at me all at once and I just kinda freak the fuck out."

Dr. Iz nodded in understanding. *There must be lots of nuts like her out there.* "Do you know other people who feel the way you do?"

Missy nodded vigorously. "Oh yeah. Tons of them."

Cha-ching! Had Dr. Iz tapped into the mother lode of climate anxiety patients in New York City? Her heart beat faster as she considered the possibilities. "What about the people closest to you? Do any of your friends have the twitch?"

Missy nodded again. "I know three other people who got it not long after me. We're all in this state of, like, suspended animation, waiting for the world to end. It's hard to focus on anything other than our certain doom. We can't go to work. It seems so pointless."

Dr. Iz's wanted to reach for her calculator. *This was too good to be true!* She could get back in the game with this gambit. And this time: no tough love. That was out the window along with Missy's teacup. Missy and her pampered ilk should all be listened to, and coddled, and encouraged to speak their truth. With proper care and stroking, this could go on for months, maybe even years. Certainly, climate change would not be resolved any time soon. There would be plenty of room for worry. "This may call for group therapy," Dr. Iz said. "Do you think your friends would be interested in seeing me? I could offer them a group discount."

"Money isn't an issue," Missy said, dismissively. "They just want to get cured."

Dr. Iz said, "That's exactly what I want, too. Heal people, heal the planet. That's practically my motto."

Missy looked at her psychologist uncertainly. "Do you know what I have?"

Dr. Iz said, "I need to do some research, but my sense is that your twitch is a manifestation of fears you have about climate change. What the exact condition is, I can't yet say."

Missy fell back in her chair. "But… you said, 'fears about climate change?' You're saying what I'm feeling isn't real?"

"Oh, my word no, Missy. Please don't think that." *Whew!* God forbid anyone thought she was a non-believer in the great secular religion of the age. She'd be canceled by the climate cognoscenti, whose drumbeating about the world's imminent destruction provided a dominant narrative for the Western world's pillars of media, entertainment, academia, and governance. Indeed, if she wanted to work her way back into the establishment's good graces, she would need to pledge her allegiance to the cause. "All I am saying," Dr. Iz continued, "is that your emotional response could stem from a particularly acute sensitivity to environmental stimuli. That makes you, in many ways, *special.*" Dr. Iz could scarcely believe she'd offered such a suck-up assessment, but there it was.

Missy blew out her cheeks and nodded. Dr. Iz's diagnosis matched her own self-assessment: *She was special.* "You're going to give me a prescription, right?"

Dr. Iz shook her head. "As a psychologist, I don't offer prescriptions, Missy. We address challenges through counseling and therapy. In the meantime, I urge you to do all you can to get your mind on other issues. Relax as best you can." Dr. Iz got up to show her out and together they walked toward the door. "Have a pleasant trip home. I know it's hot out there."

Hot? Did she say *hot?* Missy's arm jerked, banging the wall.

"And, please, dear," Dr. Iz said, "be careful of the picture frames."

2. DIAGNOSIS: CLIMATOSIS

After Missy departed, Dr. Iz restored order to the gallery of photos, certificates, and commendations on her wall and walked across her empty waiting room to the front desk, where her part-time receptionist and bookkeeper, an accounting student at Baruch College's Zicklin School of Business, was working on invoices. Crystal Martin, shading her eyes with one hand as she punched the calculator on her phone with the other, looked up as Dr. Iz approached.

"May I ask you a personal question, Crystal?" Dr. Iz asked, leaning on the credenza.

Crystal nodded affirmatively and sat back. "Shoot."

"Do you and your friends talk much about climate change?"

Crystal burst out laughing. "Are you kidding me? All the time!"

"Really?" Dr. Iz pressed.

"No," Crystal said with hooded eyes, as if Dr. Iz were crazy.

"You don't think it's a problem?"

Crystal's voice rose. "I'm not sayin' it's not a problem. I'm just sayin' it's not on my top ten list of shit I gotta worry about every day."

"I see."

Crystal gestured around her. "Dr. Iz, you know my 'hood, right? I worry about stray bullets, stepping on needles, getting to class three nights a week without having my bag snatched, and tryin' to find a charter school so my baby girl learns to read. Climate? It's... what? Too *hot?* Well, okay." She shrugged. "I'll take the heat over cold."

"So you're not thinking a climate apocalypse is going to kill you."

"Oh, hell no," she said. "Waiting for the 2 train might do me in. Some drooly kook come up and shove your ass right on the tracks."

Dr. Iz stood straight up. "You met Missy when she came in, right?"

Crystal chuckled. "Oh yeah. I bet that chick worries about nothin' but climate change."

Dr. Iz nodded. "Why do you say that?"

Crystal laughed. "C'mon, now, Dr. Iz. What else she got to worry about? I looked her up. She can't worry about money; she's rich as hell. She can't worry about rent; she owns an eight-million-dollar apartment in Tribeca. She sure don't worry about no damn job." Her voice went high. "She's an executive at her momma's company, and she's what? Twenty-two? I'll trade my problems for hers any day of the week. Straight up. Just show me the money, honey."

Dr. Iz returned to her office, flipped on her computer, called up her Chrome browser and typed "climate anxiety therapists." What she found nearly gave her a twitch: *she was late to the game!* More than a hundred climate therapists had already opened shop across the country, and business was booming. New York was a particular hotbed, with psychologists and psychotherapists setting up offices near college campuses. News articles and psychology journals indicated that therapies were still developing, but the common theme among counselors was to recognize their clients' virtue and reassure them they were good people because they cared so much about the planet. Dr. Iz recognized the logic of that advice immediately: *Repeat business.*

Missy's twitch, however, added a new dimension Dr. Iz did not see reported elsewhere. Dr. Iz believed it was a conversion disorder, in which a person develops physical symptoms brought on by emotional distress. But the fact that Missy's friends also seemed disabled by this anxiety suggested the green shoots of a possible mass hysteria. With a little nurturing, this affliction could grow into something large, terrifying, and extremely profitable.

Searching further, Dr. Iz found a possible corollary from the Middle Ages, when groups of people across Europe concerned about their environment would inexplicably dance without stopping until they collapsed, sometimes breaking their ribs, or even dying. There were numerous reported outbreaks of choreomania over hundreds of years, with some people decorating their hair with garlands, parading around naked, and engaging in sexual intercourse in public squares. It had an end-of-the-world feel to it that sounded much like the Occupy Wall Street encampment, but with a medieval flair.

Some historians attributed the choreomania phenomenon to a fear of St. Vitus, the patron saint of entertainment, who was believed to have the ability to make people dance. The more prevailing view, however, was that the epidemic was a reaction to stress and tension caused by natural disasters such as plagues and floods. Dr. Iz tapped her desk with a pencil. This could be history repeating itself, with greater possibilities for commercial exploitation.

Crystal appeared at her door and knocked on the frame. "I'm writing out the invoices for your patients this month, Dr. Iz," she said. "I'm thinkin' for Missy Crowe you need to seriously charge her ass."

"I will," Dr. Iz assured her.

"I mean, top rate—and then add 50 percent."

Dr. Iz scrunched her face. "What's on your mind?"

Crystal folded her arms and leaned against the door frame. "Dr. Iz, I couldn't pay your electric bill this month—to Crowe Power, by the way. And I couldn't put it on your credit card because it's maxed out. You've got to charge more for what you do."

Dr. Iz dismissed the idea quickly. "I don't want to chase away new clients." She pointed to her computer. "Climate anxiety is a real thing."

Crystal nodded. "Then you better make it your real thing." Crystal stepped into the office and leaned over the desk. "Make Miss Missy your poster child," Crystal said matter-of-factly. "She got arrested at a protest downtown last year and loved the attention. They had her in handcuffs and she was grinning from ear to ear."

Dr. Iz sat back in her chair. "I noticed."

"That's exactly what she wanted you to do. Notice," Crystal said, flatly.

Dr. Iz arched an eyebrow. "What if we put the word out there that I'm treating an outbreak of climatosis?"

"Never heard of it," Crystal said.

"I might have just made it up," Dr. Iz replied.

"Climatosis..." Crystal rolled it around on her tongue. "I like it. It sounds serious. What are the symptoms?"

"Extreme anxiety about the climate," Dr. Iz said. "Can be disabling. Easily spread to like-minded individuals, of whom there are probably millions. Requires intensive therapy from a licensed practitioner—like me." She paused, thinking. "There's just one problem."

"What's that?"

"Twitches related to anxiety usually go away on their own," Dr. Iz said. "There's no way of telling when."

"Then you better get moving."

Dr. Iz nodded. "That's what I'm thinking. A case like this requires consultation with other professionals."

"Like who?"

"My agent," Dr. Iz said. "Get Terry on the phone, will you? I want to see if he can get me on *Scuttlebutt Live*."

Crystal smiled. "You're going back on TV?"

Dr. Iz put an open hand over her heart and batted her eyes. "Only as a public service."

3. MISSY INACTION

Lindsey Harper Crowe had visited more than a dozen offices on her tour of Crowe Power headquarters and found few signs of life. Chairs were empty throughout the pre-war building in Lower Manhattan. Desks were cleared. Coffee pots and pantries were spotless. Even the bathrooms were pristine, with abundant baskets of untouched toiletries.

"Tampons?" Lindsey asked, as she evaluated the offering next to the sinks.

"Our Employee Equity Committee asked for them," said Jasmine Holmes, the company's senior vice-president for HR.

"Aren't we in the men's room?"

"If it brought more people to work, I'd put a dance floor in here," Jasmine said.

In her job as chairperson of the Crowe Power Company, Lindsey usually confined her activities to the twenty-fourth-floor C-suite, where executives and their assistants still showed up for work every day. Occasionally, she'd also take the spiral staircase to the twenty-fifth floor, home to the Board Room, a fitness center, the executive dining room, and the family's private dining room, known as the Crowes' Nest. Her trip to the lower floors was dispiriting, to say the least.

"For a power company, we don't show much energy," Lindsey lamented.

They turned the corner and poked their heads into the department that managed refineries and pipelines. Once a bustling cubicle farm, it had run fallow during the pandemic and ultimately turned to seed. "What other inducements have you tried?" Lindsey asked.

Jasmine ticked off her fingers. "We've offered breakfasts. Lunches. We've had sushi, barbecue, and salad bars. The only time we didn't throw out all the food was when we had Dosa Day. The guys in IT cleaned us out."

"What about happy hours?" Lindsey asked.

"Nothing happy about 'em. We've done wine bars. Jell-O shots. Tequila Tuesdays," Jasmine said. "One Tuesday, my assistant and I drank all the mezcal ourselves." She thought back and smiled. "That was our happiest hour."

They took the stairwell down to the second floor, home to what was once the Charles Crowe Conference Center, named for one of the founder's sons. "It's now the Charles Crowe Wellness Center," Jasmine said. "We converted the conference rooms to day care, a pet-sitting service, and a spa. The last one's a pickleball court."

Lindsey muttered. "Does anybody use it?"

"You're looking at her," Jasmine said. "I'm getting to be a bad-ass at pickleball."

She led Lindsey into the spotless break room, where they each poured themselves a glass of filtered water and walked to a café table.

"I know people have tools to work from home," Lindsey said. "But I don't think this is healthy. I see people on Zoom calls and I can't tell if they're listening, watching a video, texting their friends, or whether they even have pants on."

"Or having sex," Jasmine said.

Lindsey frowned. "Oh please."

"We just fired some dude in our pipeline department. He was doing his drilling at home," Jasmine said. "Microphone and pants were off, but his camera was on. You could see him and his lady friend laying all kinds of pipe." She smiled at the memory. "Most interesting Zoom call I've had this month."

Lindsey shook her head. "This is so sad," she said.

"If it's any consolation, it's not unique to Crowe Power," Jasmine said. "Everyone I talk to says their company has the same problem. The five-day week became four. Then three. Throw in holidays, the days around holidays, and the days people even *think* about holidays. You've got days out of the office for kid issues, pet issues, and bereavements. People take the day if their dog-walker doesn't show up. They take a week if the pooch dies. It's two weeks for a cat." She drifted off in thought for a moment. "What makes it worse for us? We can't demand they come to the office or they'll quit, and we can't find replacements. Nobody wants to build a career in an industry that everyone thinks is evil."

Lindsey sighed. "I'm not sure we can do anything about that."

Jasmine nodded. "Our one bright spot is CroFusion. That place is buzzin'—the office on twelve, and the lab out in Jersey City."

Lindsey brightened. "Everyone shows up?"

Jasmine sipped her water and hid behind the cup. "Almost."

Lindsey knew instinctively where this was headed. "Oh, no."

"Oh, yes." Jasmine leaned across the table. "Nobody wants to tell you this, Lindsey, but I'm three months from retirement, so I was nominated. Your daughter is MIA."

Lindsey flushed red. This was worse than disappointing; it was embarrassing. After clashing with Missy a year ago over the Crowe Power Company's supposed failures as a responsible global citizen, Lindsey offered her daughter a peace offering: an opportunity to help lead Crowe's fusion energy subsidiary, a bold and risky venture to replace fossil fuels.

The move was not without personal risk. Lindsey had expended her own credibility with Jasmine and the rest of the leadership team to make the case for her inexperienced offspring to become an executive in the most intriguing part of the company. Lindsey's stated rationale was tenuous at best: the company needed to bring some of its fiercest critics inside if it were to deal with its perceived shortcomings. The real reason was less complicated: Missy was a Crowe.

"Has she come in at all?" Lindsey asked.

"Once, from what I hear," Jasmine said.

Lindsey rubbed her forehead. "Do people talk about it?"

Jasmine paused and eyed the boss. "Well, let me think…"

Lindsey waved her hand. "You don't even have to say it, Jasmine. Of course, they're talking about it."

Jasmine said, "When your name's on the building, people are going to talk about you—for better or worse."

"So… it's a thing," Lindsey concluded.

"It's more than a thing. It's an excuse for everybody else," Jasmine said. "People say, 'If she doesn't come to work, why should I?'" She gestured around her at the empty café. "What you see is what we've got."

4. MESSAGE FROM THE MOTHERSHIP

Lindsey slowly opened a glass door to her corner suite on the twenty-fourth floor and directed her gaze to Winnie, her matronly executive assistant, seated at the front desk. "Find Missy for me, will you, please?" Lindsey said. "I need to speak with her."

"Right away," Winnie replied.

Lindsey continued into her office and stood by her phone, waiting for the console's red light to blink. When it did, she punched the button for the speaker, and Missy's voice came on, ready for battle.

"Don't even say it, Mother," Missy commanded.

Lindsey counted to three and took a deep breath. "Say what exactly, darling?"

"That I'm supposed to be at work," Missy said in a monotone. "That 90 percent of success is showing up. That you gave me some humungous opportunity and I don't appreciate it. That it's irresponsible and... like, *whatever*."

Lindsey fumed. "I thought you wanted to save the planet. You can't even get out of bed." The phone went quiet for a moment. "Do I hear *seagulls?*"

Missy, in a near-whisper, said, "Um... possibly."

"Where are you?"

"Nantucket. I came up with the girls this morning."

"Don't tell me you took a company jet."

"Re-*lax!*" Missy practically shouted. "I didn't touch your stupid plane. I took Crowe Bird II, which could stand an update, by the way. The bathroom is kinda scuzzy and—"

"Please!" Lindsey interjected. "Shut up a second!"

"What?"

"Do you hear yourself?" Lindsey asked. "You're whimpering that your private jet isn't up to par? Seriously? You shouldn't even be on it since you apparently don't even work here."

A long pause ensued before Missy said, "Did you call just to yell at me?"

Lindsey tried to calm herself. Speaking slowly in a low voice, she said, "I called to find out what is going on with you. I take it you're at Uncle Chuck's."

"We're in the guesthouse."

"Is Uncle Chuck there?" Lindsey asked.

"Hmm. Now that you mention it, I don't... really know. I didn't look," Missy said. "I've seen some of the staff over there in the main house but they're totally lame. I had to ask, like, three times for Jose to bring me one frigging latte and, well... Ah, never mind. You wouldn't get it."

"No. You're right. I probably wouldn't." Lindsey gathered herself. "So tell me. What are you doing up there in the middle of the week?"

"Well, I'm kinda, you know... working remotely?"

Lindsey laughed. "Ah, right," she said. "So you have a computer with you."

"Not exactly."

"How do you work?"

"I have a phone."

"So you're dialing in to meetings?"

"I listen in," Missy replied. Then, barely audibly, "Here and there. Twice, probably. Maybe once."

"When can I expect a report from you on how close we're getting to bringing fusion to market?"

Missy's voice took on a defensive edge. "You're getting a little aggressive there, Mother. I think that's between me and the lady I report to. You know, what's-her-face."

Okay, Missy's "remote working" concept was complete bullshit. She didn't even know her boss's name. Lindsey paced back and forth in front of her desk. "This is such a letdown."

"You don't understand, Mother," Missy said plaintively. "I want to go to the office. I really do. I know I have to show leadership and all that crap. Seriously. I've just got... this thing."

"What thing?"

"This twitch thing," Missy replied. "My right arm is not my own right now. It's owned by some, I don't know, angry climate gods. I went to see Dr. Iz yesterday in the city."

"Why on earth would you see her?"

"Because I have this massive anxiety about climate change," Missy said. "And it's not just me. It's, like, all my friends. Our lives are so pointless. The world is practically on fire, billions of people are going to die, and we fight back by using paper straws instead of plastic? It's so pathetic. We're just kinda paralyzed right now." Missy paused. "And, by the way, paper straws really suck."

In some respects, Lindsey could scarcely blame Missy and her friends for their climate anxiety. They were bombarded constantly with messages that the climate was changing in catastrophic ways, and that it was due entirely to human activities.

Lindsey gathered herself. "You could do something constructive about your climate anxiety by coming to work and helping us develop CroFusion. We're up against more competitors every day."

"You're not hearing me, Mother," Missy protested. "If I want to get rid of this stupid twitch, I *have* to relax. Doctor's orders."

"That doctor being Dr. Iz."

"Yeah."

Lindsey struggled to keep her composure. "If you're going to be a leader at Crowe Power, you can't afford the luxury of being 'kinda paralyzed right now.' Your colleagues at the leadership level aren't relaxing; they're working. And they're fighting hard for this company—as well as this cause you say you care so much about."

"I get that. I just can't do it right now," Missy said. Fatigue set in just thinking about the drudgery of going to work. "Is fusion energy really the answer?"

Lindsey couldn't contain her frustration any longer. "*Damn it,* Missy. We don't know for sure! That's your job—to figure it out and take it as far as it can go! You can't do that sitting on a beach. You have to get in here. Apply your brain to the challenge and your butt to a chair."

She clicked off the phone before Missy could respond. Losing her cool probably didn't help matters, but she was at her wit's end. Lindsey flopped onto the sofa and stared out the panoramic windows at New York Harbor. In the distance were the Statue of Liberty, Ellis Island, and Staten Island. She focused on a bright blue tugboat pushing three barges heaped with coal toward a power plant in some distant city. On that boat went one source of reliable electricity for New York, which was suffering through what would no doubt become a regular series of rolling brownouts as fossil fuel plants were regulated out of existence. This was exactly what the activists wanted, even as many of them continued to indulge in all the comforts that abundant, cheap energy provided.

For reasons of family, heritage, and the survival of Crowe Power, Lindsey needed to make CroFusion a going concern. And she needed Missy to be a part of it—for her own sake as well as the company's. There was just one question that Lindsey had in mind as she threw her head back and stared at the ceiling: *How?*

5. TEQUILA THERAPY

There was no need for air conditioning in the gray shingled five-bedroom guest house in Uncle Chuck's compound on the eastern shore of Nantucket, the summer resort island thirty miles off the coast of Massachusetts. Gentle breezes from the Atlantic Ocean wafted through the large sash windows and the open French doors of the great room, allowing fresh air to cool the chillin' assembly of Missy and her gal pals.

A drinking game suggested by Missy's childhood chum, Blair, was for the five young women lounging about to take turns downing a shot of tequila, followed by a can of White Claw hard seltzer as a chaser, every time GNN mentioned "climate change" in its coverage of a hurricane in Puerto Rico, the heat wave on the east coast of the United States, or even the rainout of the Mets baseball game in Pittsburgh. Mention of a "climate emergency" merited two shots, and "climate catastrophe" called for three. If any of the news readers or reporters said, "climate apocalypse," one had to take one large gulp right from the bottle. Missy fretted there was a good possibility the group would run out of booze before long, since there was virtually no news the reporters couldn't tie to climate.

The ladies didn't have to wait long to get guzzling. In just one half-hour, they'd already gone around the room twice. Now a sodden correspondent dramat-ically demonstrating how hard it was to hold his ground amid gyrating palm trees in San Juan shook his head in frustration as he reported on Hurricane Ralph the Drag Queen, the first storm to incorporate the switch to non-binary names for hurricanes. The correspondent asserted the storm could have been prevented if only the world took the climate emergency—two shots!—more seriously. "I'm *begging* all you listeners out there," the reporter wailed. "You must do something to dial down global warming. Anything —*anything!*—is better than nothing at all."

Missy knew exactly what to do. There was no twitch in her arm as she licked the salt off the back of her hand, threw down a shot of tequila, and closed her eyes as she sucked on a lime, followed quickly by another shot. "It's the end of the world!" she whooped. She then picked up a can of White Claw and began chugging and glugging, accompanied by a chorus of, "*Go! Go! Go! Go!*" When she finished with a wide, wet grin, her crew offered a congratulatory, "*Woo-hoo!*"

Missy slammed the can on the tile-top table, burped, and fell back on the sofa, her eyes twirling, when a familiar ringing sound pierced the fog shrouding her brain. Was that a ship passing by? She craned her neck to look out the windows and made out the top of the Sankaty Head lighthouse but didn't see any boats. Wait. *No!* That ring was from her *phone!* That fucking thing! *Hahahahaha!*

She shook her head to snap her dozing synapses into firing mode again, picked up the device from the armrest next to her, and looked at the ID through bleary eyes: Dr. Isabel Castaneda. *Uh-oh. This could be it…*

"Everyone! *Quiet!* Please," Missy commanded. Then, solemnly, "It's my doctor."

Eyes widened and all went silent as Blair reached for the remote to turn off the sound on the TV.

Missy walked quickly out of the great room and into a small library, struggling with her balance as she shut the door behind her. "Hello?" she said tentatively.

"Good afternoon, Missy. This is Dr. Iz."

Missy's heart was beating fast. "Hi."

"I wanted to check in to see how you're doing," she said.

Missy's right arm reflexively twitched. "Okay, I guess. I'm doing what you suggested and trying to relax as best I can," she said, squelching a belch.

"That's good. Are you getting some rest?"

"It's hard," Missy said, consciously trying not to slur her words. "I'm watching the news, and it's, like, crazy scary."

"I know," Dr. Iz said. "Maybe you should turn off the TV. Go for a walk. Take some deep breaths."

"Right." Missy plunged ahead. "So… do you know anything more about what I have?"

"Yes," Dr. Iz said calmly. "That's one reason I'm calling. I believe you've been stricken with climatosis."

"Oh my God!" Missy said, dropping into a club chair and slapping her forehead. "Clima—*what?* Is that Latin?"

"Sort of."

"What does it mean?"

"Climatosis is a physical reaction to your fears about climate change," Dr. Iz said. "Based on what you're telling me about your friends, I'm concerned this could be the beginning of a mass psychogenic illness."

Missy hesitated to ask the big question. "Is it, um, you know… *fatal?*"

"I don't think so," Dr. Iz said, with enough uncertainty in her voice to suggest otherwise. "But that's not to say there can't be complications. Some could be rather serious."

Missy could hardly breathe. "Like what?"

"Well, for instance," Dr. Iz said, "if someone were driving a car, and a twitch suddenly caused them to jerk the wheel, that could be very dangerous. They could veer off the road, go into a ditch, into another car, or even over a cliff."

"Oh my God!" Missy covered her eyes. "That would be horrible."

"And, as we've seen in your case," Dr. Iz added, "climatosis can be quite disabling, preventing people from normal functioning, like going to work. That could have a devastating impact on one's career, or social life, or sense of connection to society. I'm sorry to tell you this, but I'm ordering you off work indefinitely. I'm writing out a note for you right now that you can show to your employer."

Not wanting to go to work was one thing. But being *ordered* off work? Missy choked back a sob as her left hand went flying out in a sudden twitch. It smacked a lampshade, making it rattle. "How long do you think climatosis lasts?"

"I don't know," Dr. Iz said. "Since climate change is a complex challenge and there is no simple resolution, this will take some time. That means adjustment on your part."

Missy gasped for air. "I'm just… devastated. Have you seen other cases?"

"Yours is the first I know of that involves a twitch."

"That makes me, like, what? Patient Zero?"

"It looks that way," Dr. Iz said. "Given what you said about your friends, I worry about the potential for Patients Two, Three, Four, and so on. We need to contain this contagion as best we can. If history is a guide, your climatosis could spread. Before I report this to the Centers for Disease Control, I'm wondering if I could meet with you and your friends for an evaluation."

"Absolutely," Missy said. "When?"

"As soon as possible. Can your friends get out of work tomorrow afternoon?"

Missy paused, thinking. *Hmm. Do any of them work?* "I'll ask them to clear their calendars."

"Excellent," Dr. Iz replied. "How many people are we talking about?"

"Five, including me," Missy said. Then she thought of Blair, who strangely didn't seem bothered at all. "Maybe just four. I'm not sure."

Dr. Iz said. "Alright then. Let's meet in the Sheep Meadow in Central Park at three o'clock. Can you do that?"

"Absolutely," Missy said.

Climatosis, Missy mused as she hung up. It sounded kind of like bad breath. But this was obviously way worse. Missy sagged in her chair as she pondered the dire implications for her once-promising future. There was a time not so long ago that she was going to be somebody. Now? Cut down in her prime! Before she even had a chance to make an enduring mark on the world by arresting climate change through marching, or chanting, or throwing soup, or… something. How was she supposed to do that now when she had this—this terrible *thing?* She couldn't even write graffiti with her arm all fucked up!

She padded slowly back to the family room, where her crew was busy replenishing shot glasses in anticipation of their drinking contest resuming soon. How would Missy break the news that she had a strange new plague—and they were all infected?

"Guys," she said somberly, if not soberly. "It's serious."

"Oh no. *What?*" shrieked her pal, Gina Grigoryan. A high-strung heiress to a Long Island waste-disposal fortune, Gina had developed a hair trigger to alarming news ever since her pop was gunned down in a Manhattan steakhouse during her sophomore year in college. Gina leaned forward in her chair and nervously tugged on her long black hair.

"Apparently, I've got some weird fucking disease," Missy intoned. "Climatosis."

"Noooo!" Gina yelped, pulling more furiously on her tresses. "It can't be!"

Britney Hogan-Weiss, daughter of the socialist Connecticut Senator Walter Hogan, fell back in her chair. "Please tell me you're kidding! *Climatosis?* That means, like—" *Hmm. What did it mean?* Britney had no idea. "What's climatosis?"

"My twitch," Missy said impatiently. "*Your* twitch. It's from climate change."

"I could have told you," sniffed Peach, as if she had known all along. Peach was the daughter of the famed actress Lilith Anne Buckingham and her third husband, the late rock star, Yikes. She had been indoctrinated into woke celebrity politics from childhood and knew the lines by heart. "Climate change is killing us. It's just a matter of time."

"But how much time?" Gina yelped. "Is it, like, years? Months? A week? *I can't stand it!"*

Peals of squeals followed until Blair, the only person who had not been touched by the dreaded scourge, said, "Wait a second, Missy. Before we get all nuts about this: Did your doctor say your twitchy thing was caused *by* climate change? Or that it was hysteria *about* climate change?"

"Obvi, Blair, there's no difference," sneered Peach with her usual condescension. "It's climate change either way. It's all about root causes."

Missy ignored the spat and took a deep breath. "Listen up, everyone, because there's more," she said. "Dr. Iz thinks you all have it, too. She said this could be the start of some mass psycho-something. She's writing me a note that says I can't go to work until we figure this out."

As Gina, Britney, and Peach absorbed this bulletin, their arms began to twitch. Britney's left hand struck Blair, who yelped, "Hey!" Gina's arm hit a can of White Claw and knocked it over, spilling a small puddle of suds on the rug. Peach alternated twitches between her right arm and her left, as if her central nervous system couldn't decide which twitch was best.

Britney asked, "Could she write notes for us, too? I don't want to go to work until this is settled."

Blair retorted, "I didn't know you had a job."

Britney replied, "I don't. This is more for my mom. I want her to know why I can't get one just yet."

Gina squealed, "What are we going to do? I need a cure! Should we all go to a spa? There's a cool one in the Berkshires I go to sometimes."

Missy put her hands together in front of her, almost as if in prayer. She talked slowly, deliberately. "The most important thing we can do for ourselves—and for each other—is to just chill the fuck out. Alright? We can't let the stress kill us. If we do, climate change wins."

"Totally agree," Peach said, nodding knowingly.

"This calls for tequila therapy—now!" Britney declared.

Missy started typing into her phone. "I'll text Jose to make us some pizzas. Maybe he can get off his dead ass and do some work for once," Missy said. "Gina, grab the bottle, the bong, and the chips. We're going to the beach."

6. DISTRESSED GENES

A dispirited Lindsey slipped on a pair of Chanel flats and left her office with nothing more than a small clutch. She left behind a sad smile for Winnie, who was fiddling with her tangled headset.

"I'll be back," Lindsey promised.

Head down, Lindsey walked through the Hall of Fam, avoiding the frozen gazes of the spotlit portraits of Crowe Power's august leaders from the past century, ducking her head as if she didn't want them to notice her leaving. She took the small executive express elevator to the lobby before slipping on her sunglasses and heading out the door to Broad Street, the cobblestone passage that was home to the New York Stock Exchange.

Lindsey tossed her head back and inhaled the marijuana-tainted air. Pot was not for her, but a drink and a think were in her future, provided she could find a place secluded enough for no one to recognize her.

She walked past a series of bustling lunch counters and coffee shops before reaching the multi-level Broadstone Bar and Kitchen on the corner, where people were enjoying drinks behind the tall glass windows. That was far too public, and much too close to the office. She crossed the street and came upon the historic red-brick Fraunces Tavern, where George Washington bid farewell to his troops. Maybe she should pull together Jasmine, her General Counsel and former brother-in-law, Digby Pierrepont, and her CEO, Lucy Rutherford, and tell them adios, too. She could return to her previous life of shopping and day-drinking with Digby's wife, Bits, and serve on charitable boards without the burdens she carried now. Alas, Lindsey's farewell to her troops could not happen today. The tavern was clogged with visitors from the idling tour buses nearby.

She continued to Stone Street, a block of outdoor cafes offering tables in a road closed to traffic, and considered her options, none of which afforded her solitude or anonymity. Somewhere around here, she remembered, there was a bar in an unusual place. Where was it? She pulled out her phone, scanned a map, and headed over to 55 Water Street. There she found the entrance to an escalator rising up from the sidewalk. She grasped the handrail, took a step, and rode it to a level called the Elevated Acre, a lush pocket park amidst a fortress of skyscrapers. There, off to the side and almost hidden from view, was the restaurant Sky 55, with a bar in the back, its shelves of liquor backlit like a glittering jewel case. Aside from a few people finishing their lunches at tables outside, there were no other customers. This was the perfect place to get lost.

A bartender slapped a coaster on the bar and Lindsey ordered a gin and tonic, which could pass to a casual observer for a soda water with lime. The drink tasted like summer and instantly transported her back to the comforting memory of poolside parties at the family home in Winnetka, Illinois, a wealthy enclave north of Chicago, noted in pop culture as the setting of the movie *Home Alone*. Growing up, she had lived a charmed existence courtesy of Harper's, the family's department store chain. It produced gushers of money, an endless array of goods from its flagship store on Michigan Avenue in downtown Chicago, and afforded the family special status in the city. Her great-grandfather, who prized hard work, faith, and community service, built a durable dynasty that lasted for generations.

Oddly, Lindsey never felt home alone until she married Robbie and moved to Manhattan's Upper East Side. As their children Missy and Chase were growing up, Robbie made himself scarce with business travel, meetings, dinners, and, as Lindsey long suspected, illicit liaisons with a string of lovers at various locales around the city. That left Lindsey to manage the kids, the household, and her civic duties. It also caused her to seek her own companionship, which she found with Bits, her then-sister-in-law, and their circle of sedated corporate widows. She found comfort, too, in a bottle. Her beverage of choice was sometimes vodka, occasionally gin, and oftentimes wine, preferably white. Aside from an occasional binge with Bits, Lindsey believed her drinking was now largely under control, partly because she didn't have time for it.

As she sipped her drink and looked out at the gardens, she knew there was realistically no escape from her duties to the company, the Crowe family, or her daughter, annoying as Missy was. It was ironic that Missy had gone to see Dr. Iz. Lindsey recalled that when Missy was young, Lindsey bought a copy of *Get a Grip, Honey* to help her deal with her very headstrong daughter, who had learned from her father to evade responsibility by blaming every failing on somebody else. Poor grades in school? *The teacher's fault!* Lost phone? *Someone stole it!* Messy room? *Lazy housekeeping staff!* Wouldn't eat her vegetables? *The cook made them mushy!*

Back in the day, Dr. Iz had offered common sense advice on how to get children to take responsibility for themselves. The message never quite reached

Missy, possibly because Lindsey was lost in her own escapism at the time and neglected to enforce her own rules. It wasn't until Lindsey accepted responsibility for her own misery that she climbed out of her deep hole, booted Robbie, and took charge of Crowe Power before he could destroy it with his reckless spending and aimless leadership. Now she had to face another truth: Missy's behaviors were partly the result of her poor parenting. Lindsey could have done better.

Lindsey sighed and glanced out at the garden, wondering where to turn. She could still depend on Bits for emotional support, but parenting issues were beyond her experience. The wise and witty Uncle Chuck had been an enormous help as she acclimated herself to governing the company, but he and Aunt Sylvia were increasingly frail and challenged by their own difficulties. And there was Robbie, of course. Entitled, lazy, and prone to grandstanding rather than hard work, he was better left out of this. He always managed to make matters worse. He also remained embittered by his belief that she had rallied the family to roust him from his job. If pushed, he was likely inclined to pursue the opposite objective of whatever she desired, just to spite her, even if it meant working against their daughter's best interests. Lindsey thought, *he was just that much of a dick.*

As Lindsey received a second drink, her thoughts turned to Marty McGarry. The former PR chief for several large companies, including Crowe Power, Marty had suffered many an idiot executive who had skipped the difficult climb up the corporate ladder in favor of the founding family's express elevator to the top. He had also helped Lindsey in her most dangerous endeavor as company chair: to successfully fend off a series of predators seeking to take control of Crowe Power. Missy might be a more challenging puzzle; could he coax a privileged heiress who'd never had to work a day in her life into achieving some level of productivity? Short of that, could he at least use his skills as an image-maker to create the impression she was contributing to the company's success? That, at least, would remove the excuse Missy was providing for others at the company to not come to work and spare Lindsey further embarrassment.

Lindsey paid for her drinks in cash, then headed out to the gardens. She stretched and looked around for a private place to make a call. She found a bench along the eastern edge of the park overlooking the East River and downtown Brooklyn. Nestling in among the lush greenery, she reached into her clutch for her AirPods and searched for Marty's name in her contacts. She punched the screen, and Marty's voice came on, muffled by background noise.

"Miss me already, don't you?" he said, in a cheerful growl.

Lindsey feigned hurt, but she was smiling, and feeling a little buzz. "You don't call. You don't write."

"Now why would I do that?" he asked. "I knew you'd call me eventually. From what I can tell from the newspapers, the Crowe Power Company produces more corporate crises than it does kilowatt hours these days."

"I'm quite aware," Lindsey said, frostily. "Are you busy?"

"Oh, my God, yes," he said. "Working my ass off."

"Really? I hear laughter and the clatter of dishes," she said.

"I'm working remotely," Marty insisted.

"There's a lot of that going around, I hear." She smoothed her hair back and squinted into the sun. "What are you working on?"

"My second beer," he replied.

"And where might that be?"

"A bar stool at P.J. Clarke's on Third," he said. "I'm watching the Yanks get spanked."

She sighed. "Marty, you can't waste your days watching baseball."

"Oh yes I can," Marty proclaimed. "I'm pretty good at it, too."

Lindsey idly glanced at the ferries shuttling back and forth between Manhattan and Brooklyn and the helicopters launching from the helipad below. "I thought by now you'd be ready to come downtown to help me."

Marty plugged one ear with his finger. "I can't hear you."

"Oh yes you can."

"Seriously," he said. "The Red Sox just scored again, and there's a lot of bitching around the bar. Let me get to a better place." Marty rose from his stool, covered the phone, and asked the bartender to watch his spot. He headed out the door to Third Avenue, where the heavy humid air of summer in the city clobbered him like a big down pillow. "So tell me," Marty said, squinting up into the sun. "Where does it hurt this time?"

Lindsey leaned back on the bench and sighed. "This will not surprise you."

"Robbie?"

"Missy."

"Again?" Marty asked, slowly pacing the sidewalk. "I thought you got her sorted out."

Lindsey sighed. "I thought so, too. I gave her an opportunity to help lead our fusion team," she said. "It hasn't taken."

"What's the job?" Marty asked.

"Vice-President of Strategy."

"Whoa," Marty said. "That's a stretch. Isn't she right out of school?"

"Yes. Maybe the job's too big for her. I don't know," Lindsey said, biting her lip. "But she insisted. She reminded me that I jumped the line because of the family and she said she should, too. It was, she thought, her birthright. And—you'll love this—she contends she has even more claim on the company than I do because she's blood and I'm not."

"Wow," Marty said. "She inherited the entitlement gene. Sounds just like her pop."

"Sadly true."

Marty probed, "So, she got the job. What's the problem?"

"Apparently, she's immobilized by climate anxiety and can't come to work. She's seeing a therapist on the Upper West Side. You remember Dr. Iz?"

"The TV shrink? I haven't heard of her in years," Marty said. "Didn't she slap someone on her show?"

"Possibly," Lindsey replied. "I know she used to get nasty with people. That was her stock-in-trade."

"Why would Missy go see her?"

"Maybe Missy thinks she needs a slap. At this point, I'm ready to oblige her myself," Lindsey said.

Marty scratched his head. "So… what do you expect me to do?"

"Look, Marty." She sat forward on the bench and covered the phone with her free hand as a couple strolled by. "I know this isn't your thing, but I'm wondering if you could work with her. Counsel her. Coach her up a bit and get her to start focusing on something productive."

"Like what?"

"Like her job."

Marty blew out his cheeks. "I don't know, Linz. I'm a Boomer, not a Zoomer. She's in a generation I don't get."

"You have a daughter."

"Like I said."

Lindsey protested, "You worked with her father."

Marty paused. "I thought you were trying to convince me to do this."

"I am!" Lindsey insisted. "What I'm saying is, you're uniquely qualified. You know all the dark corners and weird twists of Robbie's personality. Dust off the same owner's manual. Use it on Missy. I can assure you: the wiring is pretty much the same."

Marty leaned against the plate glass window and put a foot up on the wall behind him as he recalled his tours of duty with the Crowe family, encased in great wealth for so many generations that it had lost touch with ordinary people. As hired help from a middle-class background, Marty was never accorded anything close to equal status, even by family members with no credentials other than their name. It didn't matter what their aides and counselors might have achieved on their own merits. They were Crowes. And for the most insecure among them, that meant endless efforts to reassure themselves that they were superior. While Lindsey was an exception, the odds that Missy was, too, were steep. "What would give you the idea I want to relive the glory of serving another member of your fucked-up family?"

She paused, then spoke softly, pleadingly. "Because it would really help me," she said. "And I need the help—badly."

Marty sighed. There was something about Lindsey's direct way of speaking that he found compelling. Unlike other Crowes, she never tried to apply gloss to the family bullshit. "What do I get?"

"You can be sure I would reward you appropriately," she said. Then, dropping her voice, "Maybe inappropriately, too."

Marty smiled as he remembered his last arrangement with Lindsey: an hourly fee and a fat success bonus, along with a celebratory roll in the hay that had not been specified anywhere in his contract, even the addendum. They had drifted apart when Marty's assignment was finished, as Lindsey devoted long days to running the company. Given their different social statuses, there was no chance of a lasting romance, but the mutual attraction was still there. He'd love to work with her; she was smart, sexy, and fun, and they had a shared sense of PTSD from dealing with Robbie. Managing Lindsey's spoiled spawn Missy, however, was another matter. She sounded hopeless.

"I can't make Missy successful in her job," Marty said. "She has to do that."

"I know."

Marty said nothing.

Lindsey said, "C'mon, Marty. You need a challenge. And I need you. Admit it. It's nice to be needed, right?"

"I've got a warm fuzzy feeling just thinking about it," he said, drily. He turned to look through the barroom window and put a hand over his eyes to blot out the sunny reflection from the street. He could see the TV in the far corner of the bar. The Red Sox were leaving the field, congratulating one another, apparently for a victory. Maybe investing his life in the underachieving Yankees wasn't such a great idea after all.

"Will you at least think about it?" Lindsey asked. "I don't know where else to turn."

"Of course," he said. "I'll get back to you tomorrow."

"How about coffee at Balthazar?" she said. "I'd love to see you."

Marty tried to temper her expectations. "I'm not sure you will."

7. MONUMENTAL AMBITION

As L. Robertson "Robbie" Crowe III took an elevator up to his office, the titular head of both the Star Power Company and the philanthropic Crowe Institute for the Greater Good bemoaned the fact that he had to go to the office at all. His sense of himself, sprung from superior genes and honed over years of leading large organizations, was that his greatest value to any enterprise was to think big thoughts, which he would then assign to others to execute. Such vision could not be nurtured simply by sitting behind a desk, even if it were of a size befitting a man of great power. No. Going to the office more than twice a week, wasting time in meetings with lesser beings, and reading complex reports put him to sleep, depriving the world of more of his musings.

Big ideas required sunshine and oxygen to grow. And so he spent his weekdays outdoors when he could—rollerblading along the Hudson River, bicycling in Central Park, or bodysurfing in the Hamptons. When the weather didn't cooperate, he pursued indoor sports—like liaisons with comely young staffers. Generally, such relationships began in the office, then proceeded to a suite at the New York Athletic Club or his penthouse apartment in Tribeca. They eventually concluded with a generous payoff from his one of his companies' coffers and a signed agreement to neither disclose the relationship nor sue for damages.

It was a winning formula. Surely, it worked for the women, Robbie rationalized, because it gave them a chance to see his naked genius up close and... well, naked. Ultimately, these limited engagements raised their standard of living as well as their consciousness, since they received a generous multi-million-dollar parting gift to help them past the tears. This modus operandi also worked for his business and charitable interests, since they were the ultimate beneficiaries of his large ideas, at least one or two of which might have a practical application. Alas, most of his thinking revolved around how to gain revenge on his critics, who believed his days were spent doing the equivalent of nothing.

With the assistance of his faithful and thuggish toady, Howard J. Doolin, known as Howie-Do-It, Robbie had spied on and attacked rivals and critical shareholders at the Crowe Power Company and summarily fired executives whose presence displeased him. Off with their heads, he would demand, and his board of directors would either nod or nod off in acquiescence. While his impulsive behavior prompted poor decisions that ultimately led to his own dismissal as chairman, he could still point with pride to his crowning achievement—his acquisition of Greeneron, a grab bag of green energy start-up companies.

Much to Robbie's later astonishment, one of those Greeneron firms turned out to be a company focused on fusion, the emerging darling of green technology. As a result of his agreements with his ex-wife, Lindsey, and the Fenwick administration, which had financed Crowe's fusion research, Robbie now shared ownership of some of that firm's patents through his company Star Power. In partnership with Wonderful Chairman Technologies in China, Star Power could run to the front of the pack in the race for fusion and claim the market for themselves. Best of all, as a competitor to CroFusion, it could render Lindsey's efforts worthless, and deliver the humiliation she so richly deserved for dumping him.

As Robbie strode into his Brookfield Place suite overlooking the marina in Battery Park City, his executive assistant, Ivy, stood to greet him and hand him his freshly delivered latte from the coffee shop downstairs. "Good afternoon, Mr. Crowe," she said perfunctorily.

"Ivy," he replied with a weary sigh, as if he'd been working all day. In actuality, his principal achievement thus far was lunch. He looked around briefly and shook his head. Just seeing her and this office triggered an overwhelming sense of dread that some sort of work probably needed to be done. He was exhausted just thinking about it. "What time is it?" he yawned.

She looked at her watch. "It's almost two o'clock, sir," she said.

He took a sip of his latte, which he found to be not quite the perfect temperature, but within an acceptable range. That made Ivy's job safe, at least for the moment. "What time does the Chinese delegation get here?"

"They're here," Ivy replied.

"What?" Robbie exclaimed, his eyes darting back and forth. "Where?"

"In your conference room," Ivy replied.

Robbie threw up his hands. "Why didn't somebody tell me?"

"It's on your calendar, sir," she said, quietly, but firmly.

He stepped closer to her desk. "How the hell was I supposed to know it was on there?" he asked, incredulous. "I don't look at that thing."

Nonplussed, she replied, "I emailed you about it last week. I texted you a reminder this morning. I left a voice message on your phone. And I called you again when they arrived at one-thirty."

"One-*thirty?*"

"Yes," she said. "I'm sorry, sir, that you weren't able to pick up."

He shook his head, exasperated. "And you think that all that is adequate notification?" he snorted. "You should have tracked me down and dragged me in here. I was just over at Locanda Verde. Now look at me. I'm late. And it's all your fault."

Her eyes narrowed and her jaw clenched, but she managed to hold her tongue. "As you say, sir," she said, tersely. Her expression, however, said, *What an asshole.*

Her lack of contrition made him redden with rage. "You're damn right that's what I say," he huffed. He pointed to the conference room. "Now. You need to go in there and tell them that."

Puzzled, she asked, "Tell them what, sir?"

"That you fucking blew it, Ivy," he said. "There's no way I should be blamed for being late. No way! Especially with the Chinese. Tardiness is a huge insult. They've got that whole face-saving thing."

"Face-saving—what thing?" she said. "I'm not sure what you mean."

"Damn it, Ivy! It's about showing some goddamn respect for people, which is something you ought to do!" he shouted. "Now get your ass in there and save me some face, will ya? Jesus Christ!" He threw up his hands again and muttered, "How thick can you get?"

Ivy sighed and headed toward the conference room as Robbie trailed behind, pondering once again the dumb luck that had him surrounded by incompetents, boobs, and nincompoops. Didn't anybody know how to do their job? Here he was, a man of incomparable vision—*Howie-Do-It said so!*—who saw things on a grand scale, yet nobody could keep up with his vigorous mental pace. Nor had anybody yet figured out how to turn his brilliant musings, jottings, mutterings, and streams of expletives into tangible initiatives. Did they expect him to do *everything* himself?

Robbie waited outside the conference room while Ivy announced that his eminence would enter momentarily, and that his tardiness was entirely the fault of his feeble, unworthy staff. Afterward, she exited and looked coolly at Robbie without saying a word.

Wait, Robbie thought. *Did she just roll her eyes?* The nerve of this dippy chick! That was a capital offense! Robbie considered stopping her dead in her tracks and firing her on the spot, but the Chinese were waiting. He'd deal with Little Miss Snippy Face later.

Four members of the Chinese delegation stood up as Robbie slapped on his charm mask and entered the room, smiling and waving. Robbie first nodded a hello to Harold "Hacksaw Harry" Crenshaw, the notorious hedge fund manager who served as his business advisor, before making his way to the other side of the room. There, he found that Li Deng Fu, director of Wonderful Chairman Technologies in Shanghai, had taken the chair at one end of the table, suggesting they were equals, a presumptuous affront. *I should have kept this asshole waiting another half-hour,* Robbie thought as he smiled at his counterpart.

"Li," he said, brightly, shaking hands and bowing slightly. "Pleasure to see you. Sorry I'm late, but you heard about the snafu with my staff. It was absolutely inexcusable, and I promise it will never happen again."

"No worry," Li said. He introduced his Chinese associates, a physicist named Tong Chia-Hou and an engineer, Wong Xuzhou, as well as a familiar American, the scruffy, glassy-eyed Scooter Fenwick.

"Wong and Tong. Nice to meet you." Robbie said. He then turned to Scooter and offered to shake hands. "The president's nephew, right?" Robbie asked.

Scooter cocked his head and hazily regarded Robbie as if he were gazing at a distant galaxy. "No," Scooter said. "He's my uncle."

"Right," Robbie said. "I believe that makes you his nephew."

Scooter nodded vacantly. "Yep. Yep. I see what you mean." He paused, then laughed to himself. "That's kinda funny, actually…"

Robbie didn't get the joke, if that's what it was, but pressed further. "What's your role with Wonderful Chairman Technologies, Scooter?" he asked.

"Advisor," Scooter replied. He paused, before adding thoughtfully, "That means I give advice."

"Right-o," Robbie said. "It usually does."

From what Robbie had read about Scooter Fenwick's expertise, he could advise the company about where to buy crack in New York and Washington, D.C., which strip clubs to patronize, and how much to pay in settlements if you knock up your housekeeper. It probably wouldn't take a Congressional investigation to figure out that Scooter, a law school dropout who had been in and out of rehab for many years, was cut into the action at the Chinese state-owned company for being the president's relative and possible bagman. Still, Robbie thought, he should treat him with respect. This guy might be fun to hang out with. He certainly never had any trouble getting laid.

As Robbie took his seat at the far end of the table from the Chinese delegation, Li and his team offered an evaluation of the Star Power patents they shared. Li's team had studied the material in depth for months and reached an inescapable conclusion.

"You gave us crap," Li said.

"What?" Robbie looked to Harry, who shrugged, then back to Li. "I didn't give you anything," he protested. "The president did."

"Then he gave us crap," Li said.

Robbie felt his heart fall to his stomach. "How can that be?" he asked.

Li held up a folder. "It's all old stuff—first-generation technology," he said. "Competitors—like CroFusion—are way past us, with newer lasers, pistons, miniature tokamaks, and advanced materials. I cannot believe the U.S. government spent a billion dollars for this crap. There is no value here at all."

Robbie had no idea how to respond. Since he knew next to nothing about fusion, other than his accidental role in its advancement, he was counting on his Chinese partners to provide Star Power's competitive edge. Yet it was quickly apparent they had nothing to offer. Sadly, neither did he. Lindsey must have retained the newer material as well as all the key personnel at CroFusion. By God, he'd sue her!

"With all due respect, Li, let's not rush to judgment on the worth of Star Power," Harry interjected. "Assuming your assessment is correct, there is still plenty of value here."

Scooter blurted out, "Oh yeah. Totally," he said eagerly.

Harry, surprised at this unexpected support, turned to Scooter. "Totally what?"

Scooter looked around to see people staring at him. He turned back to Harry. "You go ahead. I think you're going to say what I was going to say before I said what I said." He shook his head a couple of times, as if trying to shake his thought back into the exit chute. "I had an idea there for a second, but it's kinda gone now."

Harry nodded skeptically. *Drug-induced moment of absolute clarity, gone in an instant. Poof!* "Right," Harry said before turning back to Li, Wong, and Tong. "Well, anyway. I think there are plenty of assets to consider between our two firms. Star Power still has money in the bank—nearly a half-billion dollars from our federal grant. It also has considerable name recognition, particularly with Robbie's name at the top."

Playing to the Chinese reverence for ancestors, Harry continued, "As you know, Robbie is the great-great-grandson of one of the most impactful industrialists in history. And, of course, he is even more renowned for his own business genius." He nodded to Robbie, who suddenly sat up a bit straighter, then turned back to Li. "I think you know fusion is an incredibly hot commodity right now in the United States. Investors are looking for a way in and we can give them one.

You combine Star Power's star power with your engineering expertise, and we have the makings of a joint venture that could attract serious funding."

Li gravely shook his head. "We need one billion dollars."

Harry asked, "For what?"

"Licensing. Equipment. Personnel," Li said.

Harry shook his head. "That's fine. But I think we need to think bigger than that."

"How big?" Li asked.

"First of all, you need a number that says this is a serious venture." Harry stood up and walked to the window. "Then you also need to make a statement that says it's a big damn deal." He pointed south. "There's an island right down there, across the water from Manhattan. It's called Governors Island."

Li caught on. "Ah," he said, impressed. "The governor lives there."

"No. It's an old Coast Guard base. They're building a so-called 'climate solutions' facility out there. Thanks to some quiet discussions I've been having with the powers that be, we may have the opportunity to put a fusion campus right next door."

Li was clearly intrigued. "I see."

"That's where we would create the L. Robertson Crowe III Center for Fusion Excellence," Harry said. He let that sink in a moment, before proceeding. "The headquarters for Star Power and our joint venture would go there. Add the L. Robertson Crowe III Fusion Museum, with historic fusion artifacts, such as our original tokamak. And, to top it off, we build a towering statue looking out over the harbor toward the Statue of Liberty. This one will be called, 'The Father of Fusion.'"

Robbie was so excited he could hardly speak. "Are you talking about *me?"*

"Who else could it be?" Harry said, rhetorically. He could think of several more deserving people, such as fusion pioneers Arthur Eddington, Hans Bethe, and Ernest Rutherford, but they were long dead and in a poor position to contest the claim. So, too, were anonymous scientists toiling in fusion laboratories around the world to make advancements in fusion research. Robbie beat them all in terms of ambition and resources, as well as his desperate desire for recognition, regardless of how much it cost. Harry said to Robbie, "It has to be you."

Robbie was sold! "Fan-fucking-tastic idea!" he exclaimed. He looked to the Chinese, who were huddling at the other end of the table and animatedly speaking to each other in Mandarin. Harry leaned over to Scooter, who was excluded from the huddle.

"Do you understand what they're saying?" Harry asked.

Scooter shrugged. "Dude, no. Sorry. Only, like, when they order take-out. Even then, I'm not too sure, unless it's Kung Pao something…" He trailed off.

Li turned back to Robbie and Harry. "We are intrigued," Li declared. "We will get back to you soon about Gilligan's Island."

"It's Governor's Island."

Li regarded him suspiciously. "I thought you said the governor didn't live there."

"Right. But Gilligan doesn't either." Harry held up a hand. "It's okay. You understand the concept. I'm sure that when you think about it, you'll realize how much this makes sense for all of us."

The delegation rose, shook hands, and bowed, leaving Robbie and Harry in the conference room alone. Robbie shut the door and flopped dramatically into a chair next to Harry. Robbie looked positively giddy in the afterglow of Harry's proposal. *Whew!* The concept of a splashy headquarters, a museum, and a monument that would all bear his name was almost too good to be true! What a rebuttal that would be to all the naysayers over the years who had doubted his vision—the Planetistas, whom he bravely faced down in a confrontation on Broad Street; the Crowe Power board members who questioned whether he'd paid too much for green technology; his own family, for booting him to the curb in favor of Lindsey. This would be a giant "fuck you" to them all! *Look at me, I'm Robbie C!*

"That was positively inspired," Robbie proclaimed as he offered a fist bump.

Harry beamed and decided to push more of Robbie's buttons, if for no reason other than a little mid-afternoon entertainment. "Wouldn't that be one hell of a rebuke to Lindsey?" Harry said. "Your statue looking back at the Statue of Liberty, where she made her mark?"

"It's genius," Robbie said. "Absolute genius. I love it!"

Harry basked in his triumph. "If you can't beat her with the best technology, you can beat her with one-upmanship, right?" he said.

Robbie waved his hand. "She would never have this kind of vision." He pointed with his thumb toward the door that just closed behind the Chinese delegation. "Do we need those assholes to pull it off?"

Harry rubbed the back of his neck. "We don't need Li. He's your basic Communist Party hack. We probably don't need his scientists, either. The only one in that group we need is Scooter. But the only way to get Scooter is through the Chinese, since he's on their payroll. So consider it a group package. Buy one, get the rest free."

Robbie sighed. "Scooter seems like kind of a dope."

Harry asked, "You don't want to pay for all of this yourself, do you?"

"Not if I don't have to," Robbie said.

"Then Scooter's our gateway—to federal funds, as well as money from those who want to curry favor with the administration," Harry said. "All you have to say to extract dough out of Washington these days is 'climate change.' It's like waving a magic wand and chanting, 'hocus pocus.' Money falls from the sky."

Robbie let that sink in. He leaned back in his chair and clasped his hands behind his head, considering the ramifications of his new project. There were scientific breakthroughs to be had. A populace to be educated about fusion. Consequences for the planet. If all this came true, he could save the world! He nodded thoughtfully as he zeroed in on the issue that concerned him most. "How big do you think my statue should be?"

Harry couldn't help himself. "Colossus of Rhodes?"

Robbie blushed. "That might be overdoing it a bit—even for me," he said with a chuckle. "But we have to give the dimensions some serious consideration. It will be very important that we get the plaque right, too."

"The plaque will say whatever you want it to say," Harry said soothingly. "The winners write history, Robbie. And, with a project like this, I think it's safe to say that you, my friend, are a great big winner."

Robbie batted his eyes in gratitude for his loyal, highly paid supporter. "Who could deny it?" he acknowledged.

"Nobody alive today, that's for sure," Harry said. "But I do have to warn you. This will take some investment on your part."

"I know. We have to buy the land."

"No. We have to buy the politicians. They'll buy the land," Harry said. "You're going to need to line a lot of pockets to get this cleared by the city, state, and feds. Palms must be greased. And I guarantee you, as soon as the word goes out, the hands will, too."

Robbie sighed. He got up from the table and walked toward the window, looking out toward Governors Island, future home of the Robbie Crowe national shrine. "What else am I going to do with my money? Buy a baseball team? Get another boat? I sure don't need another vacation home in who-knows-where. I don't even visit the ones I've got." He sat down on the windowsill. "This may sound like a ridiculous problem, but after a while, you run out of things to spend your money on."

Harry pondered. "Maybe you could build a wing at a children's hospital."

Robbie turned and regarded him with a stink eye. "Right," he said.

"Just kidding," Harry said, holding up his hands.

"No," Robbie said, coming back to the table, "I think this fusion center is exactly the sort of inspirational legacy project I'd like to leave the world. Something to show how fusion can change the destiny of our planet. I mean, seriously. Who needs another hospital wing? There are already millions of 'em. This, though, would be unique—my contribution to humankind. It's something nobody else would even think of." Then, claiming ownership of the idea, as he was wont to do, he said, "I'm kind of surprised I didn't think of this before. But you know, people in future generations will surely look back and say, 'That Robbie Crowe must have been quite the visionary.'"

Harry nodded. "And they'd be right."

Robbie slapped the table with both hands. "Count me in," he said. "Figure out where I need to start sending checks and I'll start signing."

"Will do." Harry stood and began packing his satchel. "How's Missy?"

"We'll find out soon enough," Robbie said. "I put her in touch with Dr. Iz, as you suggested."

Harry smiled and stood to leave. "Perfect. Missy's in good hands."

Robbie plopped back into his chair. "Just do me one favor, will you?"

"Of course," Harry said. "What do you need, pal?"

"Can you, um… fire Ivy on your way out?" Robbie asked.

Harry looked surprised. "Seriously?"

"She needs to go," Robbie said, with a shrug. "And I really don't want to see her."

"Isn't that a bit strange, Robbie," Harry protested. "I don't work here."

"So?" Robbie said with a shrug. "You were in here with me. Just tell her I told you."

"You don't want to handle that yourself? I mean, she is your assistant."

"No!" Robbie said heatedly. "I'm sick of firing people! They get all sad or pissed off—you know, like it's my fault or something." He sighed. "Somebody else needs to do it, for a change. I'm tired of having to do everything myself."

Harry sighed. "Okay, fine." He opened the door. "I'll handle it."

"Just let me know when it's done, alright?" Robbie said. "I don't want to go out there if she's packing a box or something. It's so awkward." He pulled out his phone and punched his gambling app. *Ooh.* This was interesting…

As Robbie considered his bets on the night's baseball games, Harry popped his head back inside the conference room. "It's safe," he said. "She's gone."

A relieved Robbie smiled. "Wow. You work fast."

Harry shrugged. "She quit before I could get to her."

Robbie sagged with disappointment. "Well, hell. That kind of sucks."

"You could call her and let her know it was your idea first," Harry said.

Robbie winced. "You want to do it?"

"No," Harry said.

Robbie paused as he thought it over. "Ah. Fuck it," he grumbled, returning to his phone. "We're moving on."

"To Governors Island!" Harry said.

Robbie beamed. "Yeah, baby! Let's do this thing!"

8. A BACKUP IN JERSEY

A single tear fell down the cheek of engineer Wesley Williamson, known as PC for his resemblance to the bespectacled, dough-faced geek from the old Apple commercials. As he stood on the loading dock of his Jersey City laboratory, watching movers slam shut the roll-up door of a freight truck, he couldn't help feeling a sense of emptiness. The last components of PC's very first tokamak, the machine that made fusion energy history, were being shipped off to Star Power's warehouse in Staten Island so that PC could make room for the next generation of CroFusion technology.

The tokamak had no functional value at this point, since PC was developing several new approaches to fusion, but it was still his baby, and watching it go was like trundling one's first-born off to college. His engineering colleague Pranit Khatri, known by default as Mac, stood with him, shoulder-to-shoulder.

"You sweat and you toil, and you give everything you've got," PC said, his voice choked. "Then it's gone in a nanosecond…"

"A picosecond," Mac said.

"A femtosecond," PC countered, annoyed.

"I grant you, it was very, very fast," Mac said. He put his arm around PC's shoulder. "You were a good dad to our baby tokamak."

PC grimaced and nodded his head in appreciation. He had pursued fusion for sixteen years with the zeal of Captain Ahab. Known as both the most promising and elusive form of clean, green energy, fusion had seemed like a distant dream until PC's ingenuity helped Lindsey Harper Crowe light the torch of the Statue of Liberty with a brief jolt of electricity from his tokamak. In the year since, the competition to make fusion commercially viable more than doubled, with money pouring into the nascent industry from investors and governments around the world. CroFusion still had a lead in intellectual property, but it was shrinking, and PC's lab needed to test his pending patents on working machinery.

"Back to the future," PC said, with a sigh.

They stepped inside the lab, stacked with crates, pallets, and equipment in various stages of assembly. He headed over to a young engineer, Andrea Cohen, who held an iPad as she checked through a list of inventories.

"Progress?" PC asked.

Andrea looked up through the high-powered reading glasses that made PC think of the googly eyes he once bought at a novelty store. "The good news is that everything we've ordered is either here, in the lab next door, or on route," she said. She pointed out various crates. "All the semiconductors, capacitors, hydrogen pellets, and heat exchangers are accounted for."

PC hesitated to ask. "What's the bad news?"

"I guess you'd call it a bureaucratic snafu," Andrea said. "We haven't had the purchase orders approved for the rest of the equipment we need. Apparently, they're stuck in someone's computer."

Andrea read off the list of parts and components that were still required for CroFusion to create three fusion processes simultaneously. Since it was not clear which of the approaches under development was the best course toward commercial viability, the company had decided to spread its bets to advance a trio of possibilities. It was an expensive way to go, but Crowe Power had taken the early lead in the race for commercial fusion against well-funded start-ups in the UK, Canada, Japan, France, and the western U.S., and it did not want to relinquish it. Lindsey had promised her board, her investors, and her family that Crowe Power intended to leverage its early success in fusion into a viable business. With the Fenwick administration doing everything possible to shut down fossil-fuel-based energy, the company desperately needed new avenues for growth if it were to survive.

"This is very annoying," PC seethed as he walked slowly around the pallets and read the labels. "I'm reading every day about one company or another achieving a technology breakthrough, or issuing a new patent, or attracting new investors. We're treading water, it seems. What's the holdup?"

Andrea looked uneasily to Mac, then plunged ahead. "You'd have to ask HQ," she said.

"Who in HQ?" PC demanded to know.

"Um… Missy Mayburn Crowe?"

"Oh," PC said. To him, corporate politics was a puzzle more vexing than fusion and Crowe Power's Manhattan headquarters was a giant black hole of mystery. He had heard that people who got too close to its center of gravity were sucked into the vortex, their brains turned off, and they were never heard from again. PC's strategy had been to remain safely in remote orbit in Jersey, close enough to reach the corporate center if necessary, but far enough away to avoid its pull. The involvement of the founding family in Crowe Power made its political terrain especially treacherous. PC had the sense that Lindsey Harper Crowe was a capable leader, but her ex-husband Robbie was known as a playboy, a dreamer, and a dunce, and not necessarily in that order. PC had no idea where Missy fell on the family spectrum.

"Why wouldn't she sign them?" PC asked Andrea. "This was approved at the highest levels of the company, including the board."

"We don't know," Andrea said. "Word is—" she looked around to see if anyone was listening—"she doesn't come to work."

Mac shook his head in dismay. "We cannot wait, PC," he insisted. "Ms. Crowe is our champion. You must call her and ask her to intervene, or we are going to fall behind."

PC was aghast. "I absolutely will *not* call her."

Mac said, "She likes you! You made her a star."

"Look," PC said. "I know next to nothing when it comes to corporate politics, but I can assure you of one thing: telling the empress her daughter is not wearing clothes is career suicide. Do you want to run this lab yourself?"

"But you heard Ms. Crowe say it herself," Mac protested. "She wants fusion to be her legacy."

PC snapped. "Missy is her legacy, too. And she was there first."

Mac wearily sat down on a crate. "What do we do? If we don't act on our licenses from the national labs soon, they'll expire. Then we're back to square one. You have to do something, PC."

PC shook his head. He knew Mac was right. "Like what?" he muttered.

"PC, you need to locate your… you know," Mac insisted.

"My balls?" PC asked. "Is that what you're saying?"

"No. I know you have no balls," Mac said, shaking his head furiously. "I was thinking your, um… charm."

"Charm?" PC scoffed. "I don't have any charm."

"It is in there somewhere," Mac pleaded. "Everyone says you're a people person."

"But I'm not," PC snapped.

Mac sighed. "No," he acknowledged. "You are right again, PC. You have no people skills at all. And you have no charm."

PC threw up his hands. "What am I supposed to do?"

"If you can solve fusion," Mac said, "you can surely solve this. I think we find Missy Mayburn Crowe's mobile number and you call her. Surely, if you explain the situation to her, she will understand what's at stake."

"That's a terrible idea," PC said. "But it's the only idea we've got."

9. HEADS IN THE SAND

The phone in Missy's pocket vibrated, indicating a voice message. She pulled the phone out of her shorts and saw it was from PC at CroFusion. Why they hell wouldn't those people at the lab leave her alone—especially now? Sitting in a folding chair on the beach at Nantucket, she was on the cusp of a major insight into climate change.

Maybe it was the mushrooms working their magic, but Missy was quite certain she could see the sea level rising. The ocean water was moving higher and higher, ever upward. This had to be the "rapidly rising sea levels" she'd been reading about on Twitter! Maybe there was a glacier out there beyond the horizon that was melting like a scoop of sorbet in a punch bowl, causing the fluid to rise.

"Guys," she said, "I can see it."

Blair, laying out a blanket next to Missy's chair, asked, "See what?"

"The sea level," Missy said as she remained transfixed on the ocean. "It's, like, totally rising before my eyes. Just like they say."

Blair put a hand over her brow and squinted her eyes. "Really?"

Missy looked at her and pointed to the water. "It's right there, Blair. Look. It's getting closer and closer."

Blair shook her head. "Sorry, Missy," she said. "I don't see it."

"You have to look *harder!*" Missy insisted.

"At what? The tide?"

The tide? What? Was it high tide already? *Oh shit. Maybe that's what it was.* Missy turned back to the water, but the magic was gone. It just looked like a regular old ocean again. Oh well. She knew what she had witnessed with her own two eyes, and she promised herself she would never forget it. Just because mushrooms were hallucinogens did not make her observations any less real. They were a window to a truth that may not be visible to a closed mind.

Peach, slouched on a chair to her left, buried her feet in the sand and stared morosely into her phone. "Oh my God. You have to listen to this. A scientist at

Stanford University says the world population is growing so fast that we're running out of food."

Gina, dozing in her chair, suddenly sat up straight. "*What?*"

"We... are... running... out of food," Peach repeated, more slowly.

Gina wailed, "What about our pizzas?"

Missy leaned over and patted Gina's arm. "We're not running out today, Gina."

Peach continued reading, "This scientist says birth control should be mandatory and we should put sterilizing agents in the food and drinking water." She put the phone down, and shook her head, as if everything had just become crystal clear. "I'm totally on board with that."

"For sure," Britney said, idly, mesmerized by a video on TikTok of a dancing dog in a sombrero. "I mean, he's a scientist, right? Gotta follow the science."

"Wait a second," Blair said, falling to her knees on the blanket. "Why do you think that makes sense?"

"Because," Peach said slowly, as if addressing a child, "he predicts a catastrophic explosion. He says we have way too many people on Earth, but not for long. Listen to this quote: 'We must realize that unless we are extremely lucky, everybody will disappear in a cloud of blue steam in twenty years.'" She shook her head in mortification. "Blue steam? What the fuck!"

"Wait," Britney said, rolling off her chair onto the blanket. "Did he say, 'blue steam' or 'blue stream?'"

"What's the difference?" an annoyed Peach replied. "We'll be vaporized either way."

"Twenty years!" Gina squealed. "I'll never live to be a grandmother."

Peach harrumphed. "I'm not bringing babies into this mess just to have them die."

"If I'm not mistaken," Blair said. "I think we all die anyway."

"Not in a blue steam!" Peach insisted.

Britney shook her head in despair and crossed her arms over her chest. "People who have kids are so selfish."

Blair had heard enough. "Which people? Your parents?"

Gina twitched, knocking over her can of White Claw. "It's different now, Blair," she said, picking up the leaking can off the sand and quaffing the last ounce. "Ew, yuck," she said, spitting out the sand. "We know better than our parents did about all the damage we're causing to the planet just by living. It's like Ernesto from the Planetistas said: human beings are an affront to nature."

Blair replied, "You do understand human beings are part of nature."

Gina scoffed. "I don't know about *that,*" she said. "I mean—humans invented plastic and stuff. Fish didn't."

Blair turned to Peach. "Where did you get this story?"

Peach tapped her phone with the back of her hand. "*New York Times.*"

Blair reached out and wiggled her fingers. "Let me see." She took Peach's phone and scrolled to the top of the article, scanned the screen, then looked up in disgust. "This is from the archives—1969. How did you manage to find this?"

Peach squinted. "I dunno. I just did a search."

Blair said, "If this were true, we would have already been vaporized by now. Or not even born. According to this," she said, tapping the phone with her other hand, "America was supposed to have water rationing by 1974 and food rationing by 1980."

Gina eyed Blair suspiciously. "What are you getting at, Blair?"

Peach responded, "I'll tell you what she's getting at. She's a denier."

Blair shook her head and scrambled to her feet. "No. I'm not."

Britney snarled, "The fact that you deny you're a denier is proof right there! You're definitely a denier."

Blair opened an umbrella over the blanket. "Call me what you like, but yeah. I'm a skeptic, alright? So many of these climate horror stories seem like the same bullshit they've been peddling for years." She sat down in the shade. "I mean, fifty years ago, they were predicting a new ice age. The average temperature was supposed to drop, like, six degrees."

Gina rubbed her shoulders. "I think it's getting chilly out here right now."

Blair shook her head. "That's not what they were talking about, Gina."

Britney glared at Blair. "You need to get out of your bougie bubble, Blair. You are just totally out of it. I'd think you'd be embarrassed to even say stuff like that. The science is settled."

"Is it?" Blair snapped.

"Well, yeah! Of course it is," Britney said. "The only way you'll believe in the climate catastrophe is when we're all dead."

"Yeah?" Blair said. "When that happens, you can say 'I told you so.'"

"That's exactly what scares me," Gina said. "People like you, Blair, are going to deny, delay, and not do anything. And then, boom, it's all going to hit us at once. And we'll all be fried up like little chicken nuggets." She felt her stomach growl. "Speaking of which, I'm starving."

The gathering went silent for a moment, as the roar of another private jet flying overhead made talking useless. Finally, Missy said, "This is payback, you know. It's, like, nature's judgment against my family for exploiting fossil fuels."

She felt a vibration in her pocket and pulled out her phone to see a caller ID that said CROFUSION. Was this PC calling again? She twitched at the thought of talking about work and shoved it back in her pocket.

Gina said in a quavering voice, "My family's guilty of climate crimes, too. I mean, my dad created these giant landfills that were leaking methane all over the place. And methane's, like, one of the worst greenhouse gasses. I swear it was karma that he got gunned down in that steakhouse."

"Karma? Are you serious, Gina?" Blair said. "I thought it was some guy named Vito."

"Okay. Technically, yeah," Gina said. "But still."

Blair rolled her eyes and fell back onto the blanket. "I don't think the mob killed your dad because of his greenhouse gasses."

"I don't know," Gina grumbled. "He farted all the time."

Peach claimed the high ground. "I have to admit, my family is at least trying to do the right thing," she said. "We went all geothermal at our house in the Hamptons. And at our place in Telluride. Our condo in South Beach and my mom's penthouse in Tribeca are totally solar. Or almost. I guess sometimes, they need backup from... well, you know."

"Fossil fuels?" Blair said in a way that indicated she already knew the answer. "Is that what you're trying to say, Peach? *Fos-sil fu-els?"*

Peach glared at Blair. "You say that like you're happy about it."

"I'm not happy. I'm not sad. It's just what the deal is right now, Peach. Sorry to let reality intrude here, but something like 80 percent of our energy still comes from fossil fuels," Blair retorted. "That's not going to change anytime soon. Do you read the papers? They can hardly build windmills and solar farms these days. The activists won't let them. You might kill a toad."

Britney ignored Blair and looked at Peach. "You know, I think that's really cool your family's doing good stuff, but there's no going back on all the excesses of our parents and grandparents. The Earth's going to melt like a grilled cheese."

Gina fell prostrate on the blanket. "Oh God. Stop it! Don't talk about cheese... *please!"* she growled. "Where are those fucking pizzas? I'm *dying* here."

Missy looked back over her shoulder at the main house for any sign of activity. "I have no idea," Missy grumbled. "This is so frustrating. I'm going to text Jose and tell him to get off his butt. Anyone want anything else while I'm at it?"

They all raised their hands. "More chips, for sure," said Britney, holding an empty bag upside down and shaking it.

Gina asked, "He's gonna bring the pizzas down here, right? I don't have to walk all the way back to the house to get them?"

"God, I hope not," Peach said. "It's kinda uphill."

Missy said, "I'll tell him to bring them down."

Blair heard the creak of a hinge and looked over to see a man backing out of a screen door holding two large pans. "I think he's coming now."

"Finally!" Gina wailed.

Peach stood up on the sand and stretched. "On this 'end of the world' thing? I don't think we're going to melt," she declared. "I'm thinking maybe just the ice caps melt and that floods everything. So we're all underwater, except for, like, the Himalayas."

"We should all move to Nepal before everyone else does," Gina declared. "It'll be, like, a land rush once everyone figures it out."

"And what would we do there, Gina?" Blair asked.

"I don't know. We could open a coffee shop or something."

"Oh yeah," Blair said, drily. "There's an idea."

"What? It could be fun," Gina said, defensively.

Blair rolled her eyes and pulled a towel over her head.

Jose arrived at the blanket with the pans of pizza. Missy regarded him with trepidation. "These are gluten-free, right?"

Jose looked at her with alarm. *No comprendo…*

Missy read his panic. "Don't tell me," she snarled.

Jose shrugged his shoulders as his wide-eyed expression begged for mercy. He didn't know what she wanted, but he was quite sure he didn't have it.

Peach glowered at Jose. "You didn't think to ask?"

Missy looked to the group. "Anyone want these, or should we just give 'em to the seagulls?"

Gina protested, "But what if the seagulls are gluten-free?"

Blair smacked her forehead. "Please, Gina. Just *stop.* You're making my head hurt."

"What? I'm serious," Gina replied. "I'm trying to be considerate of the birds."

Blair ignored Gina and said to Jose, "I'll take the pizzas." She jumped to her feet, took the pans from Jose, and laid them on the blanket. Then she sat down cross-legged and pulled out a gooey slice. "Oh my God," she moaned, as she bit in. "So good." She called out to Jose as he departed. "Muchas gracias, Jose!"

The others sullenly watched Blair enjoying herself before reluctantly plunging into the pies. Missy was the last to take a piece. As she ate, she looked at her companions and sighed. Moving to Nepal was not practical. They couldn't avoid climate change. They had to do something about it, here and now. As their Sherpa here at Earth's lower elevations, Missy needed to lead them, especially now that her mushrooms were kicking in again. With her newfound clarity, maybe, just maybe, there was a silver lining in the dark cloud that was descending upon them. She would need to help them see it.

"Guys, whatever happens, let's agree: we can't lose our shit over climatosis." Missy said.

Blair, grabbing another slice, said, "Too late."

Missy insisted, "No. It's not. We can all get through this if we stick together."

There were non-committal nods and shrugs all around. "Guess so," Britney mumbled, before she felt a sudden twitch in her neck and her head shot back.

"I mean, think about this," Missy said. "We could change the course of history."

"What good is history if no one's around to hear about it?" asked Gina. "It's like that tree-in-the forest, or the forest-for-the-trees, or whatever that woodsy thing is."

Missy touched Gina on the shoulder. "People will be around, Gina. And you know why?" Missy's messianic sensibilities had returned. She declared, "Because we, the people—around this blanket—can save the world."

"It's up to us?" asked Gina, incredulously. "Are you serious?"

Blair grabbed another slice of pizza. "We're toast."

"I *am* serious," Missy insisted.

"That's what I'm afraid of," Blair said, as she plucked off a blackened pepperoni and popped it in her mouth. "How, exactly, are we going to save the world?"

Missy stood up and gazed out at the sea, which was rising and swirling and twirling again, like a Van Gogh sky. She felt consumed by a strange sense of destiny. "It's like this. We have this affliction. We can cry about it. Or we can use our own personal crises to draw attention to the horrible effects of climate change. If people like us, who grew up with, like, all the completely undeserved privilege in the world... if we can be affected by climate change, that should be a bulletin to everybody: anyone can suffer, especially poor people, and people of color, and the homeless, and transgender people."

"Why transgender people?" Blair asked.

"'Cause they always get screwed somehow," Missy said.

"That is so true!" Gina said. "They're not even allowed to go to the bathroom anymore!"

As the others tried to comprehend Gina's latest insight, Missy pressed ahead. "Think about it," she said. "Think of all the people out there—" she waved vaguely toward the mainland—"who are so selfishly going about their lives. All they worry about is their little job, or their little grocery bill, or how much they pay for gas, as if that's all that important in, like, the big picture. Who's going to even worry about paying for gas if we're all drowned, or fried, or vaporized? We need to shake them and wake them and show them that the tragedy of climate change is right here, right now." Her right arm shot straight up like an exclamation point over her head.

"That makes total sense," Peach said.

"I'm not sure what's scarier," Blair said to Peach. "What Missy just said, or the fact that you believe it."

"I think Missy and Peach are absolutely right," Britney declared. "We have to stand up for all those people out there who are too dumb to know what's going on."

"Wait a second," Blair said, dabbing the corners of her mouth with a napkin. "Aren't we, like, the worst possible spokespeople for this? Nobody's going to see us sympathetically. They'll look at us and say, 'A bunch of spoiled little rich kids. What are they whining about?'"

Missy looked at Blair. "That's exactly the point, Blair. Nobody—*nobody*—is immune. You can't buy your way out of the end of the world. It's coming for everyone."

Blair raised her hands. "I'm just sayin'. There's every possibility we look like idiots if we go public with this."

Missy glared. "Blair, did you even take mushrooms tonight?"

Blair pointed to the pans. "Just on the pizza."

Missy leaned over and grabbed her forearm, "That's why you're not seeing what's so obvious."

Blair crossed her arms. "Which is what?"

"We show the world how real this is," Missy said. "I mean, we have legit symptoms of climatosis. This isn't some theory. It's not a model that has to be proven." She held up her arm and pinched it for effect. "We're real. And we have real issues. And Dr. Iz, who's got, like, total cred, can confirm it." She looked around at her friends, who were listening closely—and clearly buying in.

"Okay," Blair said. "How are you going to spread the word? Spray-paint another building? Glue ourselves to museum walls? Sit down in traffic on the FDR and piss off all the commuters?"

Gina nodded. "We should do it topless, like Titty Rebellion."

Peach said, "Don't be ridiculous. We don't have to peel our tops off. We don't even have to leave the beach."

They all looked to Peach for the answer. She shrugged. "We make a video and post it on TikTok. Mission accomplished."

Missy jumped up from the blanket. "Perfect!"

10. THE HEAT OF THE NIGHT

Marty had been in bed for two hours but was quite certain he hadn't slept a minute. New York City's rolling brownout had finally claimed his apartment building near Lincoln Center, turning off his air conditioning. The useless fan he had acquired from Target twirled hot air in his bedroom but did nothing to reduce the temperature. All he could do was lie awake weighing the pros and cons of once again immersing himself in the Crowe family saga.

After progressively shedding his bedclothes, Marty laid atop his bedsheet in all his glory. He considered cracking open the windows, but the remarkably high volume of street noise made that a poor option. Apparently, nobody in brownout New York could sleep, since the sirens, honking horns, motorcycles, and ATVs were roaring full throttle down Broadway to his east and Columbus Avenue to his west. Surrendering to the inevitable, Marty sat up on the edge of his bed and snatched his phone off the nightstand. His weather app said it was eighty degrees outside, which was surely cooler than his apartment.

He slipped into the shorts he had tossed on the floor and a faded blue t-shirt from the New York Giants' last Super Bowl victory in 2011. He stumbled in the dark toward his living room and checked the useless thermostat: eighty-seven degrees. *Thank you, Governor Flink, for preventing fuel from getting to our power plants.* He picked up his laptop from the coffee table, dropped onto the brown leather sofa, and logged on to his computer. If he was going to consider taking on Missy as a project, he needed to know what he was getting into.

Marty found that Missy already had a sizable presence on the web. He saw photos of her as a well-scrubbed teenager at civic functions with her older brother, Chase, and her parents. Together, they created the picture of a successful, happy family—or at least, a convincing impersonation of one. A handful of shots culled from the Yale News showed freshman Missy Mayburn Crowe as a promising attacker on the lacrosse team. After a year of campus life, her story morphed from one of convention and team play to one of protest and rebellion, and she moved from the sports page to the front page. She maintained a high profile by participating in protests to show her fealty to the prevailing campus opinion on all issues of controversy—especially when it came to energy.

During her sophomore year, she joined the militant group Gas-Ex, which Marty thought sounded suspiciously like the pills in his bathroom cabinet. In fact, it was a group staging sit-ins and filing lawsuits demanding that the university divest from its profitable investments in fossil fuel companies, including the Crowe Power Company. Missy was quoted in the school paper asserting that such investments were "immoral," even if the returns outpaced the broader market and fossil fuels were better for heating and cooking than burning wood or firing up animal dung. Still, by protesting and giving passionate speeches, she could feel secure in the knowledge that her position perfectly aligned with the campus ethos. Few within the confines of Yale would disagree, at least out loud.

Marty clicked through several more pages in his search, recalling that Missy had brought her rebellious performance home in the spring of her senior year and made national news for protesting outside Crowe Power's historic headquarters in New York's Financial District. Missy was celebrated by the media for bravely spray painting a red-lettered epithet against capitalism on an adjacent office building, which resulted in her ceremonial arrest and instant release. There was no consequence for her uncivil disobedience—other than to garner fame and huzzahs from the city's climate cognoscenti.

Now that Missy had graduated from college and ascended to an executive position at the company that bore her name, Marty pondered whether he could succeed in helping her see her own self-interest in the future of Crowe Power and the revolutionary clean energy it was seeking to bring to market. If Missy were as much like her father as Lindsey suggested, the odds were steep.

Marty fell back on the sofa and reflected on his tenure at Crowe Power under Robbie Crowe. The great-grandson of company founder Homer Crowe, Robbie had proven with his time atop the family enterprise that he had little hunger for the rigors of business but a bottomless appetite for validation. Desperation to prove he had risen to the top of Crowe Power's food chain because of his vague green "vision," rather than his privileged DNA, led to a series of risky maneuvers that nearly put the company into bankruptcy. After he was ousted in a family coup and exiled to the world of foundations, Robbie's Crowe Institute for the Greater Good had flailed about for a suitable mission to save the world. Bored, he had turned his sights back on Crowe Power and forced Lindsey to relinquish Star Power to him, but progress under his rudderless leadership was scant.

If Missy were truly like her pop, Marty mused that he might need to minimize whatever damage she could inflict on the company while creating an image of her as a valuable contributor with enormous promise. He would also have to carefully curate her profile in the media to grease her path for her inevitable promotions. A Google link to TikTok, where Missy was trending, told him he was too late.

"Oh no," Marty muttered, as he sank into his couch cushions and pulled up the video. There was Missy, facing the camera, looking serious, her head jerking in spasms. "You don't think climate change is real? Check this out." The camera panned to Britney, Gina, and Peach, illuminated by the flames of Missy's firepit as they twitched and jerked around. "We're all twitching because we're freaking out about climate change. The doctor's diagnosis: we've got climatosis. Yeah, people. *Fucking climatosis*. These are the symptoms and they're getting worse. And it can happen—"she pointed to the camera—"to you."

On the side of the video, a heart indicating the number of people who had liked it stood at thirty-four thousand and climbing. There were more than two thousand comments expressing sympathy and support, five thousand bookmarks, and an untold number of shares to others afflicted or worried about catching the contagion, and the counters kept rolling up. Missy's twitch had gone viral and was apparently infecting the entire world. Surely, Marty thought, it was going to make her mother sick, too. So, sadly, would Marty's verdict on whether he could babysit another Crowe dilletante.

With sleep an increasingly remote possibility, Marty put on his gym shoes and headed downstairs. When he reached the ground floor, he turned right out of his building and headed south toward Columbus Circle. Approaching 55th Street, he could see all the way down to Times Square and its newest landmark: the Climate Countdown Clock, a towering structure at 47th Street that ticked down the time left until doomsday, as predicted by the widely quoted and frequently wrong Dr. George "Spanky" MacFarlane, director of the President's Council on Climatology. As Marty descended the hill on Broadway, he began to make out the sign and its flashing red and yellow lights:

ONLY
5 YEARS 2 MONTHS 3 WEEKS 4 DAYS 45 MINUTES 23 SECONDS
UNTIL CLIMATE CATASTROPHE!

Marty watched the seconds tick down and thought: *Maybe I don't need to buy a new car after all.* Another sign below the clicking counters noted:

The Climate Countdown Clock
is brought to you by
GEMSTONE FINANCIAL
Invest in Responsible Companies
-and-
THE DAILY REAPER
Climate News You Can Trust

Marty gazed at the clock and noted that tourists were posing for selfies in front of the sign with a feigned look of horror, putting hands around their neck in a choking motion, or pointing an index finger at their temples. Some of them had just emerged soaking wet, hair askew, from a midnight performance of the popular tourist attraction, "RAGING STORM: An Immersive Climate Change Experience." Showgoers paid a hundred dollars or more to get drenched in hurricane-force wind and water. Those lucky few in the front row were blasted with heat guns until they screamed for mercy. Reviews said it was all great climate apocalypse fun. Late night shows offering all-you-can-drink Hurricanes and souvenir life jackets were sold out for the next two years.

Another sign nearby asked:

IS YOUR BUSINESS CLIMATE COMPLIANT?
Call McGraw and Duntz
Climate Counselors-at-Law
Get with the Program

Marty took a seat on a white concrete barrier stenciled with "NYPD" in big blue letters and watched the colorful commotion playing out under the flashing lights of Times Square's electronic billboards. The causes, measures, and projections of climate change no longer merited debate; those issues had been decided, according to the victorious advocates. Whether they were right or not no longer mattered. They had transformed their pet cause into a cultural and commercial commodity in entertainment, investment advice, legal advice, media—and now, psychotherapy. Missy was just the latest exhibit in the case for catastrophe, but she surely wouldn't be the last. The "climate crisis" was bought and sold like Coca-Cola, M&Ms, and Broadway shows.

Marty watched a group of tourists pose for photos in front of the Climate Countdown Clock, waiting for the thunderous boom it sounded each night at midnight, and realized it was a waste of time—and possibly hazardous to his health—

to stand on the tracks of the climate emergency freight train. It had too much speed. He'd be better off watching the Yankees from the safety of a bar stool. At least they still won occasionally, and the beer was still ice-cold, regardless of the ambient temperature of the bar.

11. SIDEWALK SALE IN SOHO

A black car crawled down Spring Street in Soho, maneuvered around the dining shed in front of the iconic Balthazar Restaurant, and stopped at the corner. A uniformed driver sprang out of the front seat to hold the back door open for Lindsey Harper Crowe. She extended one well-turned ankle toward the sidewalk and a finely manicured hand toward the driver, who helped her out of the car, and she emerged in a summery yellow business suit. Spotting Marty, sitting in jeans and a collared shirt under a red awning extending over the sidewalk, she removed her Cartier cat-eye sunglasses and put on a dazzling smile. In keeping with the French theme of the cafe, she planted a continental kiss on both of Marty's cheeks before sitting.

"You look well rested," she purred after they ordered cappuccinos. "I hate to admit it, but doing nothing seems to suit you."

"It's not as easy as it looks," Marty said.

"Tell me," Lindsey said mockingly. "What's your secret, Marty?"

He smiled at her taunt. "I'll admit, there have been times I've been tempted to do something, but then I remember my solemn pledge to myself: Don't do a damn thing," he said. "It's all about willpower."

Lindsey nodded. "Let's put your impressive self-discipline to the test, shall we?" she said. She glanced around at the passing fashionistas going to work at the designer shops nearby to determine whether any paparazzi were lurking about. Then she reached below the table for her valise and pulled out an envelope. She slid it across the table.

"My God, did you find my GED?" Marty exclaimed.

Lindsey laughed. "It's your lottery ticket," she said. "And guess what? You won."

Marty opened the envelope and pulled out a check. Puzzled, he turned it over twice. "I see my name on it," he said. "I don't see a dollar figure."

"You know the assignment," she replied, raising her chin and eyeing him. "Tell me what it should be."

Marty held up the check and rattled it. "You think you can win me over by appealing to my sense of greed?"

"Frankly, yes," she said. She bowed her head and batted her eyes. "You are Marty McGarry, aren't you?"

"Last I looked," he said. "What you may not fully appreciate is that I do have some principles, elusive as they may appear."

"Oh, right," she said mockingly, as the waiter placed their cups of cappuccino on the table. "Almost forgot about that. Remind me what they are."

"For one thing, I don't take money under false pretenses," he said.

"Does that depend on how much money?"

He shifted in his chair. "Seriously, Lindsey. That's not the issue. I know you have plenty of dough. I'm just not sure success is possible in this case, and I don't want to mislead you by suggesting otherwise."

"I can't believe you're playing the honesty card, Marty," she said, shaking her head. "It's not your strong suit."

Marty held up an index finger and picked up his phone. "I take it you haven't seen the video."

"What are you talking about?" she asked.

Marty touched a few keys, pulled up Missy's TikTok video, and handed it over to Lindsey.

Sensing disaster, Lindsey inhaled deeply before looking at the screen. She punched the play button and on came Missy, gyrating, twitching, and talking about her climatosis. "Oh, my Lord." As Lindsey watched, she sank into her chair with dismay. "Is she bragging about this twitchy thing?"

Marty sipped his cappuccino and dabbed the foam on his lip with a napkin. "It sure looks that way."

Lindsey splayed her fingers across her forehead. "She makes it sound like a badge of honor."

"That's exactly what it is. What could be more virtuous than showing the world you believe so much in climate change that it's making you sick?" Marty said. "Missy is the climateers' Joan of Arc, a martyr to the cause."

Lindsey pointed to the screen "What do all these numbers mean on the side?"

Marty glanced at his phone. "Missy and her climatosis have gone viral. She's a global phenomenon. People have begun posting videos of their own twitching. Apparently, there's a whole lot of shakin' goin' on out there."

Lindsey was dismayed. "Is this the power of social media or the power of suggestion?"

"Both, I imagine," Marty said. "And Missy is out there, as we used to say in the newspaper business, with her tits above the fold."

Lindsey anxiously looked at her watch, remembered her next appointment, and shook her head.

Marty was relieved he could avoid rejecting Lindsey's offer. "You have to go?" he asked hopefully.

"I've got a meeting at ten. But I'm not leaving until we get this settled." She held out her hand. "Give me that check," she demanded, wiggling her fingers.

Marty handed it over, and Lindsey laid it on the table next to her cup. She reached into her handbag, pulled out a pen, and wrote a number, then handed the check back to Marty.

Marty's eyes went wide. "That's a lot of money, even for you. But especially for me."

"I'll double it if you extricate her from this climate cult," she said.

"Cult?" Marty repeated. "That might be an overstatement."

"How else would you describe it?" Lindsey asked, exasperated. She pointed to the phone. "Look at that ridiculous video. It's like something out of Jonestown. Missy and her friends drank the Kool-Aid, and now they're climate zombies, mouthing the same explanation for every weird weather event as the Planetistas. If it rains hard, it's a climate problem. If it doesn't rain, it's a climate problem. Whether it snows too much or too little, it doesn't matter. It's a climate problem either way. Too hot? Too cold? Take your pick. And if a town floods and homes are lost, it's never because developers had built houses in a flood plain. It's because of climate change. So are wildfires. They're never the result of poor forest manage-ment or badly maintained power lines or someone carelessly tossing a cigarette butt. Just look at the news, Marty. It's always a climate problem—evidence that we're heading down a slippery slope toward oblivion. It's a theory that's as un-provable as it is irrefutable, but here we are. Casting doubt, or sorting through the difficult questions, doesn't attract many clicks."

Marty studied her. "Are you saying the climate isn't changing?"

Lindsey looked around at the other tables nearby to see if anyone could hear. "Of course, it's changing!" she said, between clenched teeth. "It always has, and it always will. But they act like severe weather was invented twenty years ago. Did nobody ever see *The Wizard of Oz?*" She took a sip from her cup. "You know, I take this stuff very seriously, because I have to. I bring in people all the time to educate our leadership team about climate change. We gather every month in the board-room to hear from scientists from MIT, and Caltech, and Harvard, as well as our own research team. It's critical for our business to know what's going on out there and plan accordingly. We can't function without some intel on this issue." She stabbed the tabletop with her finger. "But here's the problem, based on what these people are telling us privately: we don't know what's going on, exactly. There are too many variables we don't understand, can't measure, and can't compute."

Marty figured Lindsey was far more educated on the issue than he was. "What does your gut tell you?" he asked.

"Our working theory is that the world is warming slowly and that human activity is a contributing factor. We just don't know how much. But nothing that we're seeing—and I'm telling you, we're turning over every rock—justifies the current hysteria. So when I see my own daughter talking about climate change as if she knows exactly what's going on and exactly why it's happening, I want to scream."

Marty sucked in his breath. "I get that."

Lindsey continued. "But here's the thing, Marty. I don't blame her."

That took Marty by surprise. "No?"

"I think she's a victim in this. There's so much pressure on our young people to toe the line of this ideology. I can't imagine what it's like for Missy. She's a symbol of the evil empire. Luring her over to the other side is quite a prize." She shook her head in dismay. "Do you remember studying the Cold War back in school? How it was a huge victory for the West when Stalin's daughter defected? These people selling windmills in our backyards and ten-foot-tall walls along the Hudson River see Missy the same way: as a trophy. They won't care one bit about her or her well-being. But they'll be glad to use her as a celebrity spokesmodel. I can see it coming now."

Marty sighed. What the hell was he supposed to do about it?

Lindsey reached a hand across the table and grasped his hand. "That's why I need your help, Marty."

Marty was leaning against his best judgment. He wanted to say, "No. This is hopeless," but he couldn't. The lovely woman sitting across from him with money, power, and every possible advantage in the world was feeling in some ways as vulnerable as the street beggars who ambled past. Yet she sounded more desperate. He studied the check, which would end any financial concerns he may have for the rest of his life. And it would have to, because there was a good chance he would be unemployable if he were identified with this fight. No company would ever hire him again.

"As much as it's about Crowe Power, Marty, it's even more about my daughter," Lindsey said. "The most important thing a parent can do in their life is to raise their children, right?" She gestured toward his phone. "There are the results. I've failed her."

Marty shrugged. "Obviously, I don't have a window into that. I wasn't around when she was growing up."

Lindsey sank. "Neither was I. At least, not enough." She winced at the painful thought of it. "Help me bring her back, Marty. She can do something more productive than twitching on the beach. She can help us move fusion closer to market. It may not be *the* solution, but it's possibly *a* solution."

Marty was hooked. "I'll do what I can," he said.

Lindsey's driver, standing nearby, signaled to her and pointed to his watch. She blotted her lips with a linen napkin and stood up. "Thank you," she said. "Please keep me posted. We don't have much time."

12. LEAVING, ON A JET PLANE

As Crowe Bird II hit thirty thousand feet, Missy touched the controls to put her seat in full recline. She pulled the shades on the windows, laid her head back on the headrest, and closed her eyes. With a new day and a relatively clear head, there was much for her to think about as she headed home.

First up was whether she should give in to her mother's totally unreasonable demand that she should show up for work. It reminded her of the ridiculous confrontation prompted by Mother's insistence, when Missy turned twelve, that she still needed to make her bed. Why that made any sense when there were plenty of housekeepers on the payroll escaped Missy, but it led to a protracted test of wills in which Missy ultimately prevailed. It helped that she had the tie-breaking support of her father, who never did anything around the house. Mother said chores built good habits, but for what purpose? To this day, Missy had no clue.

What Missy wouldn't—and couldn't—tell her mother was that her one and only day at the Crowe Power office had been deeply unsettling. Sitting in on her first meeting of the CroFusion leadership team, Missy was lost, if not completely unprepared to discuss anything regarding fusion, or even the basics of the power business. For some reason, she assumed she could sail through meetings as a benevolent family icon without having to participate. All she would have to do was bless decisions here and there with a beatific nod of her imperial head. She hadn't anticipated that as a Crowe with a fancy title, she was expected to offer more than the same name as the company founder. She had to actually know something.

Privately, she had to admit the conversation was overwhelming, if not terrifying. Lasers? Superheated plasma? Tying into the grid? Tokamak? She couldn't even spell it! *What the hell were they talking about?* Maybe this is why her father skipped out of work so often—he didn't have a clue, either. And maybe that's why her brother Chase opted to work on the other side of the world at the Crowe power plant in Tahiti rather than grind it out under the spotlight in New York. As the saying goes, better to keep quiet and let them think you're an idiot than to speak up and remove all doubt. The bitter lesson was that heckling energy companies from the outside while marching around with a sign and a bullhorn was a hell of a lot easier than working from the inside.

Missy had majored in Women's, Gender, and Sexuality Studies at Yale, taking classes in transnational feminist practices, queer aesthetics, AIDS health policies, and gender and sexuality in early education. Finding ways to somehow apply her study of the politicization of the vagina to the challenges of commercializing nuclear fusion was, to put it mildly, a bit of a stretch. Nobody in the CroFusion leadership meeting mentioned anything about "Food, Sexuality, and the Lesbian Community." Maybe this climatosis thing wasn't so bad. It gave her a possible out—and a way to contribute to the larger cause of green energy without participating in its actual development. By showing the devastating impacts of climate change that were here and now, she could be a catalyst for change. Wasn't that enough? What more did they want from her?

As Gina, Britney, and Peach enjoyed breakfasts at the table behind her in the middle of the cabin, Blair walked to the front and took the seat across from Missy. Blair leaned forward and tapped Missy on the knee. Missy twitched, as was her recent custom, then opened her eyes.

"I have to tell you something, Missy," Blair said.

Missy eyed her suspiciously. "What?"

"I'm out."

Missy sat up with a start. "Out of what?"

"This… whatever thing it is you're doing. Climatosis. Twitching. Videos. It's spiraling out of control, and I just can't get worked up about it like you are," Blair said. "Fact is, I'm busy with my day job at my dad's business. I can kind of see where all this climate stuff is all going, and I just can't give it the time or the energy."

"Just like that," Missy spat in disgust.

"I'm sorry," Blair said. "I know it's important to you."

Missy nodded and looked at Blair with hooded eyes. "It should be important to you, too. What's more consequential than stopping the destruction of the planet?"

"I'll admit, my concerns probably seem pedestrian by comparison, and maybe even a little boring to you," Blair said. "But this is my reality. My commute to the city is taking way too much time out of my day and it's wearing me out. I have to find an apartment closer to work. And I need to create a deck at work this week to present to the corporate strategy team."

"A deck? What's that?"

"A PowerPoint presentation."

Missy nodded uncertainly. "Oh. Right. Of course." Missy had at least heard of PowerPoint. "What's the presentation about?"

"You really want to know?"

Missy spread her hands out. "If you think it's more important than saving the planet."

"It is to me," Blair said. "I'm supposed to help identify new revenue streams for the company. I also have to talk about the integration of our strategic partners, ways to stimulate demand for our products, what it would take to scale, and how much capital we need through the end of next year."

Missy looked genuinely puzzled. "You may as well be speaking in Urdu." She peered at Blair. "How do you know all that stuff?"

"It's what I studied at school," Blair said with a shrug. "Applied mathematics. Economics. Statistics. Data science. Of course, it helped to study physics, too, since the development of our products requires understanding the basics of materials science and energy. Interestingly, one of the areas we're targeting for growth is fusion."

Missy sat up a bit. "Really?"

"Yeah," Blair said. "We think it's worth a bet."

Missy shook her head in wonder. She had no idea all those classes Blair mentioned were worth the bother. "Huh," she mumbled. "I always wondered why you were never around. I guess you were going to class."

"Or the library," Blair said.

"So… you were studying," Missy said, as if she had discovered a ninth planet.

Blair squinted. "I kinda thought that was the point."

Not for me, Missy mused. She was learning more about Blair than she'd ever known before. Why, she wondered, hadn't she asked her friend more questions? "Could you at least come to our meeting with Dr. Iz today?"

Blair sighed. "I suppose so," she said. "Then I have to go to work." She hesitated, then added, "And, as your friend, I have to tell you: I think you should go to work, too."

Missy flashed with anger, before realizing Blair meant well. "I know," Missy allowed. "It's just… not now. I need—" She paused. What did she need? She shook her head. "I need to get my shit together."

Blair offered her hooked little finger as a pinkie promise, and they interlocked. "Best idea I've heard in a while."

13. THE SHEPHERD AND HER FLOCK

Dr. Iz spread out a large plaid blanket on the grass in the middle of Central Park's Sheep Meadow and invited Missy and her other new patients to join her. Nearby, couples and families picnicked and sun-bathed, kicked soccer balls and threw frisbees, or played with their dogs. Dr. Iz liked the prominent positioning for her confab, since the mid-afternoon sun was suitably hot for a discussion of climate change, and the visibility of Missy and her twitching friends could generate curiosity from prospective clients. If only she could hang a shingle on one of those trees...

Dr. Iz walked around the perimeter of the blanket, introducing herself to everyone and provoking a round of nervous twitching. She couldn't help noticing that groups of young people sitting nearby were looking their way, pointing, and talking excitedly among themselves. The TikTok video was trending. *Had they seen it?* Dr. Iz wondered.

After getting settled on the blanket, Dr. Iz called her therapy session to order. She suggested they go around the circle and each tell a little bit about themselves. "I'm already acquainted with Missy," she said. "Gina, why don't we start with you."

Gina explained that she had grown up in Great Neck, a wealthy town on the North Shore of Long Island. She had excelled in its highly rated public schools and won admission to Yale. She withdrew from school for a year after her father, a waste management executive facing indictment for money laundering, was gunned down in a reputed mob hit at a Manhattan steakhouse. Not long afterward, she was diagnosed with attention deficit hyperactivity disorder. She suffered from a long list of anxieties and insecurities, but climate change was definitely in her Top Ten.

"Do you take drugs?" Dr. Iz asked.

Gina looked up at the sky. "Oh, just a little weed. Wine, for sure. Psylocibin mushrooms. Maybe LSD—"

Dr. Iz interrupted. "I'm asking about medications for ADHD. Has anything been prescribed for you?"

"Oh, right," Gina replied, with a blush. "I take Adderall."

Dr. Iz cringed. "You may want to watch mixing all those things together, Gina. It could have adverse effects for you."

Gina twitched, sending her left arm flying. "Yeah, I've heard that," she said. "Probably need to do a little better on that front." She chuckled nervously.

Dr. Iz turned to Britney. She related that she had grown up in the notoriously affluent community of Greenwich, Connecticut, where her father had spent a career in politics, working his way up from humble city manager to state representative, then to Congress, and finally, the U.S. Senate. His lifetime in public service had made him inexplicably wealthy, and the family put Britney through boarding school and an Ivy League college without financial assistance. With Senator Hogan leading the way on legislation that poured nearly a trillion dollars into the coffers of corporations selling a range of climate "solutions," Britney was miraculously awash in job offers from green, greenish, and shamelessly greenwashing companies profiting from federal subsidies. She just hadn't decided yet which shade of green she preferred.

"I mean, it's crazy what's going on out there. Some of these companies say you have to go to the office once a week, whether you want to or not," Britney said, as her right arm shot away from her side at the thought of what was obviously oppressive servitude. "It's like we're all still laboring in the coal mines."

"Right, right," Dr. Iz said, sympathetically. "I can see why that could be an impediment. How about you, Peach. I've certainly heard your name before."

Peach yawned. "Yeah, well," she allowed. "I get that a lot. It's basically because I grew up in the public eye. My mom? Lilith Anne Buckingham? She's pretty famous from her movies back in the day. And my birth father, Yikes, was famous, too, probably for the wrong reasons. He was out celebrating the day I was born at an all-night party. He was overexcited and had an accidental drug overdose. I guess he thought he was just doing coke and heroin, but somebody put some other stuff in. There was a criminal investigation and everything. But nobody was ever charged. It was all a big mess."

"So sorry," Dr. Iz said sympathetically. "Did you have any other father figures in your home life after he passed away?"

"Lots," Peach replied. "Do you ever see Page Six in the *New York Post* or TMZ?"

"Sometimes."

"They're all mentioned in there. I use apps to see what they're up to."

Finally, Dr. Iz turned to Blair, who shook her head when Dr. Iz asked about her background.

"My story's pretty boring by comparison," Blair said. "I spent the first few years of my life in Queens, where my parents started a company making components and prototypes for heavy industry. They did okay financially, and we moved to the city when I was in third grade. I have to admit, they made things pretty easy for me. But they also insisted on accountability. For instance, they paid all my expenses through school, but I had to meet certain grade standards every semester or the support would go away."

"Oh my God!" Gina said. "That's abuse."

"Not really," Blair replied. "I got my undergraduate degree and my MBA in four years."

Missy interjected. "You have a masters?"

Blair stared at her. "Honestly, Missy. What did you think I was doing?"

Missy shrugged. "I don't know," she said, blankly.

Dr. Iz looked at Blair curiously. "I haven't noticed you twitching. Do you believe you have climatosis?"

"No," Blair said, flatly. "Not at all."

"Pardon me for being so blunt," Dr. Iz said, "but why are you here?"

"Basically, because Missy asked me," Blair replied. "I'm here for support, is all. I don't have the twitch and I'm not particularly worried about climate change."

Dr. Iz looked baffled. "Why not?"

"I guess because we seem to be adapting to whatever changes are going on," Blair said. "I mean, look around you. Everyone seems to be having fun on a nice day in the park."

"Except us!" Gina wailed.

Dr. Iz patted Gina's knee. "That's because you understand what's really going on."

"Maybe so. Maybe not," Blair interjected. "I doubt any of us on this blanket understand the forces out there that are far beyond our control."

Dr. Iz bore in on Blair. This heresy was not welcome. "Like what?" Dr. Iz demanded to know.

Blair looked around at her friends, who suddenly appeared worried that she might get all science-y. This, she knew, was not going to be popular with her pals, but she plunged ahead anyway. "I've studied this because it's part of my job. But I don't think we have a good enough grasp of things to make accurate predictions on how our climate is changing. Most of the predictions they've made so far have been wrong."

Blair's friends looked pained, but Dr. Iz was intrigued. "What is it you think we don't get, Blair?"

Blair squinted. "Do you really want to get into this?"

Missy, Peach, Gina, and Britney all looked to each other and nodded. Dr. Iz decided to call Blair's bluff. "You seem to suggest you know more than we do."

"Alright," Blair said. "I don't think anyone here has an understanding of geological cycles. Or the fact that we've had many periods of warming and cooling over millions of years. I'm not sure we understand clouds, or how to measure their influence on climate. What about solar activity? And other greenhouse gases besides CO_2? Some argue we have too much carbon dioxide; others argue we're getting dangerously low, considering how important it is to vegetation. I doubt anyone here understands the cooling effect caused by aerosols."

"Aerosols?" Dr. Iz asked.

"She's talking about hair spray," Gina said, confidently.

"Not exactly," Blair said. "These aerosols come from burning coal and volcanic eruptions. One of the weird things about getting cleaner air over the past fifty years is that it lets in more sunlight, and more warmth." She noted the befuddlement on her friends' faces as they processed that news. "You see, I don't have the answers. I just have tons of questions." She looked around the blanket. "But, listen, I get it. I'm the odd one out here. I should probably shut up about it and not rock the boat. Maybe I'm not such good support after all."

Blair sat back and looked at her friends, who were twitching violently. A heretic! Right in their midst! They all knew that Blair often stood apart from the group with her opinions, but this treachery was beyond the pale. How did she get to be so smart? Why did she have to make it so complicated when the problem seemed so simple an hour ago? They looked to Missy, Blair's closest friend in the group, to address this breach of acceptable thought. Missy, unsuccessfully trying to suppress her own twitching, understood the signals. This transgression was on her to address. She stood up, arms flailing.

"Blair, can we have a word?" she said in a way that was more of a command than a question.

Blair sighed, stood up, and followed Missy away from the blanket. Finally, along a fence near a London planetree, Missy took a deep breath to calm herself and turned to face Blair.

"Do you really have to get in everyone's face, Blair?"

Blair protested. "I wasn't trying to get in anyone's face. And I'm not trying to be a jerk. I'm just saying I have questions. That's all."

"We don't need any more questions," Missy said. "We need answers."

"It sounds like you already have them," Blair retorted.

"Yes, as a matter of fact, we do," Missy said. "It's a climate crisis. That's all we need to know." She motioned toward the group. "Now you have them freaking out even more."

"I know and I'm sorry," Blair said. "They've all identified a socially acceptable reason for their anxiety. 'See! It's not my family, or my upbringing, or my job, or my shitty boyfriend. It's climate change! I'm twitchy because I care so much about the planet!' Oh, please, Missy. I just don't buy it. The carbon footprint of this group is bigger than a village in Denmark. If they want to do something, they could start in their own backyards—all twenty of the backyards they have between them."

Missy seethed. "I suppose you think I should do that, too."

Blair shrugged. "That's your call. It doesn't matter to me one way or the other."

Missy raised her chin and glared at Blair. "I think you should just go."

Blair stared hard at her. "I didn't want to come in the first place. You insisted."

Blair marched back, snatched her bag, and flashed a defiant glance at Missy and the other women, who avoided eye contact. "You'll have to excuse me. I'm getting twitchy about missing work."

As Blair stalked off, Missy sat down again on the blanket and said, "Apologies. I don't know what got into her. That was totally uncalled for."

"It's quite alright," Dr. Iz said. "Sometimes, a little knowledge is a dangerous thing."

"Isn't that the truth!" Gina said.

"She's always been a know-it-all," huffed Britney. "As if she knows… whatever."

Dr. Iz sighed. "Let's move on and talk about next steps, shall we?"

There was relief and agreement around the blanket.

"I selected the Sheep Meadow for our meeting place for a reason," she said. "Can anyone guess what it is?"

"I know," Gina said. "Because you think we're sheep."

Dr. Iz *tsk-tsk*ed. "No dear. Hardly." *Lemmings is more like it.* She scanned the blank faces of Britney and Peach and realized that no other answer was forthcoming. "It's because there's an important story here that's related to your anxieties about our environment. Back in 1979, when New York City was in the throes of a financial crisis," she said, sweeping her hand across the horizon, "this entire area was a total mess. The sheep that used to graze here had all moved on and the meadow became neglected and mismanaged. It was essentially one big dirt pile. But a handful of private citizens said, 'Enough wringing our hands. We can do something about this.' And they did. They raised money, began a restoration plan, and within a year, the Sheep Meadow was restored into the beautiful green space you see today. The Central Park Conservancy was born. Bit by bit, they reclaimed and revitalized the entire park."

Dr. Iz looked at their puzzled faces and realized they were not connecting the dots. She continued, "This, to me, is an example of what you can do, too."

Gina winced. "Excuse me, but I don't get it. What do you want us to do? Mow the grass?"

Dr. Iz shook her head. "No, no, no. I'm saying that this park was a disaster then, just like the climate is a disaster now. Right? So you can either lament that things are looking bleak. Or, like the people who banded together to save Central Park, you can say: 'You know what? We're going to make a positive contribution to our planet.'"

Gina grudgingly nodded. "Like how?"

Dr. Iz continued, "I saw your video on TikTok and I must say, I was mightily impressed. What a wonderful way to give a sense of purpose to your feelings about our world, and, in the process, find a cure for all its terrible ills. Surely, there are others out there feeling much the same as you are now. Maybe they're even twitching alone, in desperate isolation. Twitching is upsetting, I know. But it is not necessarily a bad thing. This may sound like a stretch to you, but to me, I believe it's a gift. We're lucky to have you. You're pointing out the error of our ways to all humankind—hopefully before it's too late to turn back."

That bit of pandering brought the desired result: the four remaining ladies looked quite pleased with themselves. Still, Britney lamented, "We only have, like, five more years before we're totally screwed."

Dr. Iz reached out and patted Britney's arm. "Then we need to get busy! All you have to do is look at the reaction to your video on TikTok to know there are lots of people out there who feel exactly as you do. They need to be reassured that their fears are real, and that we're all in this together. Does that make sense?"

There was nodding around the blanket. Dr. Iz continued, "You've heard of the TV show, *Scuttlebutt Live*?"

"Of course," Peach said. "My mother's been on there, like, a million times."

"Then you know it's the highest-rated morning talk show in the country," Dr. Iz said. "I spoke with a producer from the program last night who she said they'd love to have you on as soon as possible."

With that, Missy's right arm jerked in a spasm, beginning a chain reaction of twitching from Gina, Britney, and Peach. Dr. Iz nearly burst out laughing. These might be the most easily triggered people she'd ever encountered.

Missy was struck by an unwelcome thought. A drug induced TikTok video made after midnight was one thing. But now, in the hot midday sunlight of the Sheep Meadow, making a commitment to double down publicly on climatosis made her strangely uncomfortable. Was that really a good idea? Where was this going, exactly? "I don't know," Missy said uneasily.

"I understand your hesitation, Missy," Dr. Iz said. "It takes a lot of courage and a good degree of selflessness. But sharing your story with an audience of millions more people could be a great service to humanity. Think how many people out there are suffering just like you but have no idea why. They feel alone, and helpless. Just knowing there are others out there like them would give them hope."

Missy asked, tentatively, "Would you go on with us?"

Dr. Iz nearly laughed. As if she'd miss a mass solicitation for patients! "Of course," she purred.

Missy looked to Gina, Britney, and Peach and they all appeared agreeable. "Well," Peach said. "If it helps the real people out there in places like—" She paused, thinking. "Wherever real people live, I think we have no choice. We have to do it."

All eyes turned to Missy. She took a deep breath and tried to warm to the idea. "Okay, I guess."

"Excellent," Dr. Iz said. "Rest assured, I'll be with you every step of the way." *After all, I must take care of my sheep.*

14. LIVE FROM NEW YORK

It was clear from the moment the Twitcheratti arrived at the studio in Times Square for *Scuttlebutt Live* that their social media postings had generated interest far and wide. Peering in through the studio windows on Broadway near the Climate Countdown Clock was a gaggle of purportedly real people from across the nation, many of whom carried signs in anticipation of catching a glimpse of the newest stars of social media. Missy and her pals were trending, and the trend was ever upward.

"BEST TWITCHES FROM OHIO" said one placard with red-and-silver lettering and a crude drawing of a buckeye nut.

"WINONA MINNESOTA LOVES CHICKS WITH TICS," said another.

As Missy, Gina, Britney, and Peach followed Dr. Iz onto the *Scuttlebutt* set, fans outside welcomed them with a thunderous roar as the studio audience rose to its feet to offer applause and encouragement. The suddenly fab four, nervous from the attention but pleasantly surprised by the enthusiasm, flung their arms about in waves or, possibly, twitches. Each member of the group took turns saying hello to host Scuttlebutt—aka Scarlett Tuttle Butters—before taking their seats in tall director's chairs on the stage.

"Well, well, *well!*" enthused Scuttlebutt, a rotund woman in a brightly colored silk tunic, with wide flowing pants, and a mop of curly red hair. "What a welcome! Clearly, you've touched a twitchy nerve out there."

Missy blinked hard. "Wow," she said, shaking her head in wonder. "I don't know what to say."

Scuttlebutt introduced each of the ladies by name to the audience before turning to Dr. Iz.

"Alright. Let's start with a *very* familiar face—at least to longtime fans of our show—the famous Dr. Iz," Scuttlebutt said, eliciting more applause and a chant of "*Izz-ee, Izz-ee, Izz-ee.*" As the chant died down, Scuttlebutt said. "Well… You may have been gone, but clearly, you weren't forgotten."

Dr. Iz smiled and acknowledged the audience with a wave.

Scuttlebutt continued. "Dr. Iz, you were an extremely public figure for so long with books, TV, and radio. But you've been out of the spotlight for some time. I'm sure the first question on everyone's mind is: where have you been?"

Dr. Iz smiled demurely and fluttered her eyes behind her famously oversized glasses. "I've been working with so many wonderful patients here in the city," she contended. "It's been a quieter life, but a rewarding one. It's given me a chance to connect with some incredible, courageous people like Missy, Gina, Britney, and Peach." More applause followed.

"You're calling their disorder 'climatosis,'" Scuttlebutt said. "What does that mean, exactly?"

"It's very much like it sounds—an extreme anxiety triggered by the fear of climate change," Dr. Iz explained in her deeply serious therapist tone. "This fear manifests itself in physical reactions, such as uncontrollable twitching. The phenomenon is not new. We've seen evidence of similar afflictions before, such as the choreomania craze of the Middle Ages, when people fearing plagues and floods couldn't stop dancing."

"That sounds like a party—certainly more fun than twitching," Scuttlebutt said, to laughter from the crowd.

"Not really," Dr. Iz said. "They danced until they collapsed. Some of them broke ribs. Others died." A murmur went through the crowd. *"Oooh..."*

"I stand corrected," Scuttlebutt said. She turned her gaze to Missy. "Now, Missy, I understand you were stricken first. Tell us about it."

Missy nodded. "Well, it started about a month ago. I was brushing my teeth and getting ready to go to work when I got this sudden twitch, and my toothbrush went flying right into the bidet. Then I got another twitch, and another after that. Since then, I've never known when it would pop up again." She shook her head. "The sad part is that it's so disabling. I should be working, but climate change has me overwhelmed with worry for the planet." The studio's "applause" sign lit up again, and the audience dutifully obliged. *Worry... Planet... Yes!*

"That is so noble," Scuttlebutt said flatly. "But let me understand something. Your family made an enormous fortune off the very same fossil fuels cited by many experts as a key driver of our climate crisis. Does that bother you at all?'"

"Uh, yeah. Quite a lot, actually." Missy shuddered visibly. "I'm embarrassed, of course. I think maybe that's one reason climatosis hit me so hard. I'd love to go back in time and grab some of my ancestors by the lapels, or suspenders, or whatever they wore, and shake them. 'What were you thinking?'"

As the crowd roared its approval, Scuttlebutt reached out and patted Missy's knee. "That is so, so, so sensible. On behalf of Mother Earth, thank you." She then turned to the audience. "I have to advise everybody out there that these brave young ladies are not isolated cases. They're more like the canaries in the coal mine."

Gina, alarmed, blurted out, "Didn't they die?"

Scuttlebutt nodded. "Not always, dear. Sometimes they proved that everything was okay," she said calmly. "Now. Dr. Iz, you've said in the news that climatosis is contagious. And it's not necessary to be in the same room to catch it from someone else. Apparently, you can get it through Tiktok, Instagram, and DingDong." She looked offstage to a producer. "Let's show everyone our screen."

Up on a giant monitor at the side of the stage was a huge throng of people in Washington Square in San Francisco. What used to be a park for morning tai chi and other forms of exercise had been given over to otherwise healthy young people twitching and shaking, along with the city's drug addicts getting their morning fix. "They're twitching in the Golden State!" Scuttlebutt said.

The screen switched to a gathering on Boston Common, where another large group of people were flinging their arms about and jerking their heads around as they listened to a speaker standing in front of a banner that read:

THE CLIMATE CATASTROPHE IS COMING!
Stop it before it's too late!

Scuttlebutt looked at the screen, then at an index card. "There's more, too. We understand they're twitching in Tokyo and shaking in Shanghai. We have reports from Berlin, London, and Paris of more of the same." She looked up at her guests. "How does that make you feel?"

Missy looked to the others to speak up. "Kinda terrible, actually," Gina said. "I'm sorry that so many people are freaking out. But we, like, totally get it."

Britney flung her left arm out, then interrupted. "It's good in a way, too, because maybe we can all get together and finally do something about climate change."

The audience erupted in hearty applause.

"Like what?" Scuttlebutt asked.

"Well," Britney said, "like... um..." She looked to the others, who were in full twitch-mode and avoiding eye contact.

Scuttlebutt stood up and took a few steps toward her guests. "Let me put it this way. Should people glue themselves to buildings? Sit in traffic and prevent other people from getting to work? Throw Jell-O at the *Mona Lisa*?"

"I don't think they should throw Jell-O," Peach said. "It doesn't stick and kinda slides off. But tapioca pudding works well."

"And you think that's appropriate behavior?"

Britney piped up. "Under the circumstances, yes. Of course."

"We have to let the world know how we feel," Peach added. "I mean, there's a right to free speech, you know."

Scuttlebutt nodded, albeit skeptically. "So you would rank food-tossing as a First Amendment issue?"

Peach twitched. "Sure, as long as it's not cooked on a gas stove."

As Dr. Iz watched this slow-moving train veer off the rails, she quickly pulled the emergency brake. "You know, Scuttlebutt, the important thing to recognize here is that a lot of people are acting out their frustrations with an economic system that has trashed the planet."

"That's right," Peach added. "Capitalism did this."

Dr. Iz continued. "Until we fix that, I'm afraid we're not going to fix our planet."

"So true," Missy said. "It's the system we need to change."

Scuttlebutt put a finger to her chin. "To what exactly?"

Missy, Britney, Gina, and Peach exchanged glances and shrugs.

"Something else!" Britney declared.

With that, the studio audience stood as one and cheered. Shouts of "bravo!" and "yes!" filled the air, while Missy, Gina, Britney, and Peach watched the reaction with twitchy pleasure.

"Okay. There you have it. Their roadmap to the future," Scuttlebutt shouted over sustained applause. "Ladies: thank you! Good luck working out the kinks." Turning back to the cameras, she said, "Coming up after the break: what to do with that moldy cheese in your fridge. We've got some surprising answers for you, so stay right there."

Missy and her twitchy friends exited the studio and emerged onto 46th Street to shrieks, shouts, and cheers from the people who had watched the show from the sidewalk. Dr. Iz led them to a waiting black SUV, but a teenage girl stopped Missy before she could get in and asked for her autograph in a notebook. "Oh my gosh! I *love* you!" she said. "You're my idol!" Missy hurriedly took her pen in hand, then, seized by a twitch, sent it flying into the street. "Hey, that's my pen!" the girl shouted.

"Yeah, well. Get another one," Missy said. She bolted into the back of the SUV and slammed the door without looking back. *Wow,* she thought. *Now I feel like a celebrity!*

***

Marty's mouth was agape as he turned off the TV. *What the hell was that?*

As his phone rang on the coffee table, he didn't need to see the name to know who was calling. He answered with trepidation, thinking he might be fired from this gig before he even started.

Lindsey asked, "Did you see that shitshow?"

"I had to tear myself away from *Dr. Quinn, Medicine Woman,* but yes, sadly. Missy's taking her magical misery tour nationwide."

Lindsey sighed. "Please tell me nobody watches that show."

"If it makes you feel better, okay," Marty said. "It's only two million people, give or take. Three million, tops. Maybe more than that with streaming, but that hardly counts."

"Seriously?"

Marty had to admit, "What can I tell you? It's the number-one talk show in the morning."

"Really? I thought it was that other show with the nasty old bags."

"That doesn't narrow it down," Marty said.

Lindsey sighed. "This is getting worse by the minute. When are you going to talk to her?"

"I'm not sure," he said. "She's not returning my calls, or my texts."

There was a pause on the line. "I'll have Winnie suspend the payouts from her trust fund," Lindsey said. "That should get her attention."

15. THE VERDICT IS IN

President Dewey Fenwick snored softly in a rocking chair near the fireplace in the Oval Office, which was on despite the summer heat to warm his porous old bones. On a sofa nearby, the noted pollster Harrison Chambers peered through his reading glasses at the computer in his lap while the gathering of Cabinet officials from the Departments of Energy, State, and Health and Human Services eagerly awaited the results of his overnight survey.

"Bottom line: climatosis is a winner," Harrison declared.

Muted applause, smiles, and a quiet cheer of *"Yes!"* greeted the news.

"Awareness of climatosis is very high across the country—80 percent plus," Harrison said, as he looked up from his laptop. "The scores aren't as clear on what people think the President should do about it, but there's growing support on the coasts for strong government intervention. In other words, they want Washington to do something."

Vigorous nods of approval followed, led by Energy Secretary Jessica Holtgren. A petite blonde cabinet official and a former governor of Maryland, Jessica was highly prized in the West Wing for her shrewd aptitude for navigating the nexus of political advantage and financial opportunity. "And what about our donors?" she asked.

"Oh, I think you'll be very pleased. Numbers are through the roof for the president to declare a national climatosis emergency," Harrison said. "They think climatosis allows you to ram home a few things on their list that Congress would never pass."

Chief of Staff Ben Bixby asked, "What are we talking about here?"

"Well, let me see," Harrison said as he consulted his computer. "They'd like to see you pump up subsidies for their pet projects, such as green power, greener cars, greenish building modifications and the big new money-maker: resiliency, which covers just about any contractor wet dream you can imagine—seawalls and fortifications and pop-up barricades and jacked-up buildings. There are billions of dollars there. But there's also strong support for climatosis lockdowns. As you know, our biggest donors loved the lockdowns we had during Covid. They'd like to see us close schools again until we get these twitchy kids straightened out."

Ben, a Beltway swamp creature of good standing, leaned in. "What about cash payments directly to people afflicted with the twitch? I could see us sending checks timed with mail-in ballots."

Jessica clapped her hands. "Brilliant! We'll call it Climate Cash."

"Love it!" Ben ejaculated. "Sounds like a scratch-off lottery game."

Harrison checked his computer again. "I had a hunch you might go there. I polled payouts and it looks like the respondents were split down the middle. About half the people love it. The other half hate it."

Jessica scoffed, "You mean the half who have to pay hate it."

Harrison smiled. "Precisely."

"Well, sorry-not-sorry, you know?" Jessica snapped. "They can fuck off."

There were nods and smiles all around. "Where's their public spirit?" Ben muttered. He looked to the newly appointed Dr. Barclay Prince, the meticulous Secretary of Health and Human Services, and former head of an Atlanta hospital system, wearing a crisp three-piece suit. "Barclay, how bad are things out there right now? Would you say climatosis has reached the point of a public health crisis?"

Barclay nodded. "Oh, I think quite clearly it has," he said. "So many people were twitching on the subway in New York this morning that I'm told it started dozens of fistfights. They had to close the system to quiet things down. There's even talk of bringing in the National Guard."

"Excellent!" Jessica said. "Can we get them to march down Fifth Avenue? That would show how scary this is."

Ben wrote a note to himself. "I'll ask the governor."

Barclay continued. "We also have reports that absenteeism at work is the highest it's been since the start of the last pandemic. And we're starting to see an escalation of symptoms. In addition to twitching and shaking, we have unconfirmed reports of groups of young people having fits of uncontrollable laughing or crying."

The sleeping president fidgeted in his chair and mumbled what was either incomprehensible gibberish or a line from his last speech. Jessica put an index finger to her lips, warning the assembly to be quiet for a moment. Suddenly, the president's entire body twitched, and he shouted, "Step back, Jack! Or *I'll kick your ass!*" Then his head fell back on the chair and he resumed his slumber.

Jessica looked at Barclay, who sat up, alarmed.

"He talks in his sleep from time to time," she assured him. "Nothing to worry about."

"Unless he's holding the nuclear suitcase, of course," Ben said with a chuckle. "Don't want a bad dream then! It's bye-bye-bye, bye-bye Iran!" Ben turned to the patrician Secretary of State, Alexander Lewis. "Speaking of which Alex, how are other countries handling climatosis?"

Alex, a Boston brahmin whose constant Botox injections made him look and talk like a statue on the National Mall, said, "Everyone's acting true to form. Chairman Xi has ordered three-week quarantines for the families of anyone seen with a twitch. Iran's Supreme Leader has proclaimed the twitch the work of Israel's Mossad and the CIA, and declared he would chop off the arms of anyone twitching in public. France has non-stop protests, as usual, but it's hard to tell whether they're twitching, protesting gas prices, or just generally pissed off. And our friend Putin was mocking the twitch on Russian TV this morning with an exaggerated twitch of his own."

"Is that an idea?" Jessica mused.

"What?" Ben asked.

Jessica stood and walked toward the fireplace, arms folded across her chest. Standing next to the sleepy President, she nodded in his direction. "What if we reported that he had climatosis? How do you think that would go over?"

Ben said, "It could be a connection to the younger voters. You know, 'he's one of us.'"

Harrison regarded the snoozing Commander-in-Chief. "I don't think any of those young folks will mistake him for Gen Z."

"How about Gen Zzzs?" Jessica said.

"I'll poll it," Harrison declared over laughter in the room. "Discreetly, of course."

Barclay winced. "I'm not so sure that is a sound idea. Wouldn't that suggest he's feeble? Climatosis is not a condition that typically affects healthy adults over thirty. Many people could see that as a weakness. And taking into account his considerable co-morbidities, people may fear it would kill him."

Jessica turned to Ben. "What about this? You could plant a story that says a pre-existing condition of climatosis is the reason for his earlier pratfalls. The dropped ice cream cone at Martha's Vineyard. The triple somersaults down the stairs of Air Force One. Smacking that old man in the chops at the rally last week. 'See, folks? It wasn't his fault. The twitch made him do it.'"

Harrison sighed. "Let me run the numbers. I'll have a recommendation for you by tomorrow."

Barclay raised a hand, somewhat sheepishly. All eyes turned in his direction. "I have a thought here that may be a little out of step, but it's why I came to Washington in the first place, so let me try it out," he said. Leaning forward earnestly, he suggested, "Given that the country is evenly divided, what if we staked out a position in the center? We could try to unify the nation behind the idea of defeating climatosis together."

Jessica laughed heartily. "To what possible purpose?" she asked.

Barclay blushed. "I don't know. I'm thinking it could avoid further polarization," he said. He looked around the room and noticed that everyone was now avoiding eye contact. He fell back into the sofa cushions. *Was it that bad of an idea?*

Ben looked at Jessica and sighed, then turned to Barclay. "That's certainly a nice thought, Barclay. And you are a nice man for saying it. But nice thoughts are not really what we're about here. Polarization is our friend. Why would we compromise when we could use this issue to draw a hard line around our enemies? Personally, I would like to see the President take a tough stand. 'This side is right. That side is wrong. Anyone who's not sympathetic to climatosis is extreme. They're dangerous. They're basically criminals and lunatics.' I realize you're new to the capital, Barclay, but I'm sure you'll catch on soon enough.'"

Barclay grimaced. "I understand that's how the game has been played. I'm just wondering if we might try it another way."

"Why on God's green Earth would you do that?" Jessica asked, incredulously.

Barclay spoke in a voice barely above a whisper. "Because it's in the interest of the public?"

Jessica snorted. "That's a good one, Barclay! Let's see how you feel about that in a week or two," she said. "You think the other guys would be so magnanimous if they had a big fat issue like this dropped in their lap? Hardly! They'd beat us up like a rental car. That's just the way it works. If President Fenwick doesn't emerge from this pandemic as a hero, we didn't do our job." She stood over the slumbering leader of the free world and pointed. "This great leader, this incredible dynamo, must be seen as the answer to everyone's prayers."

The room quieted as everyone considered the nation's Great White-Haired Hope, who suddenly jerked again, spouted more gibberish, and resumed snoring.

Ben whispered to Barclay. "It's a really good thought," he said. "Unusual in DC, but certainly well-intended. I'll mention it to the President when he wakes up."

Barclay dolefully regarded the near-corpse. "Do you think he will wake up?"

Ben waved him off. "He's okay." He looked at his watch. "It happens every day around this time. He'll come to in time for *Celebrity Wife Swap*. You could practically set your watch to it."

As others started to gather their things, Jessica said, "One last polling question, Harrison. What did the numbers say about Missy Mayburn Crowe?"

"Oh! I'm sorry. That was very interesting," he replied.

"Tell, tell," she demanded, snapping her fingers.

"Extremely high positives, with those who like her 'concerned' or 'very concerned' about her condition. They see her as a victim, a helpless casualty of Western industrialization and our shamelessly indulgent lifestyle," he said. "She also draws extremely high negatives, with some seeing her as a spoiled child of privilege, whining about a family that is, by most accounts, a highly successful symbol of American enterprise and ingenuity. The verbatim answers from the critics include a long list of expletives, with more than a smattering of f-bombs."

"Hmm," Jessica mused. "What's the split between positive and negative?"

"About fifty-fifty," he said. "There's almost nobody in the middle. She's quite polarizing."

Ben and Jessica looked at each other and did a double high-five.

"We should invite her to the White House for a little photo op with the President," Jessica said. "Maybe create some sort of committee on climatosis. She could be on it. A young woman of her pedigree would make one hell of a trophy for Team Fenwick."

Barclay looked puzzled. "Would he go for that?"

"Of course," Jessica said matter-of-factly.

"How do you know?" Barclay asked.

Ben said, "We'll tell him it was his idea and that he just forgot."

Jessica said triumphantly, "Works every time." She turned to the famously vacuous Vice President Shrika Fugazi, who had come to the meeting late and sat at the other end of the room in wide-eyed silence throughout the conversation, petrified that someone might ask her a question. Yet, Jessica felt she couldn't ignore the most senior official in the room who was awake. "Madame Vice President? Is there anything you'd like to add before we close?"

Shrika blinked hard several times and nodded, her lips dry, her mouth agape. "Why, yes. I would like to make this point because I think it's important." She cleared her throat. "And that point is that the root cause of climatosis is climate change. And climate change, as we know all too well, is about climate," she said gravely. She leaned forward and raised an index finger to draw attention to her point. "But—and a lot of people don't get this—it's also about *change*. You hear what I'm saying? And when you put those two concepts together, climate and change, what do you get? You get climate change. So, you start by zeroing in on the problem. And that leads you to the solution, whatever that is." *Ta-dah!*

Jessica shook her head in wonder. Did anyone have any idea what Shrika was talking about? Ever? Oh well. As others in the assembly hid their eyes, Jessica drew from her vast stores of manufactured enthusiasm and said, "So well put, Madame Vice President! What can one say after words of wisdom like that? A perfect conclusion to our meeting."

16. HELLO, MY NAME IS ROBBIE

Maybe he ought to blame the scrambled eggs, or the dodgy salsa, or anything else he had ingested from the generally disgusting buffet breakfast Robbie was served at the Future of Fusion Conference at the Inter-Galactic Hotel in Midtown. Whatever it was, Robbie could barely follow the man on stage, droning on and on about advancements in plasma containment in next generation tokamaks and whatever the fuck. How was he supposed to focus on this science shit when his stomach was churning and turning like a blast furnace?

He looked up at the goateed Dr. Leonard Entwhistle, Distinguished Professor of Fusion Dynamics at Princeton University, who was talking about chart number one billion, or so. As the scientist explained why the dotted red line went up while the solid blue line went down, Robbie's eyes spun like pinwheels. He leaned over to his business partner, Harry. "You have any idea what he's talking about?"

"He says we're making progress, but there's still a long way to go," Harry said out of the side of his mouth.

"No kidding," Robbie grumbled. "Tell me something I don't know. The only question I have is, 'where's the Pepto Bismol?'" He groaned as his stomach rumbled. "I must have had a bad burrito. How long do I have to listen to this guy? He's boring the crap out of me."

"If you pick up nothing else, it helps to know the lingo," Harry whispered. "It may come in handy when we talk to investors."

Robbie grimaced. "Yeah, well. I gotta get out of here."

Harry shrugged. "Do what you gotta do. Just don't go too far. I have a guy who wants in on our deal. He's loaded and he's dying to meet you."

Who isn't dying to meet me at a conference like this? Robbie mused. *Wait till they see my statue!* Robbie got up and crab-walked down the row of people studiously watching the presentation and taking notes, and headed up the aisle toward the vestibule. There he quickly found an area of interest that stimulated his imagination: comely young conference staffers at the registration tables, smiling and wishing him a cheery good morning. He knew exactly what could make it not just a good morning, but a great morning! Maybe there was a way to get a couple of these lovelies upstairs for a little private conference. It was a hotel, after all. They had plenty of rooms…

A sleek young woman approached, wearing a tailored suit and a lovely smile. "I'm thinking you're Robbie," she said.

Robbie blushed. He was known *everywhere!* "How did you know?"

"It says so on your name badge," she replied.

Robbie looked down. "Ah, right. 'My name is.' Uh, yeah."

"Robbie Crowe, right?" she asked, brightly.

He *knew* it was more than the badge! "As a matter of fact, yes," he replied, breaking into a smile. "Do we know each other?"

"A little," she said. "Mostly, I know your daughter."

Robbie deflated like the sagging balloons at the registration table. *You stupid old fuck.* "How do you know Missy?" he asked.

"We're good friends from way back. At least, I hope we still are," she said. "Shame what's happened to her—getting climatosis and all. I know it's a struggle. If you see her, please tell her I'm still thinking of her, and I hope she gets better soon." She grasped her lapel with her own name badge and raised it. "Blair."

Robbie nodded grimly. "Right. Blair. I'll certainly tell her."

"Thanks, Mr. Crowe."

Mister Crowe? He really was over the hill, a creepy old pedo, leering at young ladies like that. Better to focus on something more achievable, like dispatching this wildly mutating chorizo. As he moved on toward the restroom, he encountered an insurmountable obstacle to his destination. Standing between him and the men's room was his ex-wife Lindsey, talking animatedly with a conference-goer carrying a thick binder. She laughed and shook his hand before they parted. As Lindsey turned toward the vestibule, Robbie quickly took cover behind a pillar, avoiding enemy observation. What the hell was she doing here? Taking credit for his fusion vision yet again? The last thing he needed was to see her. He put his back to the pillar and pulled out his phone.

"What are you doing?"

Robbie turned to see it was Harry. "Nothing," Robbie said. "Just, you know…"

"It looks like you're hiding," Harry observed.

Robbie's eyes darted around. "Lindsey's over there. What the fuck is she doing here? She must have gotten ahold of my schedule."

"You don't have a schedule," Harry said.

That froze Robbie a moment. "Well, she must have found out somehow," he insisted. "Otherwise, why would she be here? She's stalking me. I can feel it."

Harry rolled his eyes. The chances of disturbing Robbie's view that the world revolved around him seemed increasingly remote. "I wouldn't worry about it," he said. "She's probably gone by now."

"Robbie?"

They both turned to see Lindsey. "Oh. Lindsey, hey," Robbie said, with a half-hearted smile. "Didn't expect to see you here."

"Apparently not," she said. "I've been trying to reach you."

He shrugged helplessly. "Ah, yeah. Well, sorry. You know? My phone's been off."

As Harry excused himself and drifted away, Lindsey nodded toward the phone he was holding. "Looks like it's on now."

He flashed anger at being called out on his standard BS. That had always irritated him when they were married, this relentless insistence on "the truth"—as if he wasn't honest, albeit in a non-specific kind of way. "What did you want? I've got meetings back-to-back-to-back, and I've got to get to the conference and—"

She interrupted his preemptive not-guilty plea and demand for release on his own recognizance. "I wanted to talk about our daughter. She's having a public crisis."

He nodded impatiently. "Right," he said. "I've done what I can."

"Which is what?"

"I put her in touch with Dr. Iz," he said.

"*You* did that? Oh, great strategy," she said, shaking her head. "Now she's the global mascot for climatosis. What the hell were you thinking?"

He took a step forward, indignant. "You know, I really don't need the heckling," he barked. "What are you even doing here? Following me around?"

She laughed bitterly. "Why, yes! It was an elaborate ruse." She raised her eyebrows and leaned in, whispering conspiratorially. "I wrangled an invitation to deliver the conference's keynote address this morning, just on the off-chance I could encounter you in the audience."

Robbie was taken aback. "You spoke here?"

Lindsey stood back and folded her arms across her chest. "Check your program, jackass," she said sharply. "Apparently, you missed it."

Robbie gulped, before recovering his momentarily displaced superiority. "It's not like I don't already know what there is to know about this stuff," he scoffed. "I mean—"

She smiled. "Yeah, right," she said. "Surprised they didn't ask you to speak. Maybe next year they'll have a panel on how to blow a fortune on stuff you don't know, don't really care about, and will never understand. You'd be perfect." With that, she walked off.

Robbie fell back against the pillar, shaking his head. Why did it always go that way with her? It was bad enough before she started working, when she spent her days drinking her lunch with his sister, Bits, and prowling around the city's shops and museums. By the time he'd get home from the office, or from an afternoon delight, she would be plopped on the sofa, drunk and surly and accusatory, as if he had caused her misery. If she had been honest with herself, she'd know it was her fault he had to have so many girlfriends. A captain of industry under relentless pressure needed to find comfort somewhere, and he sure as hell wasn't getting it at home. Now it was even worse to see her, a haughty know-it-all, the darling of the burgeoning fusion industry. It was bad enough that she had taken his old job as chair of Crowe Power. But since her big splash demonstrating early-stage fusion at the Statue of Liberty last year, she had become unbearable, acting like she was some sort of green goddess. Wouldn't she be surprised when she saw his giant erection as the Father of Fusion on Governors Island? That would show her—and anybody else who thought he merely fell off the lucky sperm truck.

The double doors to the conference room cranked opened and the attendees bolted out as if they were cattle released from a stockade, sending Robbie into a slow jog to the restroom before the herd arrived. He quickly took care of business and emerged from the bathroom as the line was still forming. There, he found Harry, shuffling along and awaiting his turn.

"How'd you get stuck in line?" Robbie asked.

"Phone call," Harry said with a shrug. He held up a hand with his fingers spread apart. "We're due upstairs in five."

Robbie nodded and walked toward the elevator bank to wait, disgusted by the saggy-ass fashion sense of these people. Did any of these scientists have clothes that fit? Why did they all look like they were wearing hand-me-downs? Robbie shuddered at the parade of fashion faux pas and distracted himself by checking his gambling winnings from last night's baseball games. *Up three thousand bucks...* Suddenly, Harry grabbed him by the upper arm. "Let's go."

Robbie followed Harry up to a penthouse suite on the top floor, where they found notorious crypto king Todd Spinx, dressed in gym shorts and a vintage

New York Knicks jersey, spread out on a velvet sofa. A Korean woman in a light-blue dress sat at his feet, giving him a pedicure.

"Guys," Todd said as he wearily waved them in. "Make yourselves at home."

Robbie grabbed a water bottle off the buffet and sat on a loveseat while Harry took the chair across from him. Robbie glanced around at the view of Manhattan, then zeroed in on the latest wunderkind of the financial world: his terminal bedhead, trademark stubble, mismatched clothes, no muscle tone, and poor posture. He was, in short, a slob. Yet this didn't appear to be a sign of laziness. Todd had deliberately curated a look that suggested he was just crazy enough to be an eccentric genius. Certainly, many boldface-name celebrities and businesspeople thought so; they'd invested billions of dollars with him and were presumably getting something back. With degrees in physics, mathematics, and finance, and a ranking in the top quintile of the Forbes 400, it appeared there was nothing Todd Spinx couldn't master, especially the procurement of clients.

As the pedicurist switched feet, Todd said, "So cool to meet you, Robbie. Gotta say, you come from an amazing family. Homer Crowe was, like, some fucking genius, man. That dude had serious vision." Todd shook his head, almost in a reverie. "I mean, to create this vast global empire like Crowe Power that's lasted a hundred years? It must be crazy cool to be a part of a family like that."

"I certainly don't take it for granted," said Robbie.

"What I think is even cooler," Todd continued, "is that you've got your own fusion company now. Tell me about Star Power, man. Where do you see that going?"

Robbie nervously slurped his water. "I'm sure Harry has briefed you on the Crowe Center for Fusion Excellence," Robbie said. "We think it's important to show confidence in fusion with a campus that shows, you know, 'hey, this thing is real, it's established, and it's here to stay.'"

"That is so fucking awesome," Todd said. He looked at the pedicurist finishing up his toes, then turned back to Robbie. "You want her to do your feet?"

Robbie smiled with gratitude but declined. "I'm good, thanks," he said.

Todd ran a hand over his thatch of matted brown hair. "It's my only indulgence in personal care," he said, with a sigh. "I hate slowing down to take a shower or shave or any of that stuff. There's too much to do. But I can still do shit while I get a pedicure. You know what I'm saying?"

"Absolutely," Robbie said, as he began to realize that the aroma in the room was Todd.

"So listen," Todd said. He pushed his hands out in front of him, as if he were shoving all his chips to the middle of the table. "I'm all in on fusion. I dig it. My clients dig it. I can't stand these people who just bitch about climate change. I say, get off your ass and do something, man. Put your money where your mouth is, right?"

Harry piped up. "That's exactly where we are, Todd," he said.

"So what's next?" Todd asked.

Harry said, "I've got you down for five-hundred million."

Todd made a motion with his arm as if he were signing something in the air. "Done," he said. "I mean, it's a long-term bet, but I see a serious short-term payoff for the rest of my business, too. Nothing projects honesty like public do-good-ism, right? You say you want to help the planet, people just assume, 'good guy,' you know? I'm not just some blood-sucking douchebag anymore." He pointed a thumb at himself. "I'm a guy who cares. People think, 'I invest with him, and I not only make money, I save the world.' It's fantastic marketing. These ESG investors eat that shit up with a big fucking spoon, man. They don't even care about the returns, especially the public pension funds."

Harry nodded. "It probably won't hurt with the feds, either."

Todd chuckled. "Not at all."

Robbie, puzzled, asked, "Something going on with the feds?"

Todd shook his head. "A misunderstanding," he said, dismissing the possibility with a wave of his magical hand.

"Ah," Robbie said.

Todd leaned forward to explain. "Here's the deal, man. The government doesn't understand crypto, so they think I must be doing something wrong. As if 100 percent returns aren't totally achievable," Todd added. As Robbie stared at him, Todd continued, "I'm not doing anything wrong, of course. I'm doing too much right, apparently. A little money comes in. A lot of money goes out. It's like any successful enterprise. What's different, see, is I'm not like those greedy bastards out there, who just pocket all the proceeds. I'm earning to give."

Robbie's eyes widened. "Whoa! Seriously?"

Todd nodded. "Oh yeah. I want to go as fast as I can to make as much money as I can, so I can give it all away to good causes—you know, things that help everybody. People. Planet. Dolphins. Whatever."

Robbie shook his head in wonder. *What a guy!*

Right on cue, a beautiful young woman walked out of a bedroom completely naked and entirely uninhibited. She smiled at Todd but said nothing as she walked to a refrigerator, stooped over to pull out a bottle of coconut water, then retreated to the bedroom and closed the door.

What the hell? Robbie marveled. Is that what life was like for captains of crypto? *I want me some!*

Todd quickly focused back on the business at hand. "I have just one question," he said. "How quickly can I invest in Star Power? I want to make this public, so people understand I'm doing something about climate change. I'll put out a news release. Tout it on *Tonight with Jiminy Cratchit*. I'll go completely balls-out on social media. Hit it on my podcast. The works. I'm going to be your biggest evangelist, Bobby. People will be beating on your door, begging to get in."

"Wow," Robbie said, his mouth agape. "Just wow. Harry, what do you think?"

"Gung-ho, baby," Harry said. "We can set up the transfer today."

Todd smiled. "Great. I'm there."

As they stood and shook hands, Robbie was swooning. *I want to be like this guy*: a self-made genius, with women literally at his feet and others padding around the penthouse naked without a care in the world. "It's Robbie, by the way," he said.

"Did I say something else?" Todd asked. "Sorry, dude."

"No problem," Robbie said, as he regarded Todd with moon eyes. "I just have one question for you."

Todd shrugged. "Whatever you want to know, bro. My deal is, I'm an open book."

Robbie pulled Todd away toward the windows. "How do I invest in you?" Robbie asked.

Todd's eyes lit up. "Let me count the ways."

Robbie might not know how to make money like Todd Spinx, but he certainly knew how to spend it. And this guy was a sure bet.

***

Blair stood at a high-top table in the conference break area, picking at a poppy seed muffin, when Lindsey approached, holding a cup of coffee.

"I thought that was you," Lindsey said.

Blair smiled and they lightly embraced. "Hi, Ms. Crowe," she said sweetly.

"Please. I think it's time you called me Lindsey," she replied.

Blair blushed. "That may take some getting used to, but okay," she said. "I saw Mr. Crowe a little while ago. I don't think he remembered me."

Lindsey sighed. "No, he probably wouldn't. He has a lot on his mind." *Nothing good.* "What brings you here?"

"I work in strategy for my family's company, Energy Concepts," she said. "We make components for fusion and modular fission plants, mostly prototypes and parts made to spec. Hopefully, we'll get into full production as the industries mature."

Lindsey patted her arm. "That's wonderful, Blair," she said. "So happy to see you getting on with your career. I'm very excited for you."

Blair nodded, appreciatively. "Your speech this morning was great," she said. "When you talked about the obstacles we still need to overcome in fusion, those are exactly the kinds of things we're working on. In fact, we're doing things with superconducting magnets that could make sense for your company. Is there somebody there I should contact?"

Lindsey nodded, thoughtfully. "As a matter of fact, there is," she said. "Her name is Missy."

Blair sighed. "She's not talking to me," she said. "We had a bit of a thing."

"Trust me, I know how that goes. I've had a few of those 'things' with Missy myself over the years," Lindsey said. "Give it a few days and try her again. I'll do the same on my end. I think this fusion challenge is a bit overwhelming for her at the moment, especially with all these other issues going on. But if you help her help us, you could be a hero—and she could, too. That might be the boost she needs to get going."

Blair took a deep breath. "I'll give it a try."

Lindsey handed her a card. "Don't wait too long. The folks at our lab need all the help they can get, too."

17. THE JENGA PUZZLE

Marty took an Uber downtown to the gritty, glamorous neighborhood of Tribeca in Lower Manhattan, where he was dropped off at the corner of Church Street and Leonard. To get to Missy's apartment, he took a left turn at a shiny metallic bean sculpture wedged under a cantilever near the front door and entered a cavernous black-granite lobby. After a call upstairs to announce a guest, the uniformed doorman directed Marty to an elevator that whisked him up to the thirty-ninth floor and Missy's condo.

A housekeeper opened the door and led Marty through a gallery of brightly colored Georgia O'Keeffe paintings of flowers that looked like vaginas, or vaginas that looked like flowers, and here and there, a butthole. They entered a great room featuring a soaring nineteen-foot ceiling and a large outdoor terrace with a view north toward Midtown.

Missy was seated cross-legged on a white leather sofa next to a sheaf of papers, scrolling through her phone as Marty entered. She didn't bother to look up. Marty recognized the power play—it was lifted directly from Robbie Crowe's playbook on how to remind visitors who was important and who wasn't—and remained standing ten feet away without saying a word. He'd be damned if he'd look aggrieved.

Missy typed in a text message, then put the phone down and looked blankly at Marty.

"Hello," she said, offering her hand without standing. "I'm Missy."

Marty walked over and grasped her hand lightly. "I'm Marty."

"My pronouns are she/her," Missy announced. "What are yours?"

"Eenie/meenie/miney/mo," he said.

"Oh," she said, puzzled. "That's... unusual."

"In other words," he said, sitting down in a chair next to the sofa and leaning forward on his knees, "take your pick. I don't really care."

Missy regarded him suspiciously. "So," she said, "my mother sent you."

Marty nodded. "She's concerned."

"She needn't be," Missy insisted. She picked up papers from the cushion and held them up. "See all these? Letters of encouragement. Requests for speeches. Offers of product endorsements. There are a million more in my phone. The support is incredible, and it's coming from everywhere. I've got notes from Sweden. Germany. New Zealand. You name it."

"Congratulations," Marty said flatly. "You clearly touched a nerve."

Missy let the papers fall to the sofa, then picked up a sheet from the coffee table in front of her. "Here's an interesting one: a proposal for me to host a podcast on Spotify called TicTalk." She smiled to herself. "Cute. I kind of like that." She put the paper down and picked up another one. "Here's another. Would I like to become a celebrity spokesperson for the tranquilizer Kerflufflefix? Firm 'no.' I'm not ready for Kerflufflefix. But still… it's nice to be wanted." She put that paper down and grabbed still another. "'Put your twitch to good use by becoming a fighter in our mixed martial arts league.'" She balled that one up and tossed it toward a wastebasket behind her, where it bounced off the rim and fell to the floor. "I'm not into blood spatters."

These offers were getting out of hand, Marty realized. "I have a crazy idea for you."

She perked up. "What's that?"

"How about a job at Crowe Power?"

She sneered. "No thanks. I already have one."

Marty nodded. "Right. But in this case, see, you'd show up."

"Are you trying to be a smart-ass?"

"I don't try," he said. "It comes rather naturally."

"Well, right now I can't imagine going in," she declared, holding up a pile of inquiries. "I have too much to do."

Marty studied her. "Would you seriously consider any of those offers?"

"I don't know," she sniffed. "Why not?"

"Well, for one thing," he said, looking around at the elegant surroundings, "I can't imagine you need the money."

"It's not about the money, Marty," she said. "It's about giving oxygen to a movement of like-minded people around the world. There are many people in politics, media, entertainment, universities, who feel exactly like I do about this climate crisis. But we're disconnected. We need something to bring us all together."

"Like climatosis," Marty said.

Missy shook her head, in a theatrically sad sort of way. "It's not like I'm enjoying this damn twitch," she said, throwing her arm out to illustrate. "But I'm deeply gratified—no, *humbled* is a better word—that other people are finding comfort, knowing they're not alone. It's a scary thing to think you're confronting the climate catastrophe all by yourself."

"Right," Marty said, flatly. "You're apparently an inspiration."

"That, to me, makes it all worthwhile," she said grandly.

Marty didn't know how much more he could take of Her Serene Beneficence. He stood up and walked to the windows looking north over Chinatown, Greenwich Village, and Madison Square Park. Then he turned back to address Missy. "Unfortunately, you've inspired some people at Crowe Power not to go to work," he said.

Missy shrugged. "Good."

"How could that possibly be good? That's your family business."

"Maybe they have solid reasons for not going."

"Such as?"

"They're sick of despoiling the Earth."

"Ah," Marty said, sitting down again. He considered whether he should point out that Crowe Power profits paid for this sumptuous pad, its power plant on the East River provided electricity for it, its gas lines provided heat, and the company, over the past hundred years, had raised the standard of living for many of the people she now counted among her legions of admirers around the world. He suspected stating the obvious would only alienate her.

Missy eyed Marty. "What's your concern in all this?" she asked. "I know you're some sort of PR guy. Are you worried I'm hurting the company's image?"

"You're not helping."

"That's where you're wrong," she insisted. "I'm showing people that Crowe Power is human."

"Actually, it's not," Marty said, rubbing his chin.

"You don't believe it?"

"It's not a question of belief. Crowe Power is a legal entity, set up in the state of Delaware, like most companies in the Fortune 500. It doesn't have a brain, or a heart." Marty paused, thinking. *It's had a few dicks like her dad,* he thought, but he didn't want to confuse the issue. "I would agree that the people who work there care. Many of them are proud of providing an essential service."

Missy studied Marty, whom she saw as a soulless worker bee buzzing around his queen, a woman well above his station in life. *Why does Mother pay someone like this loser?* Had he ever been lauded in the *New York Times* for defacing an office building with an anti-capitalist screed? Had he ever received a standing ovation on *Scuttlebutt Live* for demanding real change? Had he ever instigated a worldwide movement of climatosians? And who the hell were the McGarrys, anyway? Potato famine refugees from Ireland? Impoverished coal miners from Scotland? Where had he gone to school? Some public diploma factory? Had he studied at the Sorbonne for even one semester? Missy had no answers, but she did have assumptions: Marty had no standing to address a woman of her peerage as if they were on some equal footing. As great-grandma Crowe used to say: he was not of her class.

Missy's housekeeper, Genevieve, poked her head into the room. "Missy, just a reminder: you have a call with Washington in two minutes."

Missy smiled and slapped her hands on the sofa triumphantly. "I think we're done here," she declared.

Marty nodded and stood up. "I have just one other question."

She looked at him blankly. *What now?*

"Where does all this go?" Marty asked.

"What do you mean?" Missy replied.

"Endorsements. TV. Politics. What's the end game?"

"There is no end game," she snapped.

"There is, actually, whether you decide it or not," Marty said. "This all goes somewhere."

She laughed mirthlessly. "Not unless I say so," she said. "I started it."

"With all due respect to your considerable powers, starting a social contagion doesn't mean you get to end it," Marty said. He pointed to the papers next to her. "Look at all the people out there who already want to make this their own. They plan to leverage this movement to get a piece of the action themselves. Wait until the politicians get involved. This can get away from you very quickly."

"I don't see how that happens," she declared.

"No, you probably can't see it, because you're in over your head, whether you get that now or not," Marty replied. "But suppose your twitch goes away. What happens then?"

Missy looked stricken. "This could go on for years," she said defensively.

"Then again, it might not last the week," Marty said. "Isn't that why you're getting therapy? To be cured? What if it works? All this could be over in a heartbeat."

Missy glared at Marty. "If and when that happens, I'll figure it out," she scoffed. "I doubt I'll need any help from you—or my mother."

Marty had heard that kind of empty boast before—from Robbie Crowe, just before he was fired. "You have my number," he said. "Call me when you're looking for a way out."

Suddenly alarmed by a sense that something was happening beyond her line of sight, Missy grabbed his arm as he walked by. "A way out from what?" she asked.

He pulled his arm free. "You'll learn soon enough."

18. COUNTER CULTURE

As Marty walked down Church Street toward Crowe Power headquarters, he ruminated on how best to tell Lindsey about his visit with her wayward daughter. Clearly, Missy was enthralled with all the attention she was getting. Once the applause stopped, which was inevitable, her attitude was likely to change. There was simply no way of telling at this point how long that would take.

With a half hour to kill before his appointment, Marty stopped at the newest franchise of Café Che, known to locals as Commie Coffee, which was making a killing bringing socialist chic to the capitalist masses of New York's most affluent neighborhoods. He entered the gleaming new store, studded with Warhol-like portraits of the revolutionary Che Guevara, and took a spot in line. As he waited, Marty noticed a man working behind the counter, wearing camouflage clothing and a black beret with a red star on the front, who looked an awful lot like Dr. Joseph Katzenmeyer, an old college classmate who had gone on to great academic honors as a professor at Bartleby.

Marty tried to catch his glance, but the man looked down, obscuring his eyes under the brim of his beret. As Marty's turn came to order coffee, he decided to give it a shot. "Joe?"

The man gulped and looked up. "Hi, Marty," he said.

Stunned, Marty said, "Interesting to find you here."

"Yeah. It's not exactly what I expected either at this point in my career," Joe said, sheepishly. "Let me get your order and I'll bring it to you." He surveyed the short line. "I can take a few minutes to chat."

Marty ordered a cup of Bolivian Jungle Roast with a splash of llama milk and took a booth in a dark corner. As Marty scrolled through his phone messages, Joe arrived with the coffee and slid onto the wooden bench on the other side of the booth. Marty thanked him for the delivery and waited for him to speak.

Joe took off his beret, placed it on the table, and nervously smoothed back his thinning curly hair. "Surprised, I'll bet," he said.

"What happened?" Marty asked. "Last I heard, you were flying high."

"That was before I issued my latest—and last—climate study," he said. "It's been all downhill ever since."

Marty leaned across the table. "What did you say?"

"Honestly, I was so stupid," Joe said, rubbing his forehead. "Last time I saw you, you may recall I was teaching science."

"Of course," Marty said.

"I was also doing research on a paper about the history of climate change. I wanted to understand fluctuations over thousands of years. Six months away from tenure at Bartleby, I published an excerpt of my findings for the *Wall Street Journal*." He pulled out his phone and pulled up the WSJ app. "Here's the piece."

Marty took the phone and looked at the headline: *Climate Change: It's Not So Unusual.*

"Yeah?" Marty said, handing it back. "I read this. As I recall, I thought you made some good points."

"So did about five thousand readers who made comments at the end." Joe looked around to see if anyone could hear him, then turned back to Marty. "But back on campus, in the land of politically acceptable versions of scientific results, they went bananas. The science was settled, they said. I was outside the boundaries of 'consensus,' which is apparently forbidden. 'Do you know what this could do to the funding for our climate studies?' They were worried I'd smudged their virtue and derailed their gravy train.

"Things spiraled quickly," he said. "I was denied tenure, blackballed in academia, and couldn't find another job to save my life. Nobody would touch me. My wife left me for some windmill mogul and moved out to a mansion on the Gold Coast. This job here doesn't pay shit—that's how Commie Coffee treats the workers of the world—but I've got to do something to get out of the house while I look for something else. I keep hoping someone will take a chance on me."

"So... you were canceled?"

Joe nodded. "Like an old postage stamp. I'm surprised the coffee shop gave me a job, but I think they overlooked my history because they're desperate for underpaid labor. Nobody wants to work these jobs anymore. I'm making $16.34 an hour, plus tips."

Marty squinted. "What did you say in the piece that was so terrible?"

"I used the year 1930 as a baseline to plot temperature fluctuations," Joe said. "It just so happens the early twentieth century was a relatively warm period—

comparable to now—so the modest increases we've seen recently don't look all that terrible. In fact, they look more like a flat line. The more standard starting point for charting temperature is 1980, a relatively cool year, to show temperatures going up like this." He ran his hand at a sharp angle into the air.

Marty shrugged. "That's it?"

"There were other points of minor controversy in the piece, but that was the gist of it," he said. "You have to understand, Marty: I wasn't denying climate change; I was just trying to provide some historical context for the data, and to warn against overstating the effects, which scientists do all the time to add some drama, whether the data backs them up or not. The funders of these studies love to see papers that suggest things are even worse than you thought. Nobody wants to fund research that goes straight to the file drawer."

Marty shrugged. "If it bleeds, it leads, right?"

"Exactly," Joe said. "The fact is, some issues related to warming have nothing to do with human activities and there's nothing you can do about them. There are other issues you might be able to influence—but it probably doesn't make sense to do so at any cost."

"I'm only a casual observer, but I'm not sure many people in power share your concern," Marty said.

"Of course not!" Joe exclaimed. "Do you have any idea how much money is at stake here? The climate industry is huge, and it's got its tentacles in everything. They want people to be alarmed so they can jam their so-called 'solutions' through. And they don't care how much psychological damage it causes to people—especially the kids, who are being indoctrinated through schools and movies and TV and the media. If young people can't sleep at night because they think the world is going to end in a few years, tough shit. In their view, people are the sole cause of climate change. That makes them expendable. As Ebenezer Scrooge said, better to get on with dying and decrease the surplus population. It's better for the planet."

Marty sat back in his bench and shook his head. "That's rather frightening, Joe."

"I wish I had a happier story for you, Marty. I don't."

Ernesto, the assistant manager of the shop, who moonlighted as a regional comandante in the Planetistas, approached the table. "Joe, I need you to work the counter."

"I'm on strike," Joe replied.

"C'mon," Ernesto pleaded. "The line is getting long."

"Long lines are good for them," Joe said. "That's part of the authentic communist experience."

After Ernesto turned away, shaking his head, Joe leaned across the table. "Marty, you're taking a chance even talking to me. If anyone sees you..."

Marty waved away his concern. "I don't care. I'm going to be canceled soon enough myself. I'd like to help you in some way if I can."

"Thanks, Marty," Joe said. "I don't know what you can do, but I'm open to ideas. Anything, really." As Joe slid out of the booth, he leaned over and said quietly, "There are lots of us in the same boat, you know. Professors, economists, finance people, politicos. We have a support group that meets in a church basement a few blocks from here. If you ever get blacklisted by Big Climate, let me know. I'll get you in."

"I might want to come anyway, just to learn something."

"Be my guest."

19. THE MOTHER OF INTERVENTION

Marty had walked through the ornate art deco lobby of the Crowe Power Company world headquarters a thousand times and never failed to admire the intricate tilework in its domed ceiling. He adored the brightly colored globe, the Latin phrases *Industria, Potentia,* and *Ingenii,* and the campy interpretation of Michelangelo's masterpiece from the Sistine Chapel, "The Creation of Adam." In case visitors failed to appreciate the company founder's place in the pantheon of early 20th Century business geniuses, God reached out not to a naked Adam, but to a mustachioed Homer Crowe, reclining on a rock wearing a three-piece business suit and a straw boater.

Whether Homer Crowe was indeed touched by God was open to debate. What was not in dispute is that he was touched intimately and often by his long-time secretary and paramour, Agnes Ludlow, who had lived with her cuckolded husband in a mansion upstream from Homer's estate in the Hudson Valley and had borne Homer twin girls. Their spawn, Annie and Fannie, were beneficiaries of a trust, as had been their children and their children's children, and the entire line of heirs had all lived quietly outside the public eye for a hundred years. That was one Crowe family crisis that Marty was glad he never had to manage.

After picking up his pass at the security desk, Marty walked through the turnstile, past the elevator bank for Crowe Power's rank-and-file employees, to an express elevator for senior executives and visitors to the company's C-suite. He rode it up to the twenty-fourth floor, triggering enough memories of encounters with Robbie to give him his own momentary twitch.

At the entrance to Lindsey's 2,000-square-foot suite, Marty used his pass to swipe the ID reader next to a glass door. He looked up to an overhead security camera and smiled for Winnie. Marty heard a click, which unlocked the door, and entered the reception area, which featured a three-dimensional logo of Crowe Power and a bronze bust of the company's heroic creator.

Winnie poked her head into the area and summoned Marty forth. He dutifully followed her through the outer office and into the inner sanctum, where he found Lindsey standing next to her desk as she talked on a speaker phone. Her general counsel and former brother-in-law, the laconic prepster Digby Pierrepont, sat in a wingback chair opposite the desk. Lindsey waved Marty in, pressed the mute button, pointed to the console, and said, "Confusion at CroFusion."

"What are the odds?" Marty asked.

"High, considering the cause," she replied.

"Missy?"

"Of course," Lindsey said, before returning her attention to the phone conversation.

The distinctive voice, which Marty instantly recognized as PC at the CroFusion lab, said, "... so, I'm sorry that I had to bring this to you, Ms. Crowe, but I really don't know where else to turn. We're stuck right now and I'm afraid we're going to lose more ground if we don't get our equipment. Superconducting magnets of this dimension are very hard to find and—"

Lindsey leaned over the phone and cut him off. "Did you try calling Missy directly?"

"I've called her number five times and left voicemails," PC said. "I haven't heard anything back. I think she's avoiding me."

Lindsey glanced at Marty and Digby and shook her head, then looked toward the speaker phone. "Don't take it personally, PC. I have found persistence with her sometimes pays off," she said. "In the meantime, I'll get things moving as quickly as possible with corporate." She bid him goodbye and called for Winnie to get Crowe Power's chief executive, Lucy Rutherford, on the phone.

"PC sounds rather exasperated," Digby said.

Lindsey nodded. "Missy has that effect on people."

Winnie shuffled to the doorway and announced that Lucy was on the line, prompting Lindsey to pick up the handset. "Hey Lucy. Can you get some purchase orders cleared for our guys in the fusion lab," Lindsey asked. "They're at wits' end, and Missy is... I don't know what you'd call her. Indisposed, I guess." Lindsey listened to Lucy briefly, then thanked her and hung up before dropping into the chair behind her desk. "Now I'm doing Missy's job, too," Lindsey said, shaking her head. "Tell me you have some good news, Marty."

"Would love to. I just don't have any yet," he said, plainly.

"I was afraid of that."

"Do you still want me to sit down?" he asked.

Lindsey motioned to the chair and sighed. "Please."

"I met with Missy this morning. And I must say, I've never met anyone so delighted to be so miserable," he said. "Missy is reveling in her climatosis. She's a big fish in the climate pond."

"Can we reel her in?" Lindsey asked.

"Not yet," he said. "She has way too much fight left. We're going to have to let this spool out a bit before we tug on the line."

Digby, a devoted fly fisherman, said, "Sounds like you're talking about a trout."

"More like a largemouth bass," Marty said.

Lindsey looked exasperated. "How long do we wait?"

"If this is her fifteen minutes of fame, I'd say she's at minute six."

"Oh lord," Lindsey muttered. She cast her gaze out the window, then looked back at Marty and Digby. "I worry this is gathering momentum far beyond Missy. If we don't nip this in the bud, I'm afraid—"

Winnie appeared at the door. "Lindsey, I'm sorry to interrupt. But your call is coming in from Washington. Jessica Holtgren is on line two."

Lindsey rolled her eyes. "As I was saying," she muttered. Lindsey blew out her cheeks and collected herself, then pointed to Marty, who was getting up to leave, and commanded him as if he were a German Shepherd. "Stay!" Marty dropped back into the chair as Lindsey pushed the button on her phone.

"Linz, darling," a voice cooed over the speaker. "It's Jessica Holtgren."

Lindsey's shoulders slumped and Digby rolled his eyes. "Madame Secretary, what a pleasure," Lindsey said.

"Please. Let's not be formal. It's Jessica to you."

"Of course, Jessica," Lindsey said. "I trust you and your family are well."

"We are, indeed, and thank you for asking," Jessica replied. "But the reason I'm calling is because I'm thinking of *you* and *your* family. I'm sure you're absolutely devastated by what's going on with Missy. The poor dear."

Lindsey sighed. "Yes, it's an unexpected challenge. We're dealing with it as best we can."

"I want to tell you that the president is concerned, too," Jessica said. "He asked that I convey his concern and assure you that he will do everything in his power to help."

That gave Lindsey pause. The last time Washington "helped," Jessica had offered a billion-dollar subsidy for the development of Crowe Power's first-generation fusion technology, only to steal it when it proved successful and hand it to the Chinese government as a failed bribe to sign a climate pact. What would the conniving Jessica and her bumptious boss conjure this time? "Thank you for your kind offer," Lindsey said. "I don't think there's much you can do at this point. It seems Missy just needs time to work this out."

She looked to Marty. *Right?*

He nodded affirmatively.

"I can tell you as a mother myself that I understand how protective you must feel toward her," Jessica said. "And while I can assure you that we only want what's in her best interests, we also recognize what a powerful figure she has become in the global fight against climate change. I'm sure you've seen that she's inspiring people around the world through her brave struggle with climatosis. The president believes she can be a tremendous ally in rallying more people to the cause of healing our planet."

Lindsey's defenses were suddenly on alert. *Uh-oh.* She turned first to Marty, who looked deeply skeptical, then to Digby, who was gravely shaking his head. Lindsey punched the mute button and asked, "Where is she going with this?"

Digby sighed. "Only one way to find out."

Lindsey unmuted the phone. "What exactly did you have in mind?" she asked.

Jessica replied, "The president has extended an invitation to Missy to become Honorary Chair of the Federal Climatosis Commission, a group he is convening next week to discuss ways to fight this dreaded affliction," Jessica said. As Lindsey slapped her forehead, Jessica said, "More must be done, and we believe Missy is just the sort of leader we need."

Missy? A leader? Lindsey looked at her advisors and held her hands out, palms up. *What do I do?*

Digby sighed. He rolled his hand in a circular motion, and quietly mouthed, "Play it out."

Alarmed, Lindsey asked, "Has Missy agreed to serve?"

"I'm delighted to tell you she accepted just a few moments ago," Jessica said. "I just want to be sure you're on board. You must appreciate how helpful this would be to our country and, of course, to your company."

"My company? How so?"

"Not that there's any direct connection, of course, because that's not the way we operate around here, but I'm sure you're aware that my department has been reviewing your application to renew permits for your oil refineries in the Gulf."

Digby threw up his hands while Lindsey, catching on, said, "Yes, Jessica. We've been awaiting approval for almost a year."

"Well," Jessica said conspiratorially, "to be completely honest with you, a positive outcome for your company is uncertain. The professionals on our team are triggered by the very idea of renewing fossil fuel processing capacity in the United States, given our nation's outsized role in poisoning the planet. Even looking at the application provoked tears and required us to bring in grief counselors. You must understand that our staffers are much like Missy—super smart, idealistic young people who want to change the world."

"To their specifications, of course," Lindsey interjected.

"Precisely," Jessica replied. "They get twitchy at the very thought of enabling more fossil fuels to feed our sick national addiction."

"You mean the fuels that still provide 79 percent of our nation's energy?"

"Whatever that number is, yes. My people would rather glue themselves to portraits in the National Gallery than approve another permit for oil refining."

"Do they realize that glue is petroleum-based?"

Jessica chuckled. "Really?"

Lindsey was losing her patience. "Jessica, you should also realize that profits from our refineries and pipelines and power plants are how we stay in business. They also pay for our advancements in fusion."

"Oh, I'm sure you can find another way," she said.

"Alright," Lindsey said. "Let's cut to the chase here. Are you telling me the permits are dead?"

"Not exactly," Jessica said haltingly. "But I would say they need critical care if they're to survive. And I think it will go a long way to show our team what a responsible company Crowe Power is if Missy serves as the honorary chair of the commission. We need someone with her passion and credibility to tell the world that fossil fuels need to go away sooner, rather than later. That's a message the whole world needs to hear. And who better than a brilliant and sensitive young woman whose family has been engaged in the energy industry for more than a hundred years? I must tell you, Lindsey, in the few conversations I've had with her, I have been mightily impressed. You did a great job."

Once Lindsey was sure the call had ended and the line was dead, she looked to Marty and Digby and shook her head. "No ifs, ands, or buts. Jessica Holtgren is a thug." Lindsey imitated a Jersey accent. "'Nice little energy company you got there. Shame if anything happened to it.' I wish I knew somebody who would stuff Jessica Holtgren in the trunk of a car. Electric, of course."

"That's beyond my scope of work," Marty said.

Lindsey flushed pink and her jaw clenched. "Jessica knows exactly what she's doing," Lindsey said. "My daughter. Poster child for her climate agenda.

I can only imagine Missy on TV, mouthing the script crafted by Jessica's operatives."

Marty sighed and looked at his watch. "I've got to go."

"Where to?" Lindsey asked.

"I'm off to see the wizard."

"Who's that?"

"The Wizard of Iz," Marty said. "I'd like to take a peek at the lady behind the curtain."

PART TWO

The Contagion Spreads

20. THE MEANING OF IZ

As Marty idly flipped through *People* magazine's inside story of the Duke and Duchess of California's "Secret Battle with Climatosis," he couldn't help noticing a common thread among the young people scrolling through their phones in Dr. Iz's waiting room. All of them looked like the spawn of one-percenters: wealthy, educated elites who were more worried about their social status than paying the rent. The climate crisis, he gathered, was a rich-people problem, with rich-people solutions.

"Marty?"

He turned to see Crystal summoning him into Dr. Iz's office as a wide-eyed patient came shuffling out, twitching violently, as if his therapy session had no impact at all. Marty, trying to remain beyond striking distance, pressed himself against the wall until the man safely passed.

Crystal led Marty into the inner sanctum, where Dr. Iz appraised him from head to toe. He was considerably older than her usual climatosis patient. There was no twitching or other obvious sign of distress. Other than a furrowed brow, he appeared calm and settled, as if he hadn't a care in the world.

"Would you like some coffee or soda?" she asked.

"A bottle of water would be great," Marty said.

"We don't do plastic here. It's bad for the planet," she said. "Would you settle for tap?"

"Of course," Marty said, as he settled into a large easy chair.

She brought him a glass of water, sat in the chair opposite, and picked up her notebook and pen. "So tell me, Marty," she began. "What brings you in today?"

"What else? Climatosis," he said, gravely.

Dr. Iz nodded sympathetically and jotted a note. "We certainly know a lot about that around here," she said. "Are you having any symptoms, like twitches?"

"No," Marty replied.

"Shakes?"

"No."

Dr. Iz nodded. "Uncontrollable laughing or crying?"

"No."

"Mood swings?"

Marty rubbed his chin. "Not really."

Dr. Iz sighed. "A sense of hopelessness?"

"Yeah. Some of that, for sure. Hopelessness," Marty said. "It feels like this thing is never going to end."

"Well, first let assure you, Marty: you're not alone," Dr. Iz said. "Many people are worried about that. Not just here, but all over the world."

Marty sighed. "What do you say to those people?"

"Every case is different," she said, "and there's not a one-size-fits-all solution. But generally, I think it's important to validate one's emotions. People are understandably upset about climate change. They see disasters all around them. They read about climate refugees fleeing areas that have become uninhabitable. They hear endless predictions of doom. There's so much that should be done, but it's not happening fast enough."

"Yeah. I get that," he said.

"There's a lot to process, Marty, and it takes time. That's why I like to stress two things to my visitors. One: be patient. It takes time, and we're not going to heal our planet all at once. And two: you're not alone. We're all in this together."

"I appreciate that," Marty said, nodding. "I have a friend who's having quite a struggle with climatosis. And I'm trying to help her out, but I'm not having much luck. I don't know if you've ever tried a different tactic to break someone out of it. But have you ever told a patient that the climate crisis is… what's the word? *Bullshit?*"

Dr. Iz blanched. Was this a set-up? Was he somehow recording this on camera? She had better be careful. "No, frankly, I haven't."

"Is it something you've considered?"

"I'm not sure how to answer that, Marty. What are you getting at, exactly?"

"I'm just wondering if people would be better served if you invalidated their emotions," he replied. "Why not tell them that their fears are exaggerated? That they're related to an advocacy press carrying water for activists, politicians, and business opportunists with an agenda? That they're being exploited and that they don't have as much to worry about as they think?"

"It's not my job to assess climate change," Dr. Iz said. "I'm a psychologist, not a climate scientist."

Marty guffawed. "Oh, come on now, Dr. Iz. That's a cop-out. I'm not a scientist either. I was a journalism major at Syracuse. But I know BS when I see it." He stood, walked over to the bookshelf, and gazed at the impressive display of diplomas, plaques, framed awards, and miniaturized billboards featuring Dr. Iz and her once-withering glare. Several photos harkened back to her glory days in broadcasting, with one shot of her in a radio booth, wearing a headset and speaking into a microphone. Others showed her on TV talk shows being interviewed by Oprah Winfrey, Phil Donahue, and Ellen DeGeneres.

"I remember when you were famous for your tough-love approach," he said. "You were the one who cut through all the psychobabble and told people what they needed to hear. It was bracing at times, but you know what else it was?" He turned back to face her. "It was necessary. *You* were necessary. People needed to hear something other than, 'I'm okay; you're okay.' Because they weren't okay. And you were great at telling them so, and getting them to face their problems straight-up. What happened to that lady?"

Dr. Iz swiveled around in her seat. "Well, obviously, I'm still here."

Marty leaned against the bookshelf and stuck his hands in his pockets. "I'm not sure. The old Dr. Iz would cut through the BS with common sense. I suspect she'd tell her patients that there's one way to know for certain if all that they're hearing about a climate catastrophe is real."

"Which is what?" Dr. Iz asked.

"It's when the celebrities and politicians who are peddling the 'climate emergency' line stop buying oceanfront mansions, flying in private jets, and acquiring multiple homes all over the world. You want to know which way the climate winds are blowing? That's your weathervane, right there. As long as it points in the direction of waterfront homes in the Hamptons selling for thirty-five million dollars, I'm not buying it."

"I understand your point of view, Marty, even if I don't necessarily agree," Dr. Iz said. "What I don't understand is why you came in to tell me this."

"Because I'm worried about a patient you're treating," he replied. "Missy Mayburn Crowe."

"I don't talk about my patients," she said curtly.

"You didn't have any trouble on *Scuttlebutt Live*."

"That was with her consent," Dr. Iz said. "I'm certainly not talking about her to you without her approval."

"Then I'll leave you with my own observation about how your therapy is working," he said. "Missy is so twisted around that she thinks being a victim is not a challenge to overcome. It's a virtue. A badge of honor. A measure of how much she cares. She believes that all this public drama is her contribution to society. How fucked up is that?"

Dr. Iz bristled. "I'm not so sure it is."

"Really?" Marty said. "What are other young people out there supposed to think if they're not twitching or crying or curled up in a ball? I gotta believe they're thinking, 'Something's wrong with me. I must not realize how horrible things are.' Is that a good outcome for them—or for us? I understand how these doomsday scenarios help people gain power over other people or make money with the latest new climate 'solution.' But I have a hard time squaring that kind of cynicism with the Dr. Iz I remember. She wouldn't sell out. She was better than that."

He walked to the door, where he paused. "I hope for Missy's sake—if not for your own—that she still is."

21. OFF-BROADWAY MELODRAMA

Missy found that the conversation over Sunday brunch was not going down as smoothly as the mimosas. As she explained her invitation to become honorary chair of the Federal Climatosis Commission, the expressions on the faces of her friends, seated at a sidewalk table of the Odeon restaurant in Tribeca, turned from happy smiles to curled lips. Peach was three bites into her niçoise salad when she put down her knife and fork and glared at Missy.

"Why are they asking you and not us?" Peach demanded. She gestured toward the others. "We have climatosis, too, you know."

Missy, digging into a Croque Madame, looked around the table and saw similar hostility from Gina and Britney. "Don't hate on me," she said with a dismissive shrug. "They probably wanted one person."

Peach fumed. "Why is that one person you?"

Missy arched an eyebrow. "Maybe because I was first?"

"Like that counts?" Gina wailed. "I think I have climatosis the worst of anybody." She twitched, flinging the spoon she had been using for her French onion soup onto West Broadway, where it landed with a clatter and was instantly run over by a truck. "I can't sleep. I can't focus. I'm a nervous wreck!"

Missy reached over and took Gina's hand. "Gina. I love you like a sister," Missy said. "But let's face it. You were a wreck before climatosis."

"Yeah. Okay," Gina acknowledged, sullenly. "But I'm even more of a wreck now."

"Fair point," Missy acknowledged.

Britney looked around the table and sniffed. "I've had climate anxiety since the first grade," she declared. "I used to go through our trash with rubber gloves, making sure nobody threw out a container that should have been recycled."

"That's very noble," Missy said, "but that's not exactly climatosis."

"Yeah, it is. It's early-onset climatosis," Britney claimed.

"I'm not sure that's a thing," Missy said.

"It's a thing!" Britney insisted. "I think I would know, since I freaking had it!"

Peach, imperious as ever, dismissed the others' claims to climatosis superiority. "I don't think anybody here has had climatosis longer than me," she said. "My mother told me I had acute sensitivity to the environment when I was a baby. I refused to take a pacifier because it was plastic. I wouldn't wear a disposable diaper; it was either cloth or I was going naked. I wouldn't even eat applesauce that wasn't certified non-GMO."

"Like you read the label?" Britney scoffed. "You were some baby genius?"

"It was just a sense I had," Peach declared, with a roll of her shoulders. "An instinct. Ask my mom. She'll tell you."

"Right. Why don't you give me her number?" Britney scoffed.

Gina shook her head. "What have you done lately?"

"I deprive myself of anything that's harmful to the environment," Peach proclaimed. "No hamburgers. No bottled water. I won't even smoke weed out of a plastic bong. It has to be sustainable bamboo."

"That's your big sacrifice?" Britney scoffed. "Is that some kind of joke?"

"It's something," Peach said. "What about you?"

Missy decided the Twitcheratti needed further sedation, so she signaled a passing waiter for another round of drinks. "Guys, listen," she said. "This shouldn't be a competition to see who's got the worst climatosis. I mean, is that really the measure of how much we care about the planet? It sounds kind of ridiculous."

They ate in silence as the waiter delivered more drinks and a convoy of cars and delivery trucks noisily rumbled down the street, flattening Gina's spoon. Peach asked Missy, "So what's the deal with the rally in Central Park?"

"Honestly, I don't know much," Missy replied. "We're supposed to talk about it in Washington next week. But I guess they're going to hold it on the Great Lawn since they're expecting about half a million people. They've got a few speakers and some bands."

"Like who?" Gina asked.

"Dover Soul and the Sluts," Missy said.

"Oh my God! I love them!" Gina cried.

"Wretched Excess is playing, too," Missy said. "So are Eugene and the Eugenics."

"That is so *cool!*" Gina said.

Peach and Britney glared at Gina. *You're not helping.*

Britney eyed Missy. "So what's your role at the rally."

"I'm one of the speakers," she mumbled.

"You're *what?"* Britney snapped.

Missy shrugged. "They want me to say a few words."

"About what?" Britney asked.

"I'm not sure," Missy said. "They haven't told me yet."

Peach pushed back from the table. "Wait a second. They're *telling* you what to say?"

"Yeah," Missy said. "What's wrong with that?"

"That's, like, government propaganda," Peach said.

"How do you know?" Missy said. "You haven't seen it."

"They're politicians, Missy," Peach insisted. "They're going to write what they want. Did they ask for any input at least?"

"Not yet," Missy said sheepishly.

Peach folded her arms across her chest and shook her head. "I don't like the sound of this."

"Me neither," Britney agreed.

Peach's jaw clenched in anger. "You're being used, Missy."

Missy flushed red. "Even if I am, so what? It's for a good cause. Don't we want to defeat climatosis?"

Peach gathered herself. "What comes after the thing in Central Park?"

Missy shrugged. "I don't know," she said quietly. "They're talking about doing rallies in other cities, like San Francisco, Seattle, and Portland. Maybe Boston and Austin."

Britney sighed. "Are you shitting me?"

Missy took a deep breath. She may as well get all the bad news out at once and be done with it. "They're also talking about a few TV appearances, some talk radio, a podcast, and possibly a book. Maybe some endorsement deals. If you ask me, it all sounds like a huge pain in the butt."

They all stared at her, speechless.

Britney downed her mimosa in one gulp. "And you're going to do all that?" she asked.

"Why wouldn't I?" Missy said. "Look, if it makes you happy, I can insist that you all come with me, at least for some of it. I mean, I can probably get you backstage passes for the rally in Central Park."

Missy's friends shot looks to one another, and Peach slapped her hand on the table. "Well, aren't we special?" Peach said. "Maybe we can get little badges that say, 'Friends of Missy.' Gosh," she said, sarcastically. "I'll be able to say I knew you when."

Missy had heard enough. "Stop it!" she said, throwing her napkin on the table. "I didn't ask for this! They called me! What am I supposed to say? *No?* This comes from the freaking president of the United States! I'm just this little… whatever."

Gina reached over and patted Missy's hand. "Don't get so angry, Missy. We're just trying to understand."

"Well, clearly, none of you do understand," Missy said. "Do you guys have any idea of all the abuse I'm getting?" She held up her phone. "I get hate messages every day from people saying I'm faking it. Or that I'm too rich to complain about climate change. Or that I should just curl up and die because I've lived this life of privilege and we need more space in the world for homeless people and refugees. It's even worse on Twitter. And you know what? I accept that. These people don't know me. They can say what they want. What I don't accept is getting it from you, my supposed friends. I take you all to Nantucket. I get you on TV. I hook you up with Dr. Iz. But nothing I do for you is ever good enough. Now I get this cool thing and all you guys can think of is what's in it for you. What the hell!" She stood up, bumping into the table and rattling the glasses.

Peach glared at her, then swept her arm across the table, sending porcelain plates, silverware, and glasses clattering to the sidewalk. "Sorry. My climatosis is acting up," she said.

As waitstaff and other diners turned to see what was happening, Gina took her mimosa glass and heaved it out into the street where it shattered on the pavement. "Mine, too!" she yelped. "I think…"

Britney took both hands and shoved everything in front of her—plates, knife, fork, spoon, glass, coffee mug, and flower vase—toward Missy and off the end of the table. "See? You might have forgotten this part, but we've all got climatosis and we're dealing with the fallout, too."

Missy shook her head in fury. "You're all nuts!"

She stormed off to her idling black car on Thomas Street. Her driver, Harvey, hustled out and opened the back door.

"I'll walk back," Missy told Harvey.

"It's two blocks!" Harvey warned.

"I need the exercise," she said.

22. THE CLIMATE UNDERGROUND

Exiled professor-turned-barista Joe Katzenmeyer guided Marty through a dark alley clogged with dumpsters, plastic bags of garbage, and scurrying rats to a stairwell at the back of St. Vitus Church in New York's Financial District. With a nod of his head, Joe indicated this was their destination and clambered down the stairs to a metal door. Using the rhythmic beat of "Shave and a Haircut," he knocked five times rapidly, paused, then rapped twice more. The door creaked open, revealing a tall man in black clothes and a clerical collar.

"Joe," the man said quietly as he opened the door wider. "Please come in."

Joe patted his companion on the shoulder and told the priest, "Father Novak, this is my friend, Marty. He's cool."

"Welcome to the Climate Underground, Marty," the priest said, extending a hand.

The priest glanced up the stairwell to see if anyone else was coming, then led them down a dimly lit corridor to a meeting room with a checkerboard floor of faded black and red floor tiles, an odd assortment of chairs and card tables, narrow slits of basement windows, and a series of jack posts holding up a sagging ceiling. Seven men and three women were seated in a semi-circle, chatting among themselves. Joe exchanged greetings, and Marty acknowledged them with nods. He noted to himself that they all looked well-scrubbed, and based on their attire, at least formerly prosperous. They also looked kind of sad. Then again, anyone seeking work with no prospects of a job would appear distressed in this dank cinderblock cell.

"I think we're all here," Father Novak said as he took a seat. "Why don't we get started."

He introduced Marty and explained that the group met once a month to support one another in their quest to find work and to share any leads about companies that would consider hiring people accused of climate change denial. As the people in the assembly had discovered for themselves, denial was a charge that carried a presumption of guilt until proven innocent and punishment was swift and often permanent. The mildest penalty was ostracism from elite circles; worse was blacklisting and cancellation. Father Novak stressed to Marty that nobody in the assembly was a denier, per se, but all had expressed skepticism, which had also become taboo.

Father Novak asked that they go around the circle and briefly say who they were and why they were there. The group included a pair of investment advisors from Gemstone, which made a splashy show of its virtue by directing money to ESG-compliant companies that offered inferior returns on investment but paid big dividends in public relations. The advisors, Fred and Ed, had lost their jobs after saying at an investment conference that they were more concerned about making money for their clients than pleasing activist "stakeholders." That stance embarrassed the virtue-signaling Gemstone chairman, and they quickly found themselves asked to a meeting with HR, where they were given cardboard boxes to gather their things.

The assembly also included three other academicians expelled from campus for failing to adhere to the prevailing climate dogma, and a journalist, Lisa Franke, who had been fired from a national newspaper for refusing to hype an alleged rise in hurricanes as evidence of a human-caused climate catastrophe. "The actual number of hurricanes had declined in recent years, as had their severity," she said bitterly. "But saying so was verboten."

Father Novak thanked the group for their introductions, then turned to Marty. "What brings you to our conclave, Marty?"

Marty said, "You've probably heard of Missy Mayburn Crowe, who's at the center of this climatosis pandemic." There were nods all around. "At the request of her family, I'm trying to help retrieve her from the clutches of some very cynical people. They have her and her friends spooked that a climate apocalypse is nearly upon us."

Lisa interjected, "Have you tried telling her about all the doomsday predictions by experts that have been wrong over the past fifty years?"

Marty shrugged. "I'm not sure it would make any difference."

"It might be helpful." Lisa pulled out her phone and began searching for a file. "Mind you, these predictions didn't come from the Weekly World News or the National Enquirer. These came from professors at Harvard, Stanford, Columbia, and Michigan. The National Center for Atmospheric Research. NASA. The

U.N. Ordinary people would hear these scary scenarios and think, 'Who am I to doubt? They're scientists. Aren't we supposed to follow the science?'"

She held the phone in one hand and used her other hand to count—at least until she ran out of fingers. "We were supposed to have worldwide water rationing by 1974. A massive famine by 1975. Dead oceans by 1980. Sunlight reaching the earth was supposed to be cut in half by 1985. The Maldives would be completely underwater by 2018. So would our West Side Highway. Britain was either going to have a Siberian climate by 2020, or maybe they'd never see snow again. Take your pick."

Joe said. "Either way was disaster. It always is with climate change propaganda."

Lisa said, "I could go on, but you get the gist," she said, dropping her phone to her lap. "Famine, floods, plagues, extinction. You name it. They were always just over the horizon."

Marty grimaced. "Okay. But I'm sure you've heard the rejoinder. What if they're right this time?"

"Like a stopped clock?" Joe said, furiously shaking his head. "That's the problem, Marty. You can't say for certain something won't happen, even if the likelihood is remote. If you say the Jets will win a Super Bowl by 2050, how can I prove you wrong?"

"I don't know," Marty said. "By watching them play?"

"Here's the problem," Joe said. "All these climate predictions are based on computer models. Outputs are only as good as the inputs, right? And while the inputs are getting better, they're still imprecise. They depend on the observational tools available, historical data that can be a little squishy, and more than a few wild guesses about what's caused by humans and what's naturally occurring. We also don't know what data we're missing because, frankly, we're just not that smart. What are the factors that we haven't thought of? To my mind, we can only judge the validity of these models by the measurable results, which are often contradictory and rarely add up."

Father Novak said, "Marty, you mentioned that the real problem for her wasn't climate change but hysteria about it. Are you familiar with dancing mania?"

"I remember a TV show about that from the eighties," he replied. "*Dance Fever.*"

"This was even more disturbing than that," Father Novak said. "Legend has it the first instance occurred on Christmas Eve in 1021, when eighteen people outside a church in a little German village danced in a 'ring of sin' and lost control of their limbs for an entire year. Centuries later, the same phenomenon occurred in a bigger way, affecting 400 people in Strasbourg in 1518. It was a summer of terrible heat, yet men, women, and children could not stop dancing for hours or even days until they collapsed in exhaustion, sometimes breaking bones or dying. Some historians called it a response to the fear of St. Vitus, who was associated with dancing, music, and entertainment. I would say it had more to do with failed harvests, floods, and diseases such as leprosy, plague, and syphilis. Those problems left people depressed, anxious, and susceptible to suggestion from their friends and neighbors. They thought if they engaged in certain rituals, they could ward off evil spirits."

"That might explain twerking," Marty said.

"Nothing explains twerking," Joe said, shaking his head.

Marty put his hands on his knees and looked around the group. "I appreciate all your comments," he said. "I'm just not sure what I can do with them. Missy is under a lot of pressure from a lot of places, including Washington."

Father Novak said, "I hate to say it, Marty, but just for her own well-being, Missy may be better off accepting the prevailing view and continuing therapy for her twitch. Resistance to the dogma around climate change may not be futile, but you see the results around you. This isn't the winning team."

23. PRESS FOR ANSWERS

President Dewey Fenwick shuffled unsteadily through a pair of tall wooden double doors into a White House conference room, prompting the gathering of reporters to rise. The room was packed in anticipation of a major announcement as he took his place behind a lectern bearing the presidential seal. He motioned with both hands for the audience to take their seats.

"Please, please," he said, dressed in a crisp navy-blue suit with a white shirt and red tie. Standing before a gallery of American and presidential flags, he began, "Now… first I'm going to make a statement. Then I'll take a few of your questions."

The reporters shifted in their chairs as the president fixed his gaze on a teleprompter.

"Alright. I think we all agree that climate change is the single greatest threat to our future," he said. "Bigger than biological warfare. More terrifying than a giant asteroid smashing into the Earth. Worse than the prospect of artificial intelligence surpassing human capability and taking over our lives." He paused for effect. "Climate change is worse because it means the climate will—listen to me carefully here—not be the same from one decade to another," he said in a throaty growl. "That's right. It could be a little hotter. It might be a little colder. We could get a lot of rain. Maybe we'll get a pile of snow—or maybe not. Seas could rise. Storms could surge. Pigs could fly, see, because the wind will be so damn strong. In other words, climate change will mean unpredictable weather, like we have now, but way, way, *way* worse." He shook his head and crossed himself. "God have mercy on our souls."

The president sipped from a glass of water before continuing. "We're already seeing the first signs of this climate catastrophe right now. We have droughts, storms, wildfires, and melting ice—including in this glass I have right here, which is melting a hell of a lot faster than it would have forty years ago. And that, my friends, is because of climate change." He paused to sadly shake his head at the tragedy of it all. "This scourge is taking a very real toll on patriotic Americans through this climatosis pandemic, with citizens in our country and around the world reacting to the threat with disturbing twitches. As your Commander-in-Chief, I will not stand idly by without taking action." He balled his right hand into a fist and shook it to show he meant business.

"So today," he said, returning to his script, "I'm declaring a National Climatosis Emergency, and I've directed my administration to take the following measures." A screen on the side of the stage turned on and listed the steps as he announced them.

"Number one—and this is a biggie—I'm asking Congress to authorize the Defeat Climatosis Act. This will allow us to send buckets of Climate Cash to people unable to work through no fault of their own. Climate insecurity should not drive any man, woman, or gender non-conforming birthing person into poverty.

"Secondly, I'm initiating a program called Operation Get Renewables Fast to speed our transition to clean energy. We're going to double down on subsidies for our dear friends in the wind and solar industries. My administration will not rest until we see windmills twirling on every mountaintop, valley and shore, and solar panels carpeting our prairies and cornfields from sea to shining sea.

"I plan to pay for that by asking Congress to levy an Obscene Profits Tax on our evildoing fossil fuel companies, which will allow us to confiscate their ill-gotten gains from bad energy and spend the money on good energy." He scanned the rows of reporters to gauge how his remarks were going over, and sensed he had another winner.

"Third, I'm asking that we send climatosis reparations to developing countries around the world to help them cope with the fact that we're discouraging the use of fossil fuels to raise their standards of living. It's my firm belief that if we're going to insist that they remain in poverty, it's only right that we funnel some dough their way. I am requesting an immediate down payment of three hundred billion dollars but, and this is a big, big 'but,'"—he held up his index finger—"these payments will not be made to the same old tin-pot dictators we've paid off in the past. No, sir. They will go only to those despots who pledge democratic reforms. And, by God, I'm going to hold them to it if it takes a hundred years."

He looked at his notes. "Alright. The last thing is that I'm establishing the Federal Climatosis Commission, which will stage informational events throughout our great land, starting next weekend in New York's Central Park. This commission, which will gather for the first time tomorrow, is comprised of experts who know how to turn crises into opportunities. I've named Missy Mayburn Crowe the Honorary Chair of this panel. As you may know, she is an heir to one of the great energy fortunes in our history. Yet even she has been stricken with this debilitating condition. I think it speaks to her courage and selflessness that she is willing to come forward to help us stop the spread of climatosis, even if it means standing in opposition to the very company that her family built."

The president paused and looked to the reporters. "Alright. I'll take a few questions, as long as you're not on the naughty list."

Shouts of "Mr. President! Mr. President!" and "Over here!" rang through the hall from the reporters, who represented major news organizations in the United States and around the world. The president put on his reading glasses and consulted a sheet of pre-approved names before calling on the venerable Bob Bobson of *YBS News*, who was seated in the front row. "Bob. It looks like you're up first."

"Thank you, Mr. President," Bob said. "You mentioned earlier that climate change is the 'single greatest threat to our future.' In your mind, is it a greater threat than nuclear bombs?"

"Oh yeah," President Fenwick said. "This nukes that."

"Worse than cancer?" Bob asked.

"Cancer schmancer," the president said with a shrug.

"What about self-replicating nanobots?" Bob persisted.

"C'mon, man!" The president scoffed. "I'll step on 'em with my shoe!"

"A giant—"

"Whoa, whoa, whoa!" the president said. "You've gotta stop this, Bob. The science is settled. Everyone agrees! Climate change is the scariest boogeyman I've seen since… what? A hood named Sugar Crisp skulked around the roller rink in Philly where I used to rent out skates. No kidding. And I've got a whole bunch of scientists getting federal funds to study this stuff who back me up."

"Have any of your experts' theories been proven right?"

"Not one." He looked offstage to Press Secretary Nadine McWilliams, who was waving her hands frantically, before turning back to Bob. "But they haven't been proven wrong, either." The president collected his thoughts, such as they were. "What kind of game you playin', man? I told you: we've got scientists on our side. Holy moly, just look at their resumes! They don't make wild guesses about things, like some of you out there. They glance at each other's stuff and say, 'yep. Looks good to me.' That's called 'peer review.' And if that's good enough for them, it ought to be good enough for you."

The president shook his head and looked at his list of reporters. "Let's move on here," he barked. "Nancy Shiffer from the *Daily Reaper*. Where are you out there, Nancy?" He put a hand over his brow to scan the room.

Nancy, seated six feet in front of him, said coolly, "Right here, Mr. President."

"Ah," he said, with a chuckle. "You're hidin' on me."

"Mr. President," she said, "there are reports today that members of the Planetistas showed up at the Norman Rockwell Museum in Stockbridge, Massachusetts to draw attention to climatosis. They threw Impossible Giblet Gravy at the Thanksgiving portrait of a woman serving turkey to her family. Is that behavior you condone?"

"No, no, no. Of course not," the president muttered. "But I understand the frustration. Sure I do."

"Do you believe they should be prosecuted for defacing artwork that's considered part of our national heritage?" she asked.

"Not at all," he said. "I mean, from what I understand, it was a mostly peaceful protest. It's not like they tossed cranberry sauce, which could stain, and maybe cause little red berries to splatter on the floor. Now that could be a little sticky, too. And… ah, hell." He lost his train of thought. "Anyway. There was a point in there somewhere."

The correspondent smiled and fluttered her eyes. "Thank you, Mr. President."

The president looked at his list but seemed to have lost his place. He turned to Nadine, his press secretary, who mouthed, "Tom." The president nodded and turned back to the room.

"Okay. I'm supposed to go to Tom next from, uh… I forget." As three reporters named Tom stood up, the president pointed to the man who stood in the second row. "I'll take the Tom in the middle there."

"Thank you, sir," said Tom, from somewhere. "Are you contemplating any measures to prevent people from getting hurt? We're getting numerous reports of people accidentally starting fights by striking others while twitching."

The president nodded. "As a matter of fact, Tom. I've asked the CDC whether we need to bring back those cute little social distancing stickies we used to have on the floors of stores and elevators, so that people don't get slugged. They're also looking into whether we should make slings available to all Americans to restrain their twitching, and whether we ought to procure billions of dollars in helmets and pads as personal protection equipment. 'Cause ultimately, there's no better way to declare a pandemic is over than to throw out all the crap you overbought, right?"

"Excellent ideas, sir," Tom said. "Thank you."

President Fenwick nodded and returned to his list but couldn't make sense of it. "Alright. Let's take one more here," he said, prompting more shouts of, "Mr.

President! Mr. President!" He looked to the crowd, pointed to a respectable-looking gentleman in the second row, and said, "You there, whatever your name is."

"Thank you, Mr. President. It's Worthington Oakes from NPR," he said.

The president stared at him blankly.

Worthington said, "Your college roommate?"

"Ah right!" the president said. "My old pal. We used to go to twist parties together."

"Mr. President," Worthington continued, "when America was overcome with anxiety during the Great Depression, President Franklin Delano Roosevelt attempted to calm the people by saying, 'The only thing we have to fear is fear itself.' Does that maxim still hold true today?"

"Nah," the president scoffed. "Different era. We've got all kinds of things to fear and my administration is committed to making sure we dig 'em all up and let people know what they are and why my opponents are responsible for them. The American people should not rest until... well, they should never rest. Climatosis is just the latest issue to emerge, but I guarantee you, there's lots more scary stuff where that came from. Fact is, climatosis has been with us for a long time. It's just that nobody talked about it."

The president paused in his reverie. "People don't realize this, but I was probably the first person in the country to ever get climatosis." There was a shuffling of chairs in the audience as the reporters settled in for another dubious tale. "You may scoff, but it's the truth. Way back in the 1940s, I remember we had an extremely hot day. I was listening to 'The Life of Riley' on the radio when my arm suddenly twitched. Just like that." He threw out his arm. "See there? And as I recall, I was thinking about how hot it was. And of course, in those days, we didn't have air conditioning like folks do now. So I know what climatosis is like. And I empathize with anybody who's come down with it." The president paused and picked up the papers on the lectern. "Okay. That's it. They're telling me I've got to go somewhere for something," he said over more shouts of "Mr. President! Mr. President! One more question."

The president started to shuffle away from the lectern, but a reporter from *Buzzniss* caught his eye.

"We hear reports that climatosis was engineered in a Chinese laboratory," the reporter said. "Do you believe that's true?"

The president stopped in his tracks and stared down the reporter. "No, sir," he said. "I believe it was made right here in America, which is where it belongs. That's what my administration is all about. Making things here."

The reporter was confused. "You want all pandemics started in the United States?"

The president scrunched his nose. "I don't want pandemics at all, jackass. But if we're gonna have 'em, I'd rather we started 'em here, on our home turf, so that we use good ol' American know-how to come up with a cure. Got it?"

"Could I ask—"

The president waved him off. "No, you can't. I've had enough of you people." As he shifted his papers from one arm to the other, his right arm twitched, sending the papers in his arm flying into the air, which prompted aides to come scurrying to retrieve them as quickly as they could, while others attended to the president.

"By golly," he muttered as he steadied himself. "I have it again!"

24. A THREE-HOUR TOUR

With one hand, Hacksaw Harry held down the site plan for the L. Robertson Crowe III Center for Fusion Excellence, and grasped his genuine Thurston Howell III yachting cap with the other, as his new boat, *My Float Option II*, approached Yankee Pier on the southern edge of Governors Island. Sitting at a large table at the stern, Harry showed Robbie the most significant features of his legacy project, as the island began filling with its usual summer crowd of tourists and day trippers.

Harry pointed to a square on the map, and then to a space on the island near a grove of trees, where young people were throwing frisbees. "Right over there," Harry said, "our project planners are thinking Star Power World Headquarters, an eight-story home to the world's most advanced fusion technology."

Robbie nodded approvingly. "Do we have any?"

"Any what?"

"Advanced technology."

"No," Harry said, "but that's just a detail at this point. We can figure that out later."

"Fine," Robbie said. He put a hand over his brow to shield his eyes from the sun as he gazed toward the island and into the future. He couldn't really envision what site Harry had in mind for HQ, especially since he was currently distracted by a pair of lovely young kayakers paddling their way past the bow. He smiled and waved to them and, for a moment, imagined inviting them over to a little picnic area in the grove to get a feel for some of that famous Robbie Crowe Excellence...

"Hey. Are you with me?" Harry said, jolting Robbie back to the task at hand. "In the middle there, we'd have the L. Robertson Crowe III Fusion Experience."

"That's the museum?" Robbie asked.

"Yep. Very interactive," Harry said. "State-of-the-art. We've got some former Disney people leading the design."

"So it is a small world after all?" Robbie asked.

"Let's hope not," Harry said with a grimace. He rose from the table and stepped over to the gunwale, with Robbie following. "And over there, on the southwestern side of the island, facing directly across from the Statue of Liberty, is your monumental achievement—the Father of Fusion."

Robbie pictured the statue in his mind. "How big are we thinking it ought to be?"

"Well, obviously, we want an erection that reflects the man," Harry said.

Robbie spread his hands out wide. "So, we're talking huge."

"Our designers have studied monuments all over the world to get a sense of the proper dimensions," Harry replied. "They're thinking a black granite base that's ten feet tall. Then, a bronze 'Father of Fusion' sculpture on top of that would stretch another twelve feet."

Robbie sank. "That's it?"

Harry looked at Robbie with a squint. "You want more?"

Robbie looked hurt. "I don't know. It sounds like you're making me a little squirt. Twenty-two feet? That seems kind of dinky—especially for such a significant achievement."

"What achievement?"

"Fathering fusion," Robbie said. "This could be a game changer for the planet, the people, everybody. Don't you think it should make people go, 'Holy shit! This *must* be a big deal!' I mean, the Statue of Liberty is, like—what?—300 feet? And what's that about? It's just some random gift from the French a million years ago about liberty or huddled poor or some crap like that. But, 'father of fusion…' that's gigantic!"

"It could be, eventually." Harry pulled out his phone and called up some notes. "You know Michael Jordan's statue in Chicago? It's seventeen feet, top to bottom."

"So?" Robbie spat. "He doesn't even play basketball anymore." He shook his head. "What about that thing up in Rockefeller Center? The guy holding the world on his back?"

"Atlas?" Harry said. He looked at his phone and scrolled. "Let's see… that's forty-five feet tall. But he's holding the world on his back."

"Then give me something to hold," Robbie said.

"Like what? You want a tokamak on your back?"

"Jesus, Harry. Take this seriously," Robbie said. "I need you to figure it out."

Harry sighed and nodded. "Alright," he said. "We'll make sure the statue lives up to your expectations."

Robbie bit his lip. "Is this thing a go?"

"Pretty much," Harry said. "Your donations are getting us the approvals we need, but they're also creating a bit of a problem."

"What's that?"

"They want more," he said. "Whatever you give, you can be sure that it's never enough. I've booked us on a quick trip out to the Hamptons next week. There's a fundraiser for President Fenwick."

Robbie shook his head. *Do I have to do everything?* "How about if I just send a check?"

"Not enough," Harry said. "Sometimes, you gotta show up."

25. CLIMATE APOCALYPSE NOW

The charter members of the Federal Climatosis Commission gathered in a White House corridor, where they were directed by Chief of Staff Ben Bixby to form a single file line before entering the Oval Office to greet the president. Missy, trembling in the presence of this almighty assembly of senators, business leaders, cabinet officials, and scholars, tried to hide her sense of intimidation with an uncertain smile. She took her assigned place between the lanky, patrician Senator Joe Kildare and the petite political dominatrix Jessica Holtgren and considered her unlikely participation.

I have no business being involved in policy at this level, she thought. *I barely nailed a B- in Perspectives on Vaginal Politics.* She breathed deeply and took solace in the fact that she was at least dressed correctly, with an environmentally friendly ensemble made of recycled polyester. Sadly, the material was ugly, scratchy, and didn't breathe. She began feeling drips of sweat roll down her back to the base of her spine. *Swamp ass? In the White House?* This was a new experience—and not a good one.

The door opened and the commissioners were ushered toward the fireplace. Missy, panicking over the idea that her jacket might soak through, felt a sudden twitch in her arm, which was thrust into a bust of Franklin Delano Roosevelt, wobbling the stand.

"Oh my God!" Missy murmured, as she reached out to steady the thirty-third president.

Jessica patted her arm and whispered to her soothingly. "It's okay," Jessica assured her. "They're removing it anyway." She leaned closer. "FDR could have stopped climate change, you know. But he made it worse, encouraging massive industrialization using fossil fuels."

Missy was confused. "Wasn't that to win World War II?"

Jessica sniffed, "Well, yes, of course. But still."

Missy showed surprise. "So… FDR is canceled?"

Jessica smiled, knowingly. "We're getting him off the dime."

"I thought that was just an expression," Missy said.

"Not in this case," Jessica said. "He's going down."

"Down where?" Missy asked.

"To the nickel," Jessica replied.

"Oh my," Missy said. *These people play hardball.*

The group lined up at the end of the room opposite the Resolute Desk, where the president spent upwards of several hours a week. Once the assembly was in place, another door opened and in shuffled President Dewey Fenwick, wearing his famous aw-shucks smile. He made his way through the line, shaking hands and saying hello to all the participants, with a photographer trailing along to record the historic moment.

When the president reached Missy, he took her hand in both of his and leaned over toward her head. *What the hell was he doing? Is he trying to kiss me?*

"You smell good," the president said, sniffing her hair, as the camera flash created a surreal strobe. "I mean, *real* good."

"Thank you, Mr. President," Missy said with a wooden smile. "I…" *I what? Use soap?* "I do my best."

The president nodded agreeably and moved on to another woman, who posed for a photo with the president while he discreetly felt her up from behind. Afterward, the commissioners were directed to two long sofas in the middle of the room, while the president took his traditional rocker near the fireplace.

Jessica said, "Mr. President, thank you so much for your time today. I'd like to begin by asking each of our commission members to say a few words about what they will contribute to our work on the Federal Climatosis Commission."

She introduced establishment pillar Hollis Blackwell, the exquisitely tailored editor of the *Daily Reaper*, America's esteemed paper of record.

"Thank you, Jessica," Hollis said tugging on his French cuffs. "Mr. President, we believe climatosis presents an outstanding opportunity to sound the alarm that the climate apocalypse is upon us now. Pardon the expression, but until people are scared shitless, our nation will never take sufficient steps to combat this scourge." He reminded the president that his newsroom had suspended all rules about so-called objective reporting—"a mythical concept, in my view"—when it helped vanquish the dreaded Orange Menace a few years earlier. He pledged to extend the same principle to *Daily Reaper* climate coverage going forward and continue to present the opinions of his environmental reporters as straight news, given all that was at stake. There was no need nor was their time to seek contrarian views on the matter, given the urgency of concocting policies and spending money.

Hollis stabbed a finger into the arm of the sofa. "We can't say when the end will come for our species. Nor can we say how it will occur. We also cannot identify with any great precision why it's happening. There are simply too many complexities we can't fathom, and that, frankly, are beyond the comprehension of our readers. Nonetheless, we can state with absolute certainty that climate change means the human race will eventually die a horrible, grisly, disgusting death—drowning from rising seas, bleeding through our various orifices, coyotes eating our entrails, and so on. And if that happens, we know who to blame." He looked down at Missy, sitting meekly at the end of the sofa. "I want to offer a little apology in advance to Missy, because we intend to name names, publish addresses, and let people know where the climate villains' kids go to school. It's an ugly job but we have to do it if we're going to eradicate climate denial."

The president nodded approval. "Desperate times call for desperate measures."

Jessica waved a hand and interjected, "Just to clarify, Hollis, you're not blaming Missy."

"Oh, goodness, no," Hollis said. "We regard Missy as a genuine hero of the Fossil Fuels Resistance. But, intelligent young lady that she is, I'm sure she would admit that her family is complicit in the destruction of the Earth. There's a penalty for that. And it must be paid in full and in advance."

Missy gulped, horrified. They wanted to blame her mother? And all her relatives? "Well," you know, "there are complicating factors. People historically have wanted oil and gas for all kinds of things, such as heating homes, cooking, a higher standard of living. There's—"

Jessica cut her off. "Yeah, yeah, yeah," she said impatiently. "You'll get your turn in a minute, Missy. Let's move on." She turned to Sydney Solberg. "As you know, Mr. President, my friend Sydney is chief executive operator of the social media platform DingDong, a competitor to TikTok."

Sydney, the fit and fashionable face of the company, turned to the president and thanked him for inviting her to sit on this esteemed panel. "I'm sure you're aware, Mr. President, that we do not—as a matter of record—censor opinions on DingDong," she declared. "We expect users to draw their own conclusions about complex issues such as the climate catastrophe once we offer them information that's been fully vetted by our Department of Veracity. And I want to thank you for the cooperation of your administration. Our team is working hand-in-hand with the FBI, the IRS, Energy, the EPA, the United Nations, and other governments around the world to distinguish fact from fiction, and we've drawn a pretty good bead on a passable truth." She shook her head, grieved. "Clearly, there's no time left for argument, with disaster hurtling our way. We will not, as a matter of principle, remove dissenting posts from DingDong. But we are burying those posts so deep on our site you'd need an archeological dig to find them. And if you do happen to stumble upon them, you'll see a label that says 'dangerous,' 'stupid,' or 'pure trash.'"

The president chuckled. "Bravo," he said. "It's not easy to keep everyone in line like that. Keep it up."

Sydney added, "I would like to thank the brilliant Dr. MacFarlane for his invaluable insights into climate change. We count on him for advice and guidance, and he delivers every time. Our team refers to him as the King Kong of Ding-Dong."

Dr. George "Spanky" MacFarlane, a middling physicist early in his career at Penn State, had morphed into the nation's preeminent climate scientist through a winning combination of glib analysis, absolute certitude, media accessibility, pithy quotes, and ruthless attacks on dissenting views. These attributes had helped him raise his profile and secure a pipeline of cash to fund studies predicting when glaciers would melt, seas would rise, and various species would be made extinct. Since his predictions were projected deep into the future when his target audience would, in theory, be dead, none of his prognostications had ever been proven right, nor had they been proven wrong. Yet, he was always considered correct, since his opinions neatly coincided with the views of his fellow travelers. "You'll be glad to know we're working with the United Nations to issue another report," Spanky said. "Our summary conclusions are all set. Now we just have to complete the study."

The president grimaced. "Don't you do the study first, then the conclusion?"

Spanky attempted to hide his contempt for such a ridiculous concept. "With all due respect, sir, that's an outmoded academic approach when it comes to a subject as important as climate change," he said. "Data is messy, and it doesn't always match up. Our job is to find the facts that bolster our conclusion as it relates to a higher truth. That's what counts."

Jessica fluttered her eyes and smiled at Spanky. "You are *sooo* wonderful. And we are so darn lucky to have you!" she said. Next up was the young movie mogul Adam Gold, head of Das Kapital Studios.

Adam, clad in two-thousand-dollar jeans, leaned forward and pushed the sleeves of his linen jacket up to his elbows. "Forgive my crazy energy here, but I am incredibly stoked," he proclaimed with a verve that suggested he had recently been snorting cocaine in a West Wing bathroom. Furiously jiggling his right leg up and down, he said, "This morning, I greenlit a film: *Wrath of Sheba, Climate Avenger*." He paused briefly to let that sink in as eyes lit up around the room. "Oh yeah! It's about this transgender woman of color stricken with climatosis who develops superhuman strength through repetitive twitching. She hunts down climate criminals and just beats the living shit out of them." He looked around the gathering to read their reaction and found they were hanging on every word.

He continued, "This leads to a showdown with the arch-villain, Fossilstein, this oily mutant white privilege creature who spits gasoline on people and sets them on fire with flames shooting out his ass." He paused. *Was it okay to say that?* Hearing no objections, he proceeded. "The climax is this epic battle for world domination—winner take all." He shuddered and fell back on the sofa, overcome with excitement. "I get freaking chills."

The president laughed. "You can't leave us hanging, man! How does it end?"

Adam sat back up. "Oh, this is great!" he enthused. "They have this classic, bloody, brutal hand-to-hand combat until Sheba summons all her superhuman powers to yank a mini-wind turbine out of the ground and slice up Fossilstein like a freaking Veg-O-Matic."

Applause broke out around the room. "That's fantastic," President Fenwick said. "Can't wait to see it."

Jessica looked at Adam with dewy eyes and shook her head. "So clever!" she said. "And so on point! Thank you, Adam." Sotto voce, she added, "Do you need money? This commission has budget."

Adam shrugged and said quietly, "If I have money to pay a big star, our message goes that much further."

She patted his leg and smiled. "We'll talk."

Around the room they went, each party outdoing the last to demonstrate their zeal. The dean of a prestigious college in New Hampshire promised to make climatosis a required course for all majors from history to mathematics. The chief executive officer of Gemstone, a leading investment bank, pledged to direct all his clients' retirement assets to support only those companies that had demonstrated a strict commitment to reducing carbon emissions and shunning those firms that hadn't, regardless of their financial returns. And General Sheri Flowerday, Chair of the Joint Chiefs of Staff, proposed banning the use of weapons that have a negative impact on climate.

"Don't they all?" the president asked.

"Pretty much," she said.

"So… what would we use to defend our nation?" the president wondered.

General Flowerday looked at him blankly. "All we've determined so far, sir, is the kinds of weapons we can't use, not what we can. Many of the weapons currently in use today have massive carbon footprints. So, obviously, they're out."

The president pressed further. "What does that leave us? Slingshots? Peashooters?"

The general looked at him, blankly.

The president shook his head. "Look. Here's the deal, General. What if the bad guys don't give a howdily-doodily about climate change and they use something like... I don't know. Bombs."

Sheri declared imperiously, "Then they're on the wrong side of history."

The president squinted. "Not if they're alive and we're dead."

Wait. *What?* Sheri blinked rapidly, processing this concept.

The president nodded. "Once you finish your plan, bring it back in for a look-see, alright? I'd like to understand how this is gonna play. Folks out there in the heartland might get a bit of agita over this one."

Missy detected an unfortunate pattern developing: Whether any of these ideas made sense or effectively addressed the problem seemed beside the point. They were all offering their bona fides to secure standing in an elite club that would shape the direction of the country—and for much of the rest of the world—for years to come. The idea she had in mind coming in—donating her appearance fees from an upcoming Climatosis Speaking Tour to the Planetistas to finance their protests—seemed like small beer compared to all these big gulps. She would need to come up with something better to keep up with this group.

Jessica walked the president through a list of symbolic gestures that her team had devised to demonstrate their commitment to climate management. One was to douse the gas-powered Eternal Flame on the grave of President John F. Kennedy at Arlington National Cemetery and replace it with a flickering electric candle powered by renewable energy. "Of course, we'll have to change the name since the wind doesn't always blow and sun doesn't always shine, and the electric candle will go out from time to time."

"Interesting," the president said. "What would you call it instead?"

"We're thinking Candle in the Wind," Jessica said.

"Ah," the president said.

"We would invite Elton John to sing at the re-dedication," Jessica added.

There were enthusiastic nods all around, especially from the president. "I love that one song he did, you know..." He hummed a few notes, then sang. "'*Get back... honky cat...*' That's what they used to call me back in the day. There was this guy at the pool hall, big hulking dude. Special K, we called him. Always wanted to fight. Anyway—" The president paused. Where was he going with this story? "I like this Candle in the Wind deal. That would show that nobody—not even presidents—can shirk their climate responsibility here, not even after they've met an unfortunate demise."

"So right, Mr. President," Jessica said. "So, so, *so* right."

The president accepted her verdict with an appreciative nod. *She gets me!*

"One last thing I would like to mention, Mr. President, is what we discussed earlier," Jessica said. "Under a series of new rules issued by the EPA, we intend to begin the process of shuttering refineries along the Gulf Coast to force the change to renewables." She turned to Missy. "Our plan includes the Crowe Power refineries in Texas, Louisiana, and Mississippi. I'm sure you agree with that, Missy."

Missy hesitated, then rolled her shoulders uncertainly. "Well, I guess so," she said. "I mean it's planet or petroleum. Right? Can't have both. Isn't that what they say?"

Smiles and nods followed from the president. *Good girl!*

Jessica offered an approving smile. "That is so courageous," she said. "It's my hope that when we announce the shutdowns at the rally, you'll endorse the decision, too. Support from a prominent member of the company's founding family would go a long way toward telling the world, 'We're driving a stake into the dark heart of fossil fuels right here and right now.' You, darling, are the tip of the spear in our war against climate change."

Missy felt all the eyes in the room staring at her. They were certainly expecting an awful lot from her. "I'll do what I can," she said.

Jessica assured her, "Don't worry about a thing. We'll prepare all the talking points for you."

The president signaled his agreement and stood up. "Thank you all for your participation in this initiative. There's just one other issue I'd like to bring up, if you don't mind," he said. All eyes turned to him. "We're not crazy, right?"

Jessica blinked rapidly. "What do you mean, sir?"

"Suppose someone comes along in a few years and proves that we were full of shit."

"That can't happen, sir," she said.

"Why not?"

"Because we'll just move the doomsday date out a few more years," Jessica said. "We do it all the time."

The president scratched behind his ear. "So… we're not going through all this rigmarole based on some sort of wild-ass guess."

Jessica said, "Oh no, sir!" There were murmurs of agreement with her all around the room. "It's more like a *scientific* wild-ass guess. We call it SWAG rather than WAG."

The president looked around the room, studying the faces. "Well, we know Spanky is the science," he said. "That's good enough for me."

As the meeting ended, Missy walked from the room in a daze. The president was on to something; they had no idea what they were talking about, yet they weren't waiting to learn more. Killing fossil fuels before other forms of energy were widely available made for good slogans and rallies, but to do so with the idea that it would force the development of renewables seemed to be a spectacularly reckless bet.

The president, heading out a different door, called back to Dr. MacFarlane.

"Hey, Spanky. What's your call on the weather this afternoon? I'm playing golf at two."

Spanky smiled. "Sunshine all day."

"You sure about that?" the president asked.

"One hundred percent!" Spanky replied cheerfully.

Jessica put an arm around Missy's shoulder and whispered: "If you don't have an umbrella handy, I suggest you get one."

26. ONE DISENCHANTED EVENING

Fifteen minutes before he was to meet Lindsey, Marty arrived early at the Chelsea restaurant Portale so that he could secure the white brick alcove in the back of the bar. The nook's single table for two would afford them privacy, and there was much to discuss.

Lindsey's arrival caused heads to turn. Dressed conservatively for a New York neighborhood that prized flamboyance, she nonetheless had a presence about her that suggested she was somebody. Most people weren't sure who, exactly, but they paid her the compliment of a second glance as she passed. *Where do I know her from?*

Marty rose to offer Lindsey a light embrace and to hold her chair as she took her seat. She ordered a glass of Gavi di Gavi while he asked for a martini and a small bowl of marcona almonds. As they settled in, Marty told Lindsey about his meetings with Dr. Iz and the Climate Underground. He told her he had dropped off a box of research materials from Joe Katzenmeyer for Missy at the front desk of her apartment, but that he had not heard whether she received them.

"Missy's going to have a huge audience for her speech Saturday in Central Park," Marty said. "They expect half a million people in the park, plus millions more watching cable news and live streaming on the internet. It's a climatosis extravaganza."

Lindsey sighed as the waiter brought their drinks and a bowl of nuts and they clinked glasses in a silent, unenthusiastic toast. "What do you suggest we do?" she asked.

He sipped his martini and eyed her. "I have to admit, I'm struggling here," he said. "I have no indication she's wavering. If she goes on stage and says what I think she'll say, you're not going to like it."

Lindsey looked around to see if anyone could hear, then leaned across the table to Marty. "I have an idea that you might hate, but I want to run it past you anyway," she said.

"What's that?"

"Pull the plug," Lindsey said.

Marty frowned. "What are you talking about?"

"It's simple. Just as the event is about to begin, Crowe Power announces an extension of these brownouts we've been having," Lindsey said quietly. "We say there's a problem with our power plant and we have to cut the juice to a swath of Manhattan that includes Central Park."

"On what grounds?" Marty asked, incredulously.

"Whatever," she replied. "A squirrel ate through the wires. A computer malfunctioned. A turbine blew. Poof. The event is over."

Marty regarded her with dismay. "Wouldn't that be rather obvious, considering your position?"

"Maybe, but so what? They can't prove it," she said. "We turn off Missy's microphone just as she's about to go on. Nobody would hear her speech. There's one other benefit, too."

"Which is?"

"It would give people a reminder of what life is like without energy."

"Well," Marty said, fingering the stem of his glass, "you're absolutely right about one thing."

"What's that?"

He looked up at her. "I hate it."

Lindsey recoiled. "Why?"

"Oh, come on, Lindsey," he said, sitting back in his chair. "Isn't that precisely the problem we have now? That there's no debate allowed about climate change? I don't think you should resort to the tactics your critics use. That's fighting the war on their terms. And that's a war you can't possibly win."

Lindsey slumped. "You're not as Machiavellian as I thought."

"Good thing for you I'm not," Marty said. Was Lindsey losing it? Maybe the pressure had gotten to her. "Is there something that makes you think Crowe Power's reputation isn't quite bad enough already?"

Lindsey raised her chin, defiantly. "Tell me this, Marty: what have I got to lose?"

"You want me to go down the list?" he said, heatedly. He ticked off his fingers. "Your daughter, for one. Washington, number two. The press would have a field day, number three. And the state would probably drag you up to Albany for hearings on what really happened." He looked at her in wonder. "Tell me again why you think this makes sense."

Lindsey waved him off. "Oh... I suppose you're right." She looked away, shaking her head. "You know what's so strange about this? When Missy was growing up, she was constantly questioning authority. Her father. Her teachers. Me. I called her 'the 67th Street Why.'"

Marty smiled. "Like the 92nd Street Y."

Lindsey nodded. "The questions were endless," she said. "'Why do I have to go to bed now? Why can't I go over to my friend's apartment? Why can't I wear these jeans?' She needed a reason before she would agree to do anything."

"What happened?" Marty asked.

"College," Lindsey said. "You'd think that an Ivy League education would cause her to ask more questions than ever. Oddly, I think that's when she suspended disbelief in fanciful ideas. I guess she decided she'd rather fit in with the prevailing ideology on campus. You know, go along to get along." She looked sadly at Marty. "And I get it. I really do. It's not easy to stand up to the crowd carrying torches and pitchforks. How can I expect her to fight back when so many of her peers are cowering, afraid to say anything that would get them shunned or canceled? It astonishes me how many big companies, even in my own industry, won't stand up for their own businesses. They mouth the same meaningless platitudes about how much they care about the planet, and how they're working to get to net zero, or how they're developing a way to magically turn moonbeams into energy."

"Surely you understand why they do that," Marty said. "They don't want to enter costly public debates, or have their workers revolt, or invite the feds in to investigate them and start rummaging through their files. 'What did you know about climate change? And when did you know it?' It can get very ugly very fast."

Lindsey shook her head. "Don't I know it. Digby has advised our leadership team that nobody can even mention climate change in an email or a text message, because all our files could be subpoenaed." She sighed. "We're in a dangerous place, Marty, and it has nothing to do with a warming planet."

Marty eyed her. "What are you thinking?"

Lindsey took a healthy swig of her wine, then leaned across the table and spoke quietly. "Alright. First, let me say, this may sound like paranoia."

Marty sipped his martini and shrugged. "That's not a promising introduction."

"Look at it this way," she said. "First, this crazy cabal of activists and bureaucrats pushes everyone into electrical power, offering the fantasy that it's created by renewable energy, right? No oil. No gas. Just clean, green electricity. Of course, we both know that's not possible, right?"

"We're at, what? Twelve percent renewables now?"

"Right," Lindsey said. "And there's no way to ramp up wind and solar fast enough to meet demand, especially when they're phasing out gasoline-powered cars and lawn mowers, natural gas-fired ovens, and every other product that uses oil or gas. What happens then?"

Marty scratched his head. "According to my high school econ class, the price of electricity goes up—rather substantially, I would think."

"A-plus," Lindsey said. "Now here's your bonus question: Who gets electricity then?"

"Whoever they want to give it to," Marty replied.

Lindsey nodded and smiled bitterly. "You're catching on rather quickly, Marty. The authorities will step in to address the crisis they created by declaring energy is a right. They'll decide how to distribute it fairly and equitably."

"By their definition," Marty said.

"The power will be entirely in their hands," Lindsey said. "Who do they favor? Who do they not? What are the sanctioned ways to use energy? What's wasteful and wrong? They won't alter the course of the climate one bit, but they'll certainly change our way of life."

"You're right about one thing," Marty said.

"What's that?" she asked.

"You are paranoid," Marty said, munching on some almonds. "But, as the saying goes, that doesn't mean they're not out to get you."

She sat back and shook her head. "Do you have a better answer?"

"Maybe they're simply naïve," Marty said with a shrug. "It seems to me that a lot of these people are on some sort of ideological bender. Make a sacrifice to the climate gods, and hope for the best. Perhaps they don't understand the consequences of their policies."

Lindsey shook her head and growled. "Don't kid yourself, Marty. They know exactly what they're doing. Energy scarcity isn't an unintended result. It's a goal."

Marty let that sink in, then signaled for the bill. "You're making me want to move to an island somewhere."

"Sorry," she said.

"But… why would they want that?"

Lindsey shook her head. "They hate capitalism for one thing, and they really don't care much for humans, either. We're messy and disobedient and we tend to want to do things our own way. They want to impose their idea of order through central planning. That's worked terribly throughout history, but they're sure they'll get it right this time, as authoritarians always do. Energy will be assigned and rationed. Who won't want to be their friend?"

"Excellent question," Marty said.

"Yes—the kind Missy used to ask," she said. "How do we help her see what's going on here? That she's being used to advance a radical agenda?" She ran her index finger around the rim of her wine glass, eliciting a slight hum. "It's one reason I want her working on fusion, and why I'm spending so much money to move it along. We have to find a way to produce abundant energy that the climate alarmists can't object to. Otherwise, I'm afraid this country's in for its darkest hours. I mean that literally."

Marty sighed. He signed the bill, pocketed his credit card, and stood. "I've left another message offering to help her with her speech. Hopefully, I'll get a chance to at least stress-test her messaging."

"I hope so, Marty," Lindsey said sadly. "Missy's in a tough spot. And we are, too."

27. I AM TANIA

Missy was so depressed she couldn't even twitch, roust herself to scroll TikTok and DingDong, or yell at the household help to do something to relieve her suffering. The script freshly delivered from the White House for her speech at the Beat Climatosis Now rally sounded like a paid political ad for President Dewey Fenwick, a commercial endorsement for his friends' windmills and solar panels, and a screed against fossil fuels that, despite their manifest evils, still turned on the heating, cooling, and lights in her apartment and every other one she could see from her living room windows. Most troubling of all, the speech concluded with a scathing attack on her family company as a "corporate climate criminal," threatening her mother with arrest.

"The measures these greedy profiteers are taking to transition to the next generation of pure, clean, wonderful green energy are far too slow to address the crisis that is right here, right now," the script read. "I say, the countdown begins today. Give these energy companies a deadline—one year—to invest in the green energy that we want now, or we start rounding up their executives and putting them in jail. And yes, that goes for the Crowe Power Company, too."

She could imagine the roar of the crowd. What a scene it would be! A huge throng of twitchy people in Central Park. A national TV audience. Celebrities flitting about the stage, touting their vacuous virtue. Politicians demanding "climate justice," whatever that means. Green financiers applauding the destruction of old energy to create new business opportunities for themselves. All of it brought to a climax by the rantings of a rebel from one of the old energy industry's founding families, followed by a closing pitch for votes for the President of the United States.

She couldn't possibly use this script. Yes, her family annoyed her. Yes, she still believed in climate change, though not quite as ardently after looking through Marty's box of materials, which contained lots of information she'd never seen before. And yes, she was still rankled by her mother's incessant complaining about her failing to show up for work. But this script amounted to a betrayal of the people she loved.

She absently turned on the TV to get her mind off the script, only to find GNN running a documentary on Patty Hearst, a wealthy young heiress to a publishing fortune who was kidnapped in Berkeley, California in the 1970s by a radical group called the Symbionese Liberation Army. Hearst's captors had thrown her in the trunk of a car and kept her in a closet. Within months of her disappearance, she had taken her captors' side, renounced her family, called herself Tania, and posed in a beret holding a gun. Then she helped her kidnappers rob a bank. The SLA guerillas had not only snatched her body, they had also taken her mind.

"Oh my God!" Missy shrieked. "That's *me!*"

Genevieve came running into the room. "Missy, are you okay?"

Missy, ashen, nodded her head. "Get me a White Claw. Now."

Genevieve scampered back to the pantry, while Missy turned off the TV and fell back onto the sofa to contemplate her dilemma. As much as she had enjoyed her celebrity, she was clearly losing control, just as Marty had predicted. She was at odds with her mother, her best friends, and now the people who were supposedly on her side, like Marty, Jessica Holtgren—even the creepy president of the United States.

As Genevieve returned with a glass of White Claw hard seltzer on the rocks, the phone in Missy's lap vibrated. She picked it up to see Jessica's name. Missy sighed and pushed a button to answer. "Hello," she said.

"Missy!" Jessica exclaimed. "How are you, darling?"

"Not very well," Missy said sullenly.

"Oh dear. Are you having a twitchy fit?"

"No," Missy said with a sigh. "I just read the script."

"Wonderful!" Jessica enthused.

"Not exactly," Missy said. "I hate it."

"Which part?"

"Well... let me see," Missy said, flipping through the pages, then slamming it down on the sofa. "I guess, just the whole thing."

There was silence on the line a moment, then, "I'm sure we could make a minor tweak or two, if necessary," Jessica said. "But I must tell you, every word in that script has been poll-tested and approved by our team. I don't think you want to let down the other members of the Climatosis Commission."

"What about this line?" Missy read, "'In 2050, scientists estimate that soaring heat will make it very difficult to live in countries such as Iran, Kuwait, and Oman.' I mean, isn't Iran kind of a shitty place to live now? Women are kind of oppressed over there."

Missy could hear Jessica creaking open a binder. "That may be, dear, but let's see here…" she said. "That line scored 88 percent favorability. So… I'm not sure what the complaint is about."

"Okay. How about this?" Missy posited. "'Capitalism and consumerism have brought the world to the brink of economic and environmental collapse. We have only ninety-six months left to avoid irretrievable climate and ecosystem collapse and all that goes with it.'"

Jessica squealed, "I *love* that passage!"

"But how do we know it's true?"

"It doesn't matter, sweetheart," Jessica said. "We know the statement *works.*"

"How do we know that?"

"Because Prince Charles said it in 2009," Jessica said.

Missy rubbed her forehead, trying to follow the logic. "The ecosystem never collapsed."

"No," Jessica said slowly, as if addressing a child. "But what happened to Prince Charles?"

"I don't follow…"

"He became king!"

Missy said, "And that proves… what, exactly?"

"My point being," Jessica said impatiently, "is that you can say all sorts of idiotic things and still rise to the top."

"Didn't he have kind of a running start on his career? He's a royal."

"As are you, my dear! There's no reason you can't become Queen of Crowe someday."

Missy felt like crying. "Not if there's nothing left of it."

"Oh, come now," Jessica guffawed. "Don't be so dramatic."

"You seem bent on driving it out of business."

There was a pause on the line. Finally, Jessica said tartly, "This is war, Missy. War has casualties. The important thing is to choose carefully which side you're on. Your family's fossil fuels business is a sinking ship. I've offered you a lifeboat. If you're as smart as I think you are, you'll hop aboard before the S.S. Crowe Power ends up at the bottom of the sea."

Missy hung up and sank into her sofa, looking blankly out at the horizon. She wasn't just a soldier in Jessica's war; she was one of her assassins. And it was all her own doing. She took three gulps of White Claw and considered life on her lonely island. She couldn't call her fellow twitcheratti after the contretemps at the Odeon. Nor could she call her mother and hear her say, "I told you so." Her father was out of the question since his judgment was deeply suspect. There was only one person she could depend upon.

She picked up her phone, tapped a contact, and listened to the ring.

A voice said, "Dr. Iz Climatosis Therapy Center."

Missy took a deep breath. "It's Missy Mayburn Crowe," she said in a voice that was almost humble. "I need to see her. Immediately."

PART THREE

A Glitch in the Twitch

28. DOCTOR IZ IN

It took some wrangling to find fifteen minutes on Dr. Iz's calendar, which was chockablock with media interviews, TV appearances, negotiations with publishers and movie studios, and meetings with her patients. As one of the nation's leading authorities on the growing climatosis pandemic, Dr. Iz was in demand. And while Missy was one of her most taxing patients, almost to the point of annoyance, she still held a special place among Dr. Iz's clientele. She was, after all, Patient Zero—as well as a walking, talking, twitching billboard for the fast-growing Dr. Iz Climatosis Therapy Center.

Missy found all eyes in the waiting room of Dr. Iz's operation studying her as she approached the desk, now run by two receptionists. Missy selected the line in front of Crystal and waited. As she looked around, Missy noticed that patients were practicing safe seating, taking chairs that were socially distanced to avoid twitch-instigated altercations.

Crystal sighed wearily when she saw Missy. "Good afternoon," Crystal said brusquely. "Here for your two-forty?"

Missy nodded.

"The doctor is running behind," Crystal said, looking down at her desk. "But she said she would squeeze you in."

Missy quietly seethed. *Squeeze me in? I'm the one who started all this!*

Crystal looked up and pointed with her pencil to the waiting area. "Have a seat. I'll call you when she's ready," Crystal instructed. "Same credit card?"

Missy nodded. "Uh-huh."

"Just so you know," Crystal said tartly, "fees have gone up."

Missy shrugged. "Fine," she said. "I'll pay whatever. I just don't want to wait."

Crystal's expression turned stern. "Neither does anybody else."

Missy found a seat in the corner away from the windows, where she pulled out her phone and scrolled through texts. In the fifteen minutes since she had left the back seat of her limo, there were already a dozen new messages from the White House press office, Jessica Holtgren, her mother, her father, Marty McGarry, and others. She wearily shook her head. This was all too much.

She looked up to see a man slouched in his seat across from her with a copy of *People* magazine open on his lap. He wasn't reading, though; he was staring at Missy, his expression accusing, if not menacing. Missy tried to avoid his glance by shifting in her seat and returning to her phone, but she could feel his eyes boring into her. As she looked up, she saw him walking over, holding his *People* magazine.

He stood in front of Missy and held it up for her to see. It featured Dr. Iz on the cover, holding her reading glasses, as a quote next to her said, "*We can beat climatosis in our lifetime*." "You started this," the man said, his voice rising. "It's all your fault."

Crystal scrambled up from behind the desk and walked over. "Mr. Kupchak, we do *not* talk like that in this office," she said. "Sit down!"

The man pointed a shaking finger at Missy. "She gave me this twitch."

"She did no such thing," Crystal insisted.

"Oh yes she did," he insisted. "She's a witch!"

A witch? Other patients discreetly looked up, but not enough to get involved. Still, Missy noticed they were all watching her out of the corner of their eyes. Did they think she was responsible for their afflictions, too?

Crystal got close to Mr. Kupchak and pointed toward the door. "I want you to leave. Now!"

"You can't kick me out. I had an appointment," the man whined.

"Not anymore," she said. "Get out."

"But I—"

Crystal leaned close and spoke so that only he could hear. "Get the fuck out before I open a can of whoop-ass."

As the man slithered past, Crystal looked to Missy. "Come with me."

Missy, her heart racing, followed Crystal past the reception desk. Crystal opened the door to Dr. Iz's office and let Missy inside, where the psychologist was seated at her desk, looking at her computer and tapping on a few keys.

Missy took a chair in front of the desk and sat, stewing, but not for long. "Uh, *hellooo*," she said in a tone that suggested aggravation.

Dr. Iz snapped out of whatever mental zone she had occupied and turned around. "Ah. Missy," she said, folding her hands in front of her on the desk. "Sorry about that. I just—" She sighed. "How are you?"

"Not great," Missy said.

Dr. Iz stood up, walked over to the conversational seating area, and indicated that Missy should take the patient chair. "Let's chat."

As Dr. Iz took her seat, she considered what it would take for Missy to beat her affliction. As Marty suggested, she could challenge the underpinnings of her concern about a climate crisis. Or she could adopt the same sort of guidance she offered the public in *Get a Grip, Honey*: Assume a degree of responsibility and quit allowing herself to be a victim. Get physically active. Eat healthy foods. Dial back on the drinking. Cut out the drugs. Get enough sleep. And meet people outside her toxic circle of friends. These young ladies all reinforced each other's bad habits and phobias. They had to break away or they'd never get well. But getting Missy well wasn't a winning strategy for the Dr. Iz Climatosis Therapy Center.

They faced each other over a table filled with fresh flowers. The windows were mercifully shut this time and the air was significantly cooler. "Feels like you have your air conditioning back on," Missy noted.

Dr. Iz shrugged her shoulders. "I'll take it while I can get it," she said. "You never know when it's going go off again."

Missy simmered. "From what I heard, they can't get shipments of gas," she said.

"Not my problem," Dr. Iz said, dismissively.

"If you're getting brownouts, then it is your problem, too," Missy said.

Dr. Iz couldn't help feeling contempt for the hypocrisy of her client. If Missy really worried about carbon emissions, she wouldn't lead a life of luxury. She would seize the opportunity to get to work in Crowe Power's fusion division to advance a promising technology. But Dr. Iz had concluded that Missy was more triggered by going to work than she was concerned about destroying the planet.

"So," Dr. Iz said, impatiently. "What's on your mind?" Dr. Iz glanced at her watch, which Missy noticed.

Missy felt the insult. "Do you have to go somewhere?"

"As a matter of fact, I do," she said. "I'm due at a taping for *Jiminy Cratchit* at four o'clock. And I've got a room full of appointments to deal with before I go."

"You have one fewer appointment than before," Missy said dryly.

Dr. Iz looked puzzled. "How do you know that?"

"Crystal kicked a guy out after he called me a witch."

"Oh no."

"Oh yeah," Missy said. "It's getting ugly out there. This celebrity stuff isn't all it's cracked up to be. Frankly, I'd prefer to be anonymous again and get my life back. But that doesn't seem possible."

"Why not?"

"Because this has gone too far," Missy said, her voice rising. "Everywhere I go, people are staring at me and either showing me a twitch and a thumbs up, or showing me the finger and shaking their head in disgust. My phone is blowing up with requests and offers and solicitations, and occasional threats. Now I'm the honorary chair of the Federal Climatosis Commission and I've got to give a big speech Saturday in Central Park."

"Well, well, well!" Dr. Iz said. "That sounds like quite an honor."

"It's not. It was written for me by the White House, and I hate it," Missy said. "Next week I'm supposed to begin a national speaking tour, attacking fossil fuels and talking about my twitch."

"What's so wrong with that?"

Missy sat forward on the edge of her chair and spoke with a clenched jaw. "I don't have the stupid twitch anymore."

Dr. Iz was taken aback. "What?" she asked, gulping. "It's *gone?*"

"Like that," Missy said, snapping her fingers, then pausing to admire her suddenly obedient arm.

Now Dr. Iz was shaken. "That's rather surprising," she said. "I certainly thought it would have lasted longer than this." Her eyes darted back and forth as she thought this through. Then she brightened. "Apparently, my therapy worked."

"Something did," Missy said, with a shrug.

"I should market my remedy," Dr. Iz said, rubbing her chin and looking away.

Missy shook her head slowly, then held up her hand and waved. "Uh, Dr. Iz? Over here." She waited for Dr. Iz to turn her way. "Could you worry about Dr. Iz Enterprises later? This is my time."

Dr. Iz turned back, blinking rapidly. "Of course, dear," she said. "Tell me. When did the twitching stop?"

Missy put a finger under her chin. "I think the last time was a week ago," she said. "I just had this weird sense that maybe I was freaking out about something that I couldn't really control. I was, like, a dog barking at the moon. I mean, we can all do our part, but I finally figured that climate isn't like some thermostat we can just dial up or down. There are a lot more questions than answers out there. I'm worried that some of the stuff they're telling us is a load of crap."

"What about your friends? Are they still twitching?"

"As far as I know," Missy said. "We haven't been talking lately." She dropped her head, sadly. "We had a bit of a fight."

"Ah," Dr. Iz said. "That happens. Especially when you're all under such intense public scrutiny and feeling the pressure."

Missy fell back in her chair. "So what do I do?"

Dr. Iz sat back. "I won't ever tell you what to do," she said. "But I can help you figure out what you want to do."

Missy sighed. "I think I should go to work. Put my head down, learn what I can, and just freaking do it."

"Do what?"

"Whatever they need," Missy said.

"And skip your speech?" Dr. Iz looked troubled. "What about all your commitments? I mean, going on tour sounds like a heck of an opportunity to bring attention to this affliction. I'd be happy to lend my support in any way I can."

"I don't know," Missy said. "I was thinking that I might just want to put out an announcement that says my twitching has stopped, I'm feeling better, I'm resigning from the commission and cancelling all these appearances."

Dr. Iz shook her head. That was a terrible idea. Missy was her poster child for a scary condition. "Is that really the right answer? You're a worldwide symbol of climatosis. What kind of signal would that send to all the other sufferers out there?"

"A good signal, I would think," Missy said. "You can get over this."

"But the climate isn't healed," Dr. Iz protested. "There are floods. Hurricanes. Storms…"

"Yeah, right," Missy said. "I know the script. It just doesn't jibe with the other things I'm reading. I'm not sure I buy that anymore."

Dr. Iz sat back in her chair, pondering. If word got out that Missy had recovered, who was going to worry about climatosis anymore? What kind of shitty pandemic was this, anyway? One you get over in a few weeks without taking any medicine or suffering any lasting consequences? Surely, there was an interest in keeping this alive—not just for Dr. Iz, but for the White House, the news media, the entertainment industry, academia, and activists pushing a climate-crisis agenda. Missy's healing was a potential disaster. "I'm not sure that saying you've recovered is the right message."

"The right message for whom?" Missy pressed.

For once, Dr. Iz looked like the one in the chair, trying to explain the inexplicable. "You have been an incredible leader—someone that other sufferers have looked up to," she babbled. "Do you want to tell them, now they're on their own? That's up to you, of course, but that strikes me as a cruel message to send at a time like this."

"A time like what?" Missy asked.

A time when I have to go on TV! Dr. Iz thought. "Look, Missy, the good news is you're feeling better, but I think you may want to consider waiting before going public," she said. "What if the twitch comes back? If you look back at the history of these mass psychogenic illnesses, you see they do recur. You probably don't want to have to explain, 'Yes, I had it. Then I didn't. Now I do again.' People may have a hard time following you. They might think you're a bit of a flake, to be completely candid with you."

"But this is the way it is," Missy said. "What's wrong with just telling the truth?"

"Nothing, of course," Dr. Iz said. "I'm just not sure that saying you're supposedly recovered is the truth. It's too early to tell. What you suggest seems rather premature to me. Now. That's just my professional opinion, of course. You don't have to take my word for it."

Missy got up to leave, shaking her head. She was no closer to a solution than she had been when she walked in. She might even be further away, trapped in a worldwide web of climatosis that she had spun herself. As she passed through the waiting room, she stopped before she reached the door and turned back to the reception desk. She leaned over it so that only Crystal could hear her.

"Can I ask you about something?" Missy said.

Crystal looked around her, then decided this was not the place for a conversation. She walked around the credenza, took Missy by the arm, and escorted her to the hallway near the elevator. "What do you want?" she asked.

Missy gulped. *What did she want?* "I… I want your opinion." She looked over her shoulder toward the office, then back to Crystal. "You see what goes on here. Do you think there's anything really wrong with these people?"

"Yes," Crystal replied.

"What?" Missy asked.

Crystal folded her arms across her chest and regarded Missy with a harsh glare. "Climatosis. You should know."

"Have you seen anyone recover?"

"Not so far," Crystal said. "Why?"

"Do you think she wants anyone to recover?"

Crystal raised her eyebrows. "Of course. Why wouldn't she?"

"I'm starting to wonder that myself."

29. LOSING HER GRIP

With yet another rolling brownout scheduled to make her apartment on the Upper West Side unbearably hot for sleep, Dr. Iz made a practical decision about her on-and-off relationship with Harold "Hacksaw Harry" Crenshaw: it was back on, along with the electricity in his two-story Park Avenue apartment.

Harry's bedroom was chilled to a frosty sixty-seven degrees—perfect for snuggling under a blanket and drifting off to dreamland. She entered wearing a silk nighty that she had brought for the occasion, crawled under the sheets, and laid on her side to face Harry, sitting back with one arm behind his head on the pillow and the other gripping the remote. He was focused on the television, which he had turned to *Late Night with Jiminy Cratchit*.

"Hey, Izzy," he said, quietly. "When are you on?"

"Second guest," she said, nestling in. "Right after some comedian named Ballzy."

"Was he?"

"Not in the least."

Harry turned off the sound as the frenetic Jiminy bounded onto the stage in his sneakers to deliver his opening monologue, a predictable hash of safe political potshots at the usual suspects. "You mind if I mute this asshat?"

"I wouldn't mind if you muted the whole thing—including my part," she said, with a yawn. "I'm not sure you're going to like what I had to say."

He looked over with a start. "Uh-oh. Why not?"

She sucked in her breath and bit her lower lip. "I went off script a little bit," she said.

"Oh no," he said. "Is the old Dr. Iz resurfacing?"

"You tell me after you see it," she said. "I might have been a bit blunt."

She pulled the blanket up over her shoulders and sighed. Apart from the occasionally chaotic scenes in her waiting room, things couldn't have gone better for her business, at least until today. Her office was gushing cash with new clients competing for time on her calendar, and her hourly rate had doubled. Her reentry into public life as a priestess of the climate prophecy had restored her to a position nearly as visible and respected as she had been in her heyday. Much as the public revels in the downward spirals of its falling stars, it dependably cheered stories of redemption, and Dr. Iz was once again riding high. Suddenly, overbooked restaurants miraculously found prime tables for her and her guests, interview requests poured in from major media, and publishers made competing offers with huge advances for a next book from Ground Zero of the climatosis pandemic. Still, she had been deeply unsettled since Marty McGarry had challenged her treatment of Missy. That was only made worse by her consultation with Missy today, in which her advice to hide her recovery bordered on malpractice. Dr. Iz had panicked at the thought that the climatosis contagion would be over all too quickly. More disturbing was the feeling she had after Missy left: she had betrayed her patient's best interests.

After immigrating from Cuba in a leaky boat as a child, young Isabel Castaneda had found the transition to a new country, a new culture, and a new language destabilizing. She pursued a career in psychology because she genuinely wanted to help people work through difficult feelings she sometimes had herself. Somewhere along the way, as she got a taste of the rewards celebrity could bring and became the fabulous Dr. Iz, her motivations changed. She paid the price for her ambition with a stunning fall from grace.

Now she feared another calamity was coming, one that had nothing to do with whether the climate was changing or not. This climatosis charade had been overplayed, and she knew it. She had been making things worse for people, rather than better. She was encouraging people to act out their worst fears—and now to not even admit they were getting better. It was more profitable for them to suffer. And it was more attention-getting to ride the circuit of talk shows with ill-informed clowns like Jiminy Cratchit, a former stand-up comedian who had transitioned into a humorless national scold. "At some point," she said, "I'm going to have to actually treat this affliction with something other than coddling."

Harry looked at her as if she needed a shrink. "Why on God's green earth would you do that? Won't it go away on its own?"

"It has already, at least for Missy."

"Oh no."

"Oh yeah. That could bring the whole thing crashing—"

Harry cut her off and unmuted the TV. "Hold that thought. You're on."

She looked at the screen, where her segment was beginning. A beaming Dr. Iz walked onstage, waving to the applauding studio audience. Jiminy Cratchit bounced up from his desk to give her a light embrace and a kiss on the cheek, then directed her to a seat next to the un-ballsy Ballzy. She greeted him, sat down, and looked around. With a wave and a nod, she acknowledged the audience, who sat at safe social distances to avoid getting clocked by a twitching neighbor.

"Alrighty then," Jiminy said, as the applause subsided. "So glad to see my dear friend Dr. Iz again. As I'm sure everyone knows, she's enjoying an incredible career renaissance by leading our fight against climatosis." He turned to her and held up a copy of *People* magazine. "So tell us. How goes the battle? Can we really beat climatosis in our lifetime?"

She sighed. "It's an uphill climb, Jiminy, but I think it's possible." She went on to explain that outbreaks of climatosis, especially among the young, affluent, and highly educated, had been reported throughout Western Europe, as well as Australia and New Zealand, and countries along the Pacific Rim, from Japan to Singapore. The number of people afflicted was climbing every day, fueled by a growing chorus of experts predicting doom. "Of course, the evidence is all around us that they very well could be right. Who's to say that this particular hurricane or that particular drought wasn't the result of human-caused climate change? One of my clients saw a photo of a dead penguin and she couldn't stop crying for three days. So, yes, people are distressed, and understandably so. They're bombarded with bad news about the climate every day—and they think it's their own fault."

Jiminy nodded thoughtfully. "Isn't it?" he asked. "I mean, a lot of experts I've listened to are saying we're simply paying the price for a decadent lifestyle."

"I've heard claims that this is simply a reckoning," Dr. Iz acknowledged, "but I'm not sure I'm comfortable with that."

"Really?" Jiminy said. "It drives me crazy that there are still people out there denying climate change is happening. You know the type. Flat-earthers. The people with the tin-foil hats." The audience laughed. "It's like that crazy uncle you encounter at the family picnic with a couple of beers in his belly who says the whole thing's a hoax. I find those kinds of people deplorable. Don't you?"

The applause sign lit up as Dr. Iz noted his point with a nod. "You know, it's interesting, Jiminy," she said. "I didn't really pay much attention to the actual science behind climate change until people started coming to me for therapy. That prompted me to do a little digging into the subject. And, believe it or not, I found there were a number of very respected scientists out there who doubt all the doomsday predictions. They say there's no cause for panic, that things are happening much slower than predicted, and that we're adapting to the changes that are taking place."

There was a low murmur of surprise and even some boos from the studio audience. Jiminy said, "You can't possibly be saying you listen to those people." He shook his head in despair. "I've given up on those crazy skeptics. It should be obvious to all of us now that a climate crisis is at hand and we have to make big changes in our lifestyle if we're going to beat it. It's like that episode of *Seinfeld* where Kramer is marching in the fight against AIDS. We all have to wear the ribbon."

"And beat up the people who don't?" she asked.

Jiminy laughed. "If that's what it takes, hell yes!" The audience erupted in more applause. Jiminy continued, "How do we get everybody on board and convince them to do what's necessary?"

Dr. Iz crossed a leg and leaned closer to the desk. "Well, I don't realistically expect that people who are busy with their lives are going to develop expertise about orbital variations, tilts in the earth's axis, and glaciation cycles," she said. "But, for the average person, I would say you don't need to be a weatherman to know which way the wind is blowing when it comes to climate change. There's one surefire way to know whether the seas are really rising and are about to swallow us all."

Jiminy leaned forward eagerly, cupping his hand under his chin. "And what is that, pray tell?"

"All you have to do is keep an eye on the wealthy politicians, business leaders, and celebrities who profess to be experts on the topic," Dr. Iz said. "Are they selling their beachfront houses and buying something in the hills? Are they trading 20,000-square-foot mansions for little apartments with tiny carbon footprints? Are they still heating and cooling multiple homes, collecting fleets of Bugattis and race cars, and buzzing around to climate conferences in private jets? Or do they just peddle that BS so that the rest of us can work it out? That's an easy way to tell whether these doomsday predictions are something that should give you a twitch."

Jiminy blanched. "You know, if I didn't know better, I might take that personally."

Dr. Iz replied, "I'm not pointing at anyone in particular, Jiminy. I mean, I read that you recently purchased a huge home on the ocean in Martha's Vineyard where, I take it, they're not building a ten-foot seawall around the perimeter."

Jiminy simmered. "Not as far as I know."

"One might say that our behavior, rather than our rhetoric, suggests what we really think about the issue. But that's not just on you. That's on everybody."

Jiminy looked offstage, steaming. Then he turned back. "If you want to kill your career again, it might be easier just to slap someone."

"Maybe I just did?" she said, with a wry smile.

As the crowd hooted its disapproval, Jiminy announced they'd take a short break. "We'll be right back," he said. Then, sneering at Dr. Iz, he said, "Some of us will, anyway."

As the crowd cheered, Harry turned off the TV. "What the hell, Izzy?"

"Yeah. I know," she said, sinking into her pillow. "They told me to leave and said I could never come back."

He propped himself up on one elbow. "Understandably so. Why did you do that?"

"I don't know, but it felt good," she said. "I couldn't stand him sitting there, so smug, so secure, pointing fingers at everyone else. An hour after our taping, he was flying off to Cabo in a private jet for a buddy's birthday party."

"Sounds like somebody has unresolved anger issues," he said.

"Possibly," she replied. "He was one of the people who pounced on me when I had my trouble years ago. Condemned me, shunned me, wouldn't take my calls. Now he's magnanimous, welcoming me back because he thinks I'm reinforcing the same bullshit he sells every night. I couldn't resist."

"Well, you're not just killing your golden goose," he said. "You're killing mine, too."

"Mine might be dying anyway, and maybe that's a good thing," she said. "The more I understand about the root causes of climatosis, the more I'm convinced we're making it worse, scaring the crap out of people for no good reason."

Harry rolled over on his back and looked up at the ceiling, shaking his head. "There are plenty of good reasons. I've got investments in a bunch of businesses that stand to make a shit-pile of dough from climate change. Can't you at least wait a little bit longer?"

"Wait for what?"

"Let me close this deal for Robbie Crowe's Fantasy Island," he said. "We need to keep our foot on the gas, so to speak, to keep up the sense of urgency. That's the only way my funding goes through. I've got a hundred million dollars coming to me in this deal alone. Once that's tied up, you can say whatever you want. Until then, could you please cool it?"

Dr. Iz popped up. "Wait a second. What kind of deal do you have with Missy's father?"

"Nothing, if you're going to torpedo it on national TV," he replied.

"Is that why you told her father Missy should see me?" Dr. Iz asked.

Harry sat up. "I make no apologies. You needed the business," he said. "This climate crisis is the greatest business opportunity to come along in a generation. I knew you'd sense that immediately, and you'd treat her accordingly. I was right on both counts."

Dr. Iz's mouth fell open and she shook her head. "You mean, because I'd been chastened by my own experience, I wouldn't confront Missy about her fears."

Now it was Harry's turn to get indignant. "As a matter of fact, yeah. That's exactly what I thought," Harry said. "At least until tonight."

"I see," she said. She got up on her knees and faced him. "So I should thank you for your remarkable cynicism?"

He nodded. "Absolutely. Is it any different than yours?"

"How about some advice instead?" She swung her right arm back, then brought her open palm hard across his face in a thunderous slap.

"What the hell?" he said, rubbing his cheek.

She scrambled up out of bed. "Sorry," she said. "I felt a twitch."

She gathered her glasses and a book off the nightstand and dashed out of the room.

30. SENDING OUT AN SOS

While sorting through a pile of background materials for Missy to peruse before her speech, Marty assembled three stacks of reports on his coffee table. The first—and shortest—was comprised of the most coherent and credible reports about climate change. The second concerned the promise and limitations of fusion as an alternative to fossil fuels, which, after Lindsey's assessment, suddenly felt more urgent to Marty. The third and tallest stack was a sure cure for insomnia: a reject pile, destined for the recycle bin, that no normal human could possibly read without punching their ticket to dreamland. By the time he got to a government report on predictions about rain deluges, Marty was dreaming that he, Lindsey, and Missy were herding animals onto an ark. Sadly, they were missing unicorns.

A siren outside roused Marty from his slumber, and he forced himself to resume his research. He had initially found the most recent report from the influential International Panel on Climate Change a candidate for pile No. 3. But after slogging through a warning to make certain "adaptive actions do not worsen existing gender and other inequities within society," he came across a chapter outlining the panel's predictions for temperature increases through the end of the century: roughly one-to-two degrees Celsius. If he were not mistaken, that was less than half of what they'd predicted just a few years ago. Had anyone reported this?

Marty leafed through his stacks of material, looking for a news story on this significant change in scenarios. He found nothing. He opened his laptop and tried a search. All his queries about climate change and temperature predictions turned up links to government entities and fundraising activists, including the Planetistas, the Klimate Korps, and the Fossil Fuel Abolition Fund, all of which insisted: the end is near, donate here. The drop-down menus of frequently searched questions offered by the search engine was no help either:

Is climate change irreversible? (*Yes. Buy an electric car anyway.*)
Is it too late to save the planet? (*Only chance to survive: support the Big Green Deal.*)
How long do humans have left? (*Maybe ten years—if we stop all carbon emissions immediately.*)
What country is best to live in as the planet heats up? (*One with nude beaches.*)

The search was exasperating. Marty plugged in new search criteria and clicked on "News" at the top. Surely, the ever-vigilant news media had not ignored the IPPC finding as an inconvenient truth.

It took more digging but buried deep in the *Daily Reaper*'s story touting "startling news" about the looming catastrophe requiring "immediate drastic action" were oblique references to a significant reduction in the projected temperature increase. Apparently, the IPCC report in 2014, considered the previous last word on such things, had predicted an increase of up to five degrees Celsius from pre-industrial levels by 2100. While the *Reaper* quietly reported that figure obsolete, it still assured the citizenry there were plenty of reasons to panic. Somehow, the climate change that we would all experience would be more harrowing than previously believed. There would be even more searing heat! Even higher surging seas! Toastier winters without ice, threatening the food supply, the water supply, shorelines—*gaaahhh!*

Marty sank back into his sofa. He remembered the days when the local TV weatherman was a bow-tied comedian, wearing a plaid sportscoat with a water-squirting flower in his lapel, who would jolly his viewers with predictions that abundant sunshine and warmth would follow the cold misery they were currently experiencing. Forecasts were corny but useful, even if you still had to flip a coin on whether to chance going to the baseball game that night. Now, with the major news organizations hiring legions of "climate reporters" to scour the globe looking for extreme events, the weather was no laughing matter. It was an incitement for twitching.

Marty's phone vibrated, indicating a text message. He snatched the phone off the couch and saw it was from Missy.

MMC

Dr. Iz coming up on Jiminy Cratchit.

Marty looked at his watch and turned on the TV. With a half-hour to go before Jiminy Cratchit, Marty watched the eleven o'clock news and wondered if he hadn't fallen asleep again.

First came the bulletin that former Vice-President Chad Hanger had collapsed after working himself into a frenzy during a panel discussion at a climate confab in Aspen. When asked whether earlier predictions of warming hadn't been wildly exaggerated, Hanger bolted from the stage screaming, "Oceans are boiling! Rain bombs are falling! Run for your lives!" His spokesperson said the former Veep's attack had been the result of hyperventilation, and he was treated at the scene with a paper bag.

The second story involved presidential nephew Scooter Fenwick, who was identified in yet another paternity claim, this one made by a pole dancer, Hotzie Totzie. It was reported that Ms. Totzie's son, born the previous day in Newark, would be named Scooter Fenwick the fifth, or sixth, as soon as an accurate count could be made of how many Scooter Fenwicks there were out there.

Marty hit the mute button. Hadn't he heard all those reports before? He turned to ESPN for sports highlights, then switched back to Channel 7 for Jiminy Cratchit. What he saw was startling. Dr. Iz's old belligerence was back, seemingly with a vengeance. Whatever was bugging her—whether it was his visit, Missy's visit, or something else—it looked like suicide-by-talk-show. His phone buzzed again, with another missive from Missy.

MMC

R U up?

Marty hit Missy's number on his phone, and she picked up after one ring.

"Now that," she said, "was totally weird. What was she doing?"

"A stunt for ratings?" Marty said. "I couldn't explain it otherwise."

"I need to see you," she said. "Do you have time tomorrow?"

"I'll make time," he replied.

"Good," she said. "This rally is freaking me out."

31. SPEECH AT THE BEACH

Even a man of Robbie's wealth could not recall a time when lunch had cost him fifty thousand bucks. But that was the going price for the *"Let's Dewey Again!"* fundraiser at the Todd Spinx estate in Amagansett, Long Island.

As Harry put it, "You're buying influence, not a lobster roll." Robbie, he said, should consider the lunch tab a down-payment on his plans for Governors Island. Fifty grand would pay him back many times over in legal cover, subsidies, regulatory waivers, land acquisition, permit approvals, and anything else he might need. Once donations were accepted in Washington, so were phone calls.

Inside the estate's fifteen-foot hedges, a white canvas tent set up over the tennis courts housed the luncheon setting for two hundred of the president's closest and wealthiest friends. Pre-prandial libations were served from two bars by the pool, a champagne fountain, and a martini luge, featuring dry gin cascading over an elaborately carved block of ice designed to reflect a melting Earth. Robbie snagged a glass of a locally produced sauvignon blanc from a passing tray and sidled up to Harry, wearing his standard Hamptons uniform: ivory gabardine slacks, Gucci suede loafers, an open-collar white shirt, and a blue blazer.

"Have you met our partners?" Harry asked, clinking his wine glass with Robbie's.

"Sorry," Robbie said, absently. "Our partners in what?"

"The three-billion-dollar L. Robertson Crowe III Center for Fusion Excellence," Harry said.

"*Three?* I thought it was two."

Harry shrugged. "We've run into cost overruns."

"We haven't even broken ground," Robbie said.

"We have a lot of hungry mouths to feed, Robbie," Harry said. "Plenty of people here are taking a bite."

Robbie stared at Harry in disbelief. "What did you do?"

"It's not what I did," Harry said. "It's what our political pals did when they agreed to back the plan. Once their donors got a whiff of this deal, they all wanted in." He nodded toward a group of beefy men holding blue cans of beer, fea-turing the likeness of a famous football linebacker wearing lipstick and mascara. "You got your heads of the construction union, the maritime union, the building trades, electrical workers, you name it. Expect a lot of overtime." He nodded to-ward the veranda, where a well-dressed man and woman were admiring the view of the beach.

"That's Beatrice Pooter—the master contractor for our project," Harry said. "All her suckling subcontractors get a teat." Harry swiveled and turned his back to a woman enjoying an orange-colored cocktail. "The woman in the white dress behind me? That's the mayor's girlfriend. She's opening Maybelline's on the first floor of Star Power HQ."

Robbie said, "What's that?"

"Either an oyster bar or a steakhouse," Harry said. "She hasn't decided whether it's surf or turf."

"I didn't know we're having a restaurant."

"Neither did I until this morning," Harry said.

Robbie peered over Harry's shoulder at Maybelline. "What restaurants has she run?"

"None," Harry said, with a shrug. "She runs a homeless shelter in the Bronx. But she always wanted to have her own place, bless her heart." He clapped Robbie on the shoulder. "C'mon, man. Be happy. This is a huge success story. Robbieville is coming along just fine."

A roar of engines and the approach of whirring helicopter blades caused Robbie and Harry to turn, just in time to see Marine One landing on the lawn. As it settled onto the grass, a door opened and a pair of marines in full dress descend-ed the steps. They lined up to salute the president, who exited the plane wearing aviator sunglasses and his trademark navy windbreaker bearing the presidential crest. The last to jump out of the chopper was Scooter Fenwick, who stumbled as he hit the grass and landed on the lawn. *Where the hell was he, anyway?*

Harry nudged Robbie. "Scooter gets a cut, too."

Robbie was aghast. "What does he add?"

"A couple zeroes to his bank account," Harry said. "Maybe his uncle's, too."

"For what?" Robbie asked, exasperated.

"Breathing in," Harry said.

"That's it?"

"He breathes out, too—when he's not in cardiac arrest," Harry said. "Look, Robbie. It's no skin off our nose. Scooter gets paid from the Chinese cut."

"I thought they were out."

"Nah. Everybody's in, and they're all greased up. It's a fucking orgy, man." Harry put his arm around Robbie's shoulder and pulled him away from the crowd. They walked toward the bathhouse. "There's just one little wrinkle."

Robbie sighed. "Do I want to hear this?"

"The Chinese want a second statue," Harry said.

Robbie shook his head. "No way."

"A smiling Chairman Xi," Harry said. "Fusion now has two daddies."

Robbie practically spat. "That's ridiculous. What has he done?"

Harry nodded in sympathy. *About the same as you.* "I told them your statue had to be taller."

"By how much?" Robbie asked.

"Inch and a half."

"It's a thirty-foot statue," Robbie said. "Nobody's going to know the difference."

Harry set down his drink on a high-top table and put his hands on Robbie's shoulders. "Look at me," Harry said. "You know you're the bigger man, in every way. And it will say so somewhere on the plaque. I'll make sure of it."

Robbie shook him off. "I wish I could say this didn't bother me. But this doesn't sound like it's my project anymore. All this money flying around. Can't people go to jail for stuff like this?"

Harry scoffed. "Not in the great State of New York. You put the right checks for the right amounts in the right pockets, and you're practically guaranteed immunity. It's not the letter of the law, but it's certainly the spirit. Excelsior, man! It says so on the state flag."

The president of an electrical workers' union approached, holding his blue can of beer. He slapped Harry on the back. "Yo, boss. How they hangin'?"

Blue-blooded Harry slipped into blue-collar Harry. "All good, Bruno. How ya doin'?"

"Can't complain, ya know?" he said, with a chuckle. "What good would it do?"

"Nuttin'," Harry replied.

Bruno asked Harry if they could have a word, which sounded like a *woid,* and pulled Harry aside. "I got the thing for the thing."

Harry nodded. "Good."

"I'm thinkin' fitty."

"Works for me," Harry said.

Bruno looked around to see if anyone else could hear him. "And the finder's fee."

Harry nodded. "Understood."

As Bruno waddled off, Robbie asked, "What was that about?"

Harry said, shaking his head in amusement. "You don't want to know," he said. "But I'll tell you this much. The only way to build Robbieville on public land is to make it a government-sanctioned money-laundering operation. The donor cash comes in one door; the contracts go out the other. In and out it goes, in perpetuity." Harry gazed off into the sky. "There's a lovely symmetry to it."

Robbie and Harry made their way through the crowd to say hello to the host, Todd Spinx, attired in his trademark resale-store style: camouflage cargo shorts, a Mets jersey, and flip-flops showing exquisitely pedicured toes. Robbie thought: this man couldn't look any weirder if he tried. Yet he seemed to be trying very hard.

"Dude," Todd said to Robbie, "I got your money just in time. I was able to squeeze you in on a high-speed rail project in California."

"That's fantastic," Robbie said with a big smile. Then, "Isn't it?"

"Oh yeah. Huge deal. Train will run from Cerro Gordo to Bodie."

"Cerro—?" Robbie said. "I've never heard of those places."

"Yeah, well," Todd said, "you probably wouldn't. They're technically what you'd call 'ghost towns.'"

"Wait. What?" Robbie said. His brow furrowed. "Why would a train run between ghost towns?"

"It's as close as we could get to big cities," Todd replied with a shrug. "And you never can tell. These places could come back if they ever find gold again. The important thing is that it gets built. It doesn't really matter if anyone ever uses it or not. You dig? It's a huge statement."

"About what?" Robbie asked.

"Oh, come on. You know."

Robbie didn't know, but he nodded anyway. If it made sense to Todd, a certified financial genius, it must be real.

Todd leaned in. "Look, Robbie, if it makes you feel better: You're not just going get all your money back. You'll make a fucking *killing*, man."

Robbie brightened. "I like the sound of that," he said. "When do I start seeing returns?"

Todd sniffed. "As soon as I get some new investors."

"I see," Robbie said. Then, thinking, said, "Or… wait. Maybe I don't."

"Money comes in. Money goes out," Todd said, impatiently. "It's a very simple business model." Todd slapped Robbie on shoulder. "Catch you later, dude. I gotta go say hello to the prez."

Robbie turned to Harry as Todd sauntered away. "Did that make any sense to you?"

Harry shrugged. "Perfect sense. It's a pyramid scheme."

Robbie blanched. "I'm screwed?"

"Depends."

"Depends on what?" Robbie asked.

"If you're at top of the pyramid or the bottom," Harry said.

"I'm not sure where I am."

"You might be in deep shit," Harry said. "How much did you invest?"

"Two hundred fifty million."

Harry spit his wine. "Why didn't you ask me? I would have warned you."

"I thought he was legit," Robbie whined. "Or you wouldn't have brought him in."

"I brought him in to put his money into *our* project. Not the other way around." Harry drained his wine glass and handed it to a passing waiter. He put his hand on Robbie's shoulder and guided him toward the tent. "Look. He probably won't hurt you. Not intentionally, anyway. We're partners. Or at least we will be once he wires us the money."

Robbie blanched. "He hasn't done that yet?"

Harry shrugged. "Like he said. He's gotta wait for others to kick in." Harry saw Robbie's concern. "I wouldn't worry. I get the sense he likes you. He'd probably hose somebody else first."

Mollified, at least for the moment, Robbie sensed as he headed to lunch that he had landed in a financial mosh pit. Everything was in excess—sand and sea, good vibes and big bribes, sockless shoes and strapless minidresses. The president was on the premises, and they were all bumpin' uglies under his protective embrace. No wonder everyone was in such a good mood. These folks were, literally and figuratively, inside the tent. The system, for them, wasn't just working well. It was *great!*

After a lunch of lobster salad and scallop bisque, the president rose from the head table. He picked up a microphone and tapped it with his fingers. "Hello... hello... This thing on?" Assured it was by Chief of Staff Ben Bixby, the president continued. "I want to thank all of you for coming out today. What a wonderful place to spend time with so many good friends. And of course, I want to offer special thanks to our host today… " *Who the hell was that, anyway?* Some kid he saw a minute ago. A crypto guy. *Tim somebody? Tom?*

Todd stood up and waved to the president to refresh his memory. "Right here, sir," he said.

"Yeah," the president said. "There he is. That fella there. A dear, dear friend. Thanks so much… you." *Ah, hell. Whatever his name was.* The president looked around at the tables filled with his people. Love washed over him like the juniper juice sluicing down the icy martini luge. Dewey do it again? The answer was obvious!

The president commented on the fine weather, the lovely surroundings, and the generosity of the assembly. "Thanks to your support, we've been able to achieve great, great things together over the past few years. And now, with your contributions today, we're going to accomplish even more." Everyone rose to their feet and roared approval.

The president smiled and waved, and then motioned for them to sit down. He then asked an aide whether his remarks were being recorded. Assured they were not, and that phones were turned off, he pressed ahead.

"They say in every crisis there is opportunity, and I think that's never been clearer than it is today with the devastating spread of climatosis," the president said. He looked out over the audience. "There is no greater resource in our country than our wonderful young people. It's heart-breaking to see so many of them afflicted with this twitchy deal. Where's my good friend, Robbie Crowe?"

From a table in the middle, Robbie tentatively raised his hand.

"Stand up, young man!" the president commanded. As Robbie stood, feeling all eyes upon him, the president said, "Some of you, no doubt, are aware that Robbie's beautiful daughter, Missy, has been stricken with climatosis." Heads shook in dismay and a groan of sympathy arose from the crowd. "Now I met this fine young woman at the White House not too long ago. And as I understand it, she's been rendered unable to work by this heinous contagion. But she's an incredibly brave young lady, and I've been able to enlist her in the cause of defeating climatosis once and for all." More applause followed on cue.

"One way we're going to do that is through her father's tireless—and I mean *tireless*—efforts to advance fusion technology, which could go a long way to replace fossil fuels. I smell four or five million green jobs, maybe six or seven. And these aren't just any old jobs that cause a person shame and disgrace, like those in the oil and gas industry. These are jobs any decent person can be proud of when they go home at night. They can look at their family across the kitchen table and say: 'Honey, I did something today for our planet.' So thank you, Robbie Crowe, for your magnificent innovations in fusion. A grateful country salutes you."

Applause rang through the tent, and Robbie turned and waved.

The president, annoyed, said, "Alright, pal. That's enough."

Robbie blushed and took his seat.

The president continued, "Our nation's youth are scared by the climate apocalypse, and who can blame them? They know their parents and grandparents and great-grandparents have done everything possible to ravage our precious Earth with gasoline-powered vehicles, coal-fired power plants, and homes heated by natural gas—cranking out carbon emissions like there's no tomorrow. Well, guess what, folks? There *is* no tomorrow if we keep doing what we're doing."

The crowd applauded somberly as President Fenwick warmed to the topic. "Now we have an opportunity to tap the brakes before we all go flying over the cliff. And I intend to do that by getting rid of all these old energy businesses. That will allow you folks to create new ones to take their place. I'm going to shut down every damn fossil fuel facility in our country that I can. We're going to make everything in this nation electric—cars, heating, cooling, you name it. I don't care if you're roasting weenies or toasting marshmallows. I'm one-hundred percent AC/DC." A sudden burst of applause came from a table of twelve well-dressed men in the corner, who jumped to their feet and cheered.

When the applause died down, the president continued. "Now, some of my friends in Congress say, 'Dewey, old boy, you can't do that. You can't shut down our nuclear facilities, our coal plants, our gas plants. We don't have enough electricity from renewables and we never will!' Okay. That's their opinion. But see, that's why I'm planning to ask Congress for a trillion dollars in clean, green energy, to provide cash to struggling companies, like yours, that make windmills, solar panels, and electric cars, that provide insurance and financing and marketing to the fast-growing climate industry. We're calling my spending proposal the Healthy Families Act, so that people don't get the idea that we're wasting their money on some climate boondoggle." He chuckled, as if that were far-fetched. "And if, for some unforeseen reason, we can't produce all the electricity we need, then by God, we're just going to have to pick and choose our priorities."

The crowd stood and applauded heartily. It was just what they wanted to hear.

The president again motioned for them to retake their seats. "Okay. Here's the deal. I don't think we can get the sort of energy conservation we need voluntarily. Fact is, we've got too many selfish, pig-headed people out there who won't play ball. So, under the powers vested in me by the Climatosis Emergency Act, we're just gonna tell 'em, 'Here's what you gotta do.' Seriously."

"Do we really need shops open for eight or ten hours a day?" he asked. "I don't think so. Why not just two or three? And who says a restaurant has to open for breakfast, lunch and dinner? Pick one, I say, and that's it. Let's set the hours for folks to buy a loaf of bread or a pound of coffee. There's no reason these stores and offices need lights on all day, wasting valuable energy for no reason at all. You get in, you get out, you go home within the hours allotted for people to drive an electric car. And once you're home, through the advancements of our new Smart Home Intelligence Technologies program, we can decide whether your car can be recharged that day or whether you need to wait a while. We can also tell you where your temperature ought to be set. None of this, 'ooh, I'm too warm,' or 'ooh, I'm too cold' crap. Toughen up, people! We're all gonna have to give a little to stop this degradation of our beloved planet. No price that we pay is too high."

An aide walked up to the president and whispered in his ear. The president nodded and turned back to the crowd. "They're telling me I'm getting a little ahead of the news here, so you're going to have to wait until after the election to hear the rest."

The crowd rose again in unison, roaring its approval, while Scooter darted from table to table, scooping up envelopes.

Harry leaned over to Robbie. "What could go wrong with a plan like that?"

Robbie shook his head in dismay. "I don't know… Everything?"

32. PIER PRESSURE

When Marty met Missy at the end of Pier 26 abutting the Hudson River, the first question on his mind was whether she intended to leap into the turbulent water below. Missy was all a jumble—shifting her stance from one foot to the other, her hands fidgeting, her eyes darting around under a hoodie as if desperately searching for something, but she had forgotten what it was. Was she hoping for a speedboat to whisk her out of town? A raft to paddle to Jersey? Whatever had happened to the triumphant Missy he met in their first encounter had left her shaken, not stirred.

They walked over to a set of wooden chaise lounge chairs to get out of the way of the joggers, skateboarders, and walkers rounding the end of the pier. Marty slid a backpack off his shoulder and set it on the ground. He sat on the side of his chair to face Missy as she explained the meeting in the Oval Office, the plans for the Beat Climatosis Now rally, her scripted remarks attacking her family's company, and her growing sense of unease about the whole thing.

"Let me just get this out of the way," she said. "You were right. Okay?"

Marty nodded in a properly somber way. "I take no satisfaction from that." He cocked his head, thinking. *Well, maybe a little bit.* This, however, was no time for gloating. If there were ever a chance to bond with Missy, it was now. He needed to listen.

Missy pulled her knees up under her chin and hugged her legs. "I took a long walk this morning along the river, trying to think this thing through. And then I noticed something down there," she said, nodding toward the Battery Park City neighborhood. "They've hung a bunch of blue banners from light posts. And the banners say how high the water could get because of climate change. It would take another thirty years, and a massive storm, and a huge rise in sea level, but the water will supposedly go way over our heads."

Marty nodded. "What did you think about that?"

"I thought, that's inconceivable. I also thought, shit, man. I'm being hung out there just like those banners—to scare the hell out of people. 'Look at what happens if you don't go along with our crazy scheme around climate change.'"

Marty sighed. "I agree."

She shot him a look. "You do?"

"Climatosis is a gift to these folks," he said. "It makes a nice, neat cover story. It's not some abstract concept like computer modeling that few people understand. It's a problem you can see. The fact that it hit a member of a family that's a household name in fossil fuel energy makes it that much better. You're the perfect vehicle for their messages. 'See, folks. The climate crisis came for the worst offenders first. And you're next.'"

Missy stretched her legs out and laid back. "I don't want to do this rally on Saturday," she said. "But I can't see any way out of it. This whole twitching thing is kind of my deal. I mean, I started it. And it was crazy at first, exciting, even, in a weird way."

"So it appeared," Marty interjected.

"But then it took off way more than I ever thought possible," Missy said. "Now look where we are. I've got the creepy, crepey President of the United States inviting me to the Oval Office and sniffing my hair and telling me he's counting on me."

"Heady stuff," Marty said. "So to speak."

"And it's not just him who's pushing me," Missy continued. "It's this whole group of people on the commission, from the media, education, Hollywood, big tech—even the military. What am I supposed to tell them? 'Hey, guys. I don't feel like doing this anymore? Carry on without me?' There are going to be, like, millions of people watching. They've been talking about it on the news and on social media all week."

Marty settled back into his chair and they both looked out toward New Jersey, and the ferries, tour boats, sailboats, and tugs passing in between. Marty said, "You may find this hard to believe, but there was a time when I, like you, was going to change the world. I carried banners with stencils of clenched fists and chanted, 'Power to the People.' By power, I wasn't thinking gas and electricity."

"What happened?"

"I moved on, as a lot of us did," he said.

"You compromised your principles."

"Not entirely," he said. "One of my core principles was paying rent. Another was eating. With four hungry mouths to feed, including my own, saving the world wasn't number one on my list any longer. I needed a job."

Missy reached out a hand and touched his chair. "I don't want you to take this the wrong way," she said, "but I don't actually need a job."

Marty turned. "Yes, you do."

She guffawed. "What? You think I'm going to starve?"

Marty swung his legs around and faced her. "I didn't say you needed a paycheck," he said. "I said you needed a job—a mission to prove your self-worth. I know enough about your family to realize that at some point, it's not enough to be a Crowe, bathing in the reflected glory of some distant ancestor. Hand-me-down genes can wear out fast. You need to create your own persona. Your current mission doesn't suit you."

"Why not?"

Marty sucked in his breath. "You said it yourself: you're being used. Your fellow travelers are happy to leverage your name, and probably your fortune, to drive their agenda. But it's more than that. They love to see you grovel. The wealthy heiress, whose family made a pile from fossil fuels, on her knees, begging for mercy. They're pulling you down to a level where they can feel not just equal, but superior. You've come over to their side."

"I am Tania," Missy said, sadly.

"Patty Hearst?"

Missy shook her head. "In some ways, yes. The difference is they didn't kidnap me; I volunteered. Stupidly, as it turns out. The more I've studied climate change, the less I seem to know. I didn't realize until this week that I was just echoing the views of the loudest people in the room. Same for my friends, like Peach, Britney, and Gina. What the hell do we know about it?"

Marty pulled the backpack off the ground and handed it to her. "Speaking of which—"

"What's this?"

"More material to help you get smart before you take the stage," Marty said. "Might be useful background."

Missy slouched in her chaise. "I've read so much already, it's made my head hurt. And it won't make any difference, anyway," she said. "The speech is done. Jessica Holtgren and her flying monkeys wrote it."

"You don't have a say at all?" Marty asked.

"Apparently not," Missy replied. She sagged back into her chaise, folded her hands, and closed her eyes. "I just want this to be over."

Marty said, "You know what I do for a living, right? I've written a lot of speeches for a lot of people. Why don't I at least take a look at what they gave you. I could bring my friend Joe over—he knows the topic backwards and forwards.

Maybe we can tweak it a bit." When she didn't reply, Marty pressed. "What does it say now?"

"Oh, it's this weepy tale about how I got the twitch and what it means and how it's a symbol of the struggle we all face. And that we need to make big changes now if we're to prevent more people from suffering my fate." She shook her head. "There's just one big problem."

"What's that?"

"I don't have the twitch anymore."

Marty paused, absorbing that bulletin. "You're kidding."

"It's gone," she said with a sigh. She snapped her fingers. "Arrivederci, baby."

"But… I saw you twitch a moment ago."

"I'm faking it," Missy admitted. "Dr. Iz told me I shouldn't tell people."

"Of course she said that," Marty replied. "It could kill her business."

Missy sighed. "Then she went on TV and practically killed her business herself. I don't know what to do now."

He clapped his hands together. "Here's a crazy idea. What if… you go to work?"

"I know even less about fusion than I know about climate change."

Marty said, "Let me help you ease you into it. No pressure. I'll ask PC if he can come to your apartment for a little off-campus tutorial. He can walk you through the basics. The guy's a genius."

Missy looked alarmed. "That's what scares me. What if I ask a dumb question?"

"Guaranteed," Marty said. "You will. But you've got to start somewhere."

33. BURNING DESIRE

Through the lenses of advanced telescopes and microscopes, PC had visited more exotic worlds than almost everybody on the planet. Yet he had never seen a locale as distant from his own as Missy's apartment. With size, space, light, and dimensions so completely unlike his cramped Jersey City studio, Missy's habitat appeared as remote as GN-z11, a galaxy in the Ursa Major constellation, thirty-two billion light-years away. The top of the Jenga Building seemed further away than that. He had entered the Twilight Zone.

As PC said hello to Missy and began to carefully roll up his umbrella, Missy's housekeeper—a housekeeper!—appeared and reached out a hand. "I'll take that for you," Genevieve said, taking the umbrella from his hand. "Would you like a glass of wine, Dr. Williamson?"

PC chuckled. *Wine? On a weekday?* "Sure," he replied with a grin.

Genevieve asked, "What kind of wine would you like?"

"Oh, I don't know. Anything, I guess," he said. "Do you have… apple?"

Genevieve arched an eyebrow. "I don't believe so." She looked to Missy. "I could send out for some… I think."

"Go with the pinot," Missy said under her breath.

PC trailed slowly behind Missy as she led him through the gallery of Georgia O'Keeffe paintings. He stopped at a portrait of an opening flower, and studied it, his mouth slightly agape. He was struck less by the brilliant splash of color than the intricate engineering structure of the ovule and stigma, the curves of which suggested both elasticity and strength.

"Do you like it?" Missy asked.

He put a finger to his chin. "I feel like I've seen it somewhere before. I just can't recall where." He shook his head, trying to rattle the memory into place. "I'm sure it will come to me."

Missy nodded as they moved on. "You spend a lot of time in the lab, PC?"

He nodded vigorously. "Pretty much all day every day."

"Uh-huh."

She led him into the living room and indicated the sofa, where they both sat facing the tall, panoramic windows overlooking the city. As dusk descended, the lights of Midtown took on an added shimmer through the light rain, with the scalloped edges of the Chrysler Building etched in white light, and the cascading tower atop the Empire State Building bathed in bright red. PC shook his head in wonder at the view.

Genevieve brought the wine and set it on the coffee table. Missy picked up her glass and raised it to PC, who smiled awkwardly. He picked up his glass by the stem and was instantly distracted by the purplish hues, wondering how long the skins of the grape must have been kept in the barrel to create such a rich color, and thinking—

Missy reached over and clinked his glass, startling him, and said, "Cheers."

He nodded, and said, "Ah. Right." Then he took a tiny sip. *Whew!* "That's kinda strong."

Seriously? Missy wondered. "Would you like something else?"

"No, no," he said, taking another swig, and then clearing his throat. "This is, um… really good."

Missy shifted in her seat to face him and ran a hand through her hair. "I hope you don't take it personally that I haven't been out to the lab," she said. "I know you've been working very hard to advance the cause. I've just been busy with other things that are kinda wrapping up now."

"I'm sure there's a lot on your plate," he said blandly. *Staying this rich must take at least a little work, doesn't it?* Then again, how would he know?

"So tell me," Missy said, "where do things stand? Are we making progress?"

"Not as much as I would like," he replied. "I'm a bit stymied."

"Stymied?" Missy asked.

"Oh yes. I'm stymied." He went on to say that competition to make fusion energy commercially viable had intensified significantly. Announcements were coming daily about money pouring into the industry from governments, corporations, and private investors. Breakthroughs were celebrated regularly, too, with new records every week for heat generation, duration, and temperature. While PC's original tokamak had proven successful in lighting the flame on the Statue of Liberty, it was not yet proven that the process could be dependably replicated. Under his direction, CroFusion was pursuing several approaches simultaneously to see which worked the best. "The fact is, we've lost some ground in recent months. But if I can source a few critical components, I think we could get back in the game very quickly."

"What kind of components?"

"The one I'm focusing on right now is magnets."

"Seriously?" Missy said. "My friend Blair has a company that makes magnets. Energy Concepts. Have you heard of them?"

PC nodded excitedly. "Of course. Who hasn't?"

"Well, I hadn't until a week ago," she said. "Would you like me to connect you?"

"Absolutely!" he said.

Success! Missy might have made her first contribution to CroFusion. This called for more wine! She refilled her glass, and PC's as well, then quickly typed a text message to Blair asking to see her. Turning back to PC, she said, "You really love what you do, don't you?"

"Of course. It's the greatest passion of my life," he said, blinking back a tear.

Missy wondered how one could get so moved by life in a laboratory. "It's never, you know... boring?"

"Working on fusion?" PC was aghast. "Quite the contrary. It's rather thrilling."

"How so?" she asked.

"Wow... where do I begin?" he said, looking up at the high ceiling. "Start with the concept of harnessing the power of the sun and the stars here on earth. That, in itself, is mind-blowing. Then there's the challenge of containing this superheated plasma in a way that's self-sustaining. And if you can do all that, then there's the promise of the most abundant source of energy the world has ever seen, yet it doesn't contribute greenhouse gasses to the atmosphere. What more could you ask?"

"That it works, I guess," Missy said.

"Oh, it will work!" PC said. "I'm sure of it. Fusion is incredibly challenging, and at times, seemingly unattainable, yet we inch a bit closer every day." He shuddered with excitement before slurping up more wine to calm down. "We are on the verge of something very profound and powerful that could change our lives forever. When this takes, fossil fuels will become a thing of the past."

"I never knew hydrogen could be so exciting," she said.

He was stunned by such naivete. "Seriously? Why, it's my favorite element."

"I'm pretty sure you're the first person I've met who has a favorite element," she declared.

"Oh yes," he said, folding one leg over the other and settling back into the sofa. "I'm fond of some of the heavier elements, such as plutonium and uranium. And, I have enormous respect for metalloids, like silicon."

"Who doesn't?" Missy said, nodding absently.

"Not to mention actinides, which I think are really underappreciated."

"It's just not fair," Missy said, pulling her knees up under her chin and feeling a buzz from her wine.

PC raised an index finger. "But you just can't beat hydrogen," he said. "No, ma'am. It's number one on the periodic table and in my heart."

"How so?"

"It's the lightest and most abundant element in the universe," he said. "At first glance, you might think, 'oh, there's nothing particularly distinctive about it.' After all, it has no color, no odor, no taste. And its sheer ubiquity makes it seem rather common." He shifted in his seat to face her, took a healthy swig of the pinot noir, and put his glass down. "But here's the thing. When you superheat hydrogen isotopes, they fuse together into this—" he twirled his arms in the air—"wild, swirling plasma."

Dancing, prancing isotopes? What the hell was he talking about? Yet Missy was drawn in, if not enthralled. *I want to go to a plasma party.* "How does that happen?"

PC, finally feeling relaxed in this exotic place, picked up his glass again and took a generous sip of his wine. "Start with tritium, okay? It's an extremely rare, radioactive isotope. You can only find trace amounts in the atmosphere. But then you introduce it to deuterium, which is abundant. Nearly all the deuterium in the world was created in the Big Bang nearly fourteen billion years ago."

"Of course," Missy said, as if she knew.

PC was in his element. He sat forward on the sofa, excitedly. "See, when you mix the tritium and deuterium at the right temperature, they fuse together, generating enormous heat. You get that, right?"

"I'm struggling a bit—physics and chemistry are not my strong suits—but yes. I'm following you. This is fascinating," Missy said, feeling the heat herself. She was finding this weirdo strangely attractive. He—*we!*—could save the planet!

He leaned forward, conspiratorially. "I don't talk about this much. But tritium," he said, quietly, "is my very favorite isotope."

"Really?" Missy said, sipping her wine. "Why is that?"

"I guess because it's the oddball," he said. "It's kind of awkward. A loner. I think I understand it better than all the others. All it needs is to spend time with deuterium in the right atmosphere, and then…" He trailed off, his head shaking.

Missy was in suspense. "Then what?"

"Magic happens," PC declared, with a devilish chuckle.

Missy never heard anyone talk about an isotope like that. "Whoa," she said.

"What about you?" he asked.

Missy stretched an arm across the back of the sofa. "I'll be honest. I don't really have a favorite isotope. In fact, I don't think I could even name one," she said. "But I'm really intrigued by the idea of a swirling, twirling plasma party with a Big Bang."

PC's eyes widened and he gulped. This was moving in unexpected ways well outside the confines of his laboratory. "I just remembered where I've seen that flower before," he said.

She leaned closer. "Where was that, PC?"

He blanched. "The Museum of Modern Art. I went there with this woman I knew when I was getting my doctorate and she helped me appreciate certain aspects of the—" he trailed off, suddenly rattled. "Oh... never mind."

She looked at him seductively. "No. Please continue. I think I know what she was talking about."

"You do?" he asked nervously.

"Would you like a refresher?"

He looked at her and felt his brain had twirled and swirled into a plasma-like mush. It had finally dawned on him where this interlude could lead, and that was most likely career disaster. A liaison with Missy could be more difficult to contain than a fusion experiment. "You know what?" He stood up. "I've got to go."

"What?" she exclaimed. "What's the hurry?"

"Sorry," he said. "Early day tomorrow. We're setting up our lasers. I've got to supervise the team, and—" He walked quickly toward the door, calling back over his shoulder. "I don't want them to get overheated." *Like me!*

34. PERSONAL MAGNETISM

Feeling energized from her encounter with PC, Missy decided she would break out of her bubble and make her way to Blair's office in the former Garment District on foot. She found it liberating and a bit unsettling to see the city from an unaccustomed point-of-view. Manhattan wasn't nearly the same experience from the sidewalk as it was from the back seat of a limo, where she was typically focused on her phone and rarely looked out the window.

She headed north from the Jenga Building through northern Tribeca and the throngs of men unfurling blankets of Gucci knockoffs on the sidewalks near Canal Street. She crossed into Soho over broken curbs and walkways, past blocks of boutiques, hotels, cafes, and graffitied walls, and across Houston Street to Greenwich Village. From there, she wound through the majestic marble arch in Washington Square Park, past the apartment towers on Fifth Avenue, and up Broadway, where drug merchants with folding tables and walkie-talkies populated every corner.

Inside an old dress factory on 32nd Street, Missy was directed by building security to a rickety freight elevator, which she rode to the tenth floor. There she found the cavernous red-brick laboratory of Energy Concepts. Blair met Missy at the entrance with a smile, a hug, and a cup of her favorite chai.

"C'mon," Blair said, taking her by the hand. She led her through a labyrinth of wires, cords, tubes, and machinery to her desk, which her father had made in his shop from an old door and a pair of sawhorses. "Welcome to my luxurious suite," Blair said, as they sat down on swivel stools. "As you can see, we don't spend a lot on furniture."

"Wow," Missy said. *People actually work here?* "How often do you come in?"

"Pretty much every day—unless I'm out talking to customers," Blair said. "Who knows? Maybe you'll be one of them." She saw Missy's discomfort with this trip outside her comfort zone and tried to make her feel more at ease. "It's so good to have you here!"

"Yeah. Well…" Missy took a deep breath. "It wasn't an easy trip. It required a lot of soul-searching over the past few days. And I realized I've been kind of a jerk. No, wait." She paused, thinking. "I've been a total jerk. And all I can do about that now is say I'm sorry."

Blair reached out and patted Missy on the knee. "I'm sorry too, Missy. We both said some stuff. Hopefully we can move past all that. We could have exciting things to work on together." She reached over her desk and picked up a piece of film that looked like audio tape. She handed it to Missy. "Like this."

Was Blair kidding? "I have no idea what this is," Missy said.

"I'd be stunned if you did," Blair said. "It's called HTS, for high-temperature superconductor—a critical component in fusion. My dad and his team have been developing this with researchers at MIT. Based on what I know about CroFusion, I think it could help you."

Missy stared at the tape in her hand. "You realize I'm pretty stupid about this stuff at this point. What does it do?"

"You know what plasma is, right?"

Missy nodded. "Yeah. PC explained it a bit. That swirly, twirly goo."

"You have a more impressive grasp of technology than I thought."

"Seriously?"

"No," Blair said. "But it's a start. What this does is, it contains the goo, as you call it, in a more confined space. This magnet is thinner and more powerful than the alternatives, and it helps the fusion process operate at much higher temperatures. That reduces the required cooling, which is important for a whole bunch of reasons."

Missy's eyes were spinning. "I'll have to take your word for it," she said. "I'm not sure what any of that means, exactly,"

"The people at your lab will."

"Oh my God. Are you kidding?" Missy said. She leaned in and spoke in a near-whisper. "This will arouse PC in more ways than one."

Blair laughed. "Bring me in. Let's see if there's any there, there."

Missy suddenly felt empowered. "I can make that happen," she said, proudly. She tapped a note into her phone, then turned back and forth on her swivel stool and looked around. "I can't believe we're in a place like this. What are we doing here?"

"We're inventing the future," Blair said. "That's pretty cool, don't you think?"

Missy nodded. "I'll probably think so once I get up to speed. I have a lot of catching up to do."

Blair smiled. "First things first." She slapped the desk. "Are you ready for your big speech on Saturday?"

Missy dolefully shook her head. "No. At this point, all I want to do is get it over with."

Blair winced. "Really?"

"Absolutely," Missy said. Then, sensing Blair's puzzlement, asked, "Why? What are you thinking?"

Blair shrugged her shoulders. "Just that you may never have a bigger stage in your life," she said. "Why don't you take advantage of it?"

Missy sighed. "Because in all my soul-searching, I realized one thing about myself."

"Which is?"

"I'm a coward," Missy said.

Blair started to object. "No, Missy. You're—"

Missy stopped her. "It's true. I haven't been leading a revolution. I've been following it, and going with the flow. My mother used to say, 'if all your friends jumped off a cliff, would you follow them?' And the answer is, 'yes. I would.' That's exactly what I'm doing now."

Blair puzzled over this. "What does your mom think about the speech?"

Missy sighed. "I don't know. We haven't been talking."

Blair shook her head. "That's so sad. I used to talk to my mother every day, even if it was nothing more than a little text message. There are days I could use some motherly advice," Blair said, her voice catching. "Sounds like you could use some now."

Missy's head sank. "I hear you. It's just—"

Blair held up her hand. "I'll tell you what it 'just' is, Missy: nothing terribly important. It's pride. It's stubbornness. It's all those trivial things that get in the way of people who love each other talking to each other. And if you should be talking to anyone right now, it's her. I'm not one for giving advice. But I would strongly suggest this: call her."

Missy sighed and looked off vacantly.

Blair picked up a couple of iron magnets from her desk. "Remember this from school?" she said. She took the magnets and pushed the ends together but couldn't close the gap. "The poles repel because they're too much alike. Just like you and your mom."

Missy looked skeptical. "I always thought I was more like my dad."

Blair chuckled. "I can see a bit of that, but no. You and your mom are way more alike. But look here," Blair said. She flipped one of the magnets over, and they smacked together. "All it takes is a little adjustment in position. Then you connect."

Missy scoffed. "You know what annoys me?"

"What?"

"You're always right."

35. A MOTHER AND CHILD REUNION

The last vestiges of Missy's childhood were no longer evident in her former bedroom in the family's five-story townhouse on East 67th Street. All her mementos were gone. Where, exactly, Missy couldn't even guess. All she knew was that her little nest on the third floor had been swept clean of its feathers. In their place was an exercise studio, as impersonal to her as an Equinox gym. She shook her head in mourning. *What a gut punch this is.*

As she stood in the doorway, feeling like a guest in her old home, she looked around at the mats, free weights, elliptical trainer, large-screen TV, and the framed black-and-white photos of Manhattan that had replaced her posters. Was this her mother's way of putting some distance between them? It made her sad, and wistful for the more protected and anonymous life she had led not so long ago. She could use a plush toy about now.

"There you are."

Missy turned to see her mother. Missy regarded her warily, before embracing her lightly, almost defensively.

"You like my studio?" Lindsey asked with a smile.

"It's okay, I guess," Missy replied. "What happened to all my stuff?"

Lindsey glanced around the room and folded her arms across her chest. "Don't worry, darling. Everything's boxed up in the basement—all your scrapbooks, and yearbooks, and photos and trophies. I think there's even a signed poster of Justin Bieber in there."

Missy covered her eyes in embarrassment. "Oh my God. Seriously?"

"It's all ready for delivery whenever you like," Lindsey said.

Missy shuddered and looked back into the room. "Is this some kind of statement about me?" she asked, meekly. "Like, I'm out of your life?"

Lindsey scoffed. "Not at all. You're very much in my thoughts. It was just… time. The room didn't work as a museum. I decided I'd either have to string a velvet rope across the doorway or put it back into circulation." She glanced around the space and gestured with her arm. "I love it like this. The light is great in here. The acoustics are perfect for music while I'm working out. And," she said, putting a hand on Missy's shoulder, "it reminds me of you."

Missy looked skeptically at her mother. Was she being sarcastic? Or was that a little tear in her eye?

"Come on," Lindsey said. "Let's chat."

Lindsey led Missy down the staircase to the second-floor study, an elegant but comfortable room that Lindsey used for reading, talking to friends, or watching television. Here, family photos remained on view, though anything depicting Missy's father had been dispatched like Missy's stuffed bear. A maid brought water and tea and mother and daughter sat on the sofa at opposite ends. "So," Lindsey said, "Your big speech is Saturday night. Are you ready for it?"

Missy's chin set. "Are you?"

"I don't have to give it," Lindsey said.

"Does it bother you that I do?" Missy sked

"I'll be frank with you: it did," Lindsey said, idly pushing back her hair. "I even considered shutting off the power to Central Park."

Missy looked at her in astonishment. "You could do that?"

"Of course," she said. "It wouldn't be hard."

"But you're not going to?"

"No," Lindsey replied before taking a deep breath. "I've come to terms with it. Whatever happens up there is your responsibility, not mine. You created this platform. You deserve to stand on it and say what you believe."

Missy was perplexed by this unexpected reaction. "Do I have the right mom here?"

Lindsey laughed. "Your one and only."

"I don't get it," Missy said. "Why are you so calm about this?"

Lindsey reached over and put her hand on top of Missy's. "You may find this difficult to believe, dear," she said, "but I don't expect you to be an echo chamber for me—or, for that matter, anyone else. Not your father. Not our company. Not your friends. Not the president of the United States. If you say what's on your mind, and what's in your heart, I'm sure you'll do fine. All I would suggest is that you tell it like it is."

Missy eyed her mother suspiciously. "What is this, mother? Reverse psychology? Some kind of weird sales pitch?"

Lindsey laughed. "Not at all," Lindsey said, shaking her head vigorously and spreading her hands out. "I want you to say what you think. Seriously."

Missy still wasn't buying it. "And how did you come to that conclusion?"

Lindsey withdrew her hand and sat back. "It came to me yesterday, when I was working out in your old room. I was reflecting on you, and the kind of person you were when you were growing up. And I thought about how you were always questioning authority. Teachers. Staff. Your father. Me."

"I thought you hated that," Missy said.

"I've found it annoying many times, true," Lindsey conceded. "What parent wants to endlessly debate a child about eating their spinach or cleaning their room, especially when you know it's often nothing more than a delay tactic. But as you grew up, I came to respect—sometimes grudgingly—your fierce independence. Every child needs to find the right distance from their parents. But it was more than that with you. It was an essential part of your decision-making. You really needed to understand why something had to be done in order for you to do it. I had to think hard, at times, about my answers."

Missy got up from the sofa and walked around the room slowly, glancing idly at the paintings by Monet and Degas, the vases of freshly cut flowers, and the array of books on the coffee table and on the shelves. She started to turn back to her mother, but something caught her eye. There, on the shelf right next to her, among books by Sartre, Jung, and Freud, was a hardcover copy of Dr. Iz's first book, *Get a Grip, Honey*. "Oh my God. There it is." Missy laughed to herself and pulled the book off the shelf and held it up. "Did you ever read this?"

"Cover to cover," Lindsey said.

"Why?" Missy asked.

Lindsey rose from the sofa and walked over to Missy. "It was my reference manual for raising a stubborn child." She held out her hand to take the book from her, opened the cover, and flipped through the well-worn pages. "There's a chapter in here about dealing with kids who get under your skin because they question everything you say."

Missy folded her arms across her chest. "What was her advice?"

Lindsey chuckled. "Basically, it was to answer the damn questions. Sometimes, that called for more patience, or time, than I had." She sighed. "I was often in a hurry to get somewhere."

"Like where?" Missy asked.

Lindsey looked down at the floor. "Like somewhere else," she replied. "There were times I just had to… get out." She took a deep breath. "I probably shortchanged you in doing so, and I'm ashamed of that. I didn't always give you the explanations you needed or deserved."

Missy nodded. *Wow. I never heard that before…*

Lindsey flipped through more pages in the book. "There was also this," she said, holding the book open for Missy to see. "Chapter Three: Dealing with Anxiety."

"What was I anxious about?"

Lindsey sucked in her breath. "This wasn't about you. This was about me," she said. "I was in a bad place. There's some stuff in here about cognitive-behavioral therapy. It prompted me to see a therapist who helped me understand the source of my own anxieties. I didn't have a twitch, but I was self-medicating in ways that were, shall we say… counterproductive."

Feeling solicitous toward her mother, Missy put a hand gently on her back. "How did you get rid of your anxiety?"

"I divorced it," Lindsey said, with a rueful laugh.

Missy pulled back. "You're saying Dad was to blame?"

"Only indirectly. He is who he is, and I realized a long time ago I couldn't change that," Lindsey said with a sigh. "My stress came from trying to become someone I'm not just to please him. All I could think of was: 'What am I doing wrong?' It was a futile, and ultimately destructive effort." She paused, considering how far to go with this. "I hung in there because of you and Chase and the hope that I could somehow coax our marriage back to life. Obviously, that didn't happen."

Missy flopped down in an easy chair. "Jesus, Mom. That is so bleak."

Lindsey shook her head. "Not really," she said. "It forced me to do an honest assessment of where I was in life, and to take stock of my relationships—the good, the bad, and the horrible. My breakthrough came when I realized I needn't twist myself into a pretzel to please others. I am what I am, and I got comfortable with that. No apologies. I'm in a better place for it."

Missy sank low into the chair and pressed her fingertips together in front of her face, contemplating how her mother's journey corresponded with her own. Lindsey put the book back on the shelf and sat down on the ottoman across from Missy. She reached out and patted Missy's knee.

"So, tell me. These people you're working with in Washington," Lindsey said. "Do they like you?"

She chuckled mirthlessly. "Are you kidding? They *love* me."

"Really?"

"Like a deer head mounted on the wall," Missy said. "They're very proud of their trophy—as long as it stares blankly into space and never makes a sound."

Lindsey pursed her lips. "How does that make you feel?"

Missy raised her chin. "Honestly? Not so hot."

"I'm not surprised."

"It was exhilarating at first," Missy said. "All the attention. All the buzz. All the invitations to places you'd never go otherwise. I mean, it was totally cool to sit in a meeting in the Oval Office with the President of the United States and all these big-name people. But… it took me a while to figure out there's a price for that."

"More than you want to pay?" Lindsey asked.

Missy sighed, reflecting how she got to this place. "You know, while you were going through your crap with Dad, I was having my own problems. Growing up in this family was not easy," she said. "Everyone makes assumptions based on your name and where you live about who you are and how easy you have it. You want to prove you're not that different, that you're just like them, and that you fit in. So you ingratiate yourself in so many ways that you get trapped in their expectations. How you're supposed to look. How you're supposed to act. How you're supposed to think. And that's where I am. In a prison of my own making."

Lindsey reached out and took Missy's hand and gently squeezed it. "I know the situation all too well," Lindsey said. "Breaking out is not easy, dear."

Missy laid her head back on top of the chair. "You know, when I started joining protests back in school, I finally felt like I fit in. I wasn't this stereotype of a privileged person who was somehow oppressing everyone around me," she said. "I didn't know how I had personally polluted the world, since I had never worked a day at the company. But I was, like, totally overwhelmed with guilt."

"About what?"

"About being born, I guess," Missy said. "But when I was out there protesting, I was part of the crowd, joining the revolution that was going to pull down the people in power in favor of… I don't know. Them, I guess. And then, last year, when I spray-painted that building on Broad Street, I was so damn proud of myself—for about a day and a half. It took me a while to understand it was just performance art, and all I was seeking was applause from people I didn't know, but who loved to see me bow and scrape and show that I had adopted their view of the world. They wanted to bring me down a peg in the name of equity. And I went along, willingly." She shook her head. "It never occurred to me until recently that some of these people were enjoying watching me suffer."

Lindsey nodded. "Of course. They will if you let them."

"It's even worse with climatosis," Missy said. "I basically invented it—subconsciously, I think. Maybe this twitch started because I wanted to show how much I cared about the planet. But then it got out of hand. It became this ridiculous competition to show who cared the most. I don't even have climatosis anymore. But now I'm stuck."

Lindsey pondered Missy's dilemma. "Since you invented it, maybe you can uninvent it."

"How?"

"You have your big speech on Saturday. That could be your chance to do a reset."

"I can't even imagine that," Missy said.

Lindsey put the tip of her index finger under her chin, regarded her daughter, and said, "Try."

36. SCIENCE FRICTION

The revised script from the White House proved little better than the first version, despite Missy's suggested changes, and it was in some ways worse—a story with so many holes that it might as well have been drafted by Gina, Britney, and Peach while passing around the bong. She looked to Marty and Joe Katzenmeyer, who were sitting across from her at her dining room table, peering through their reading glasses, while making notes on their printouts of the script.

"So," Missy mused as she looked at her script. "Can I say this? 'The melting of Artic Sea ice is causing the sea level to rise.'"

Joe looked up over the rims of his glasses and blinked hard a few times. Then he carefully slid his glass of ice water across the table. "Let me answer that by asking you a question, Missy," he said. "When the ice melts in my glass, do you think the water will rise? Will it suddenly lap over the rim and leave a puddle on the table?"

Missy paused a moment to think it over, then made a mark on her script. "That's a no." Glancing down again, she asked, "What about this? 'The number of hurricanes is increasing because of the impact of humans on climate change?'"

Joe returned to making notations on his own printout of the script as he replied. "No," he said. "The number of hurricanes is the same, or lower. And the impact of humans on climate has not been verified. It's a theory. It's not proven. And it's certainly not quantified."

"Do we have more droughts?" she asked.

"No," Joe said.

Missy checked that off. "More strong tornadoes?"

"No."

Missy made another check. "Fewer polar bears?"

"We have more," Joe replied. "There's more open ice. More plankton. More seals. More dinner for polar bears. They're feasting up there."

"What about this?" Missy asked. "'We have to follow the science?'"

"The science? Yes," Joe said. "The science fiction? No."

Missy slapped her pen on the table. "This speech is terrible. If I take out all the BS, there won't be anything left except, 'Good evening and good night.' Why should I bother doing this at all?"

"The speech isn't for you, Missy," Joe said. "It's for all the people who've been marinating in climate orthodoxy for so long it's become a matter of faith."

"Is any of it true?" she asked.

"Parts," Joe said. "Just not enough to justify the overheated response." He pulled out a chart and handed it over to Missy. "You have to look at the course of history. See this? It covers the past six hundred million years." He pointed with a pencil. "The red line here is temperature. The blue line here is carbon dioxide. As you can see, they don't move in tandem. That's because there are lots of other things going on besides carbon concentrations. We need more research to understand what those things are."

Missy sat back in her chair. "But they say we can't wait for that. We should get rid of fossil fuels just in case their hunches are correct."

Marty reached into his satchel and pulled out a fact sheet. "We'd need to replace seven billion barrels of oil, thirty-one trillion cubic feet of natural gas, and five hundred million tons of coal. That's just for this country in one year."

"Where would we get our energy?" Missy asked.

Marty shrugged. "Sunshine and gentle breezes?"

Missy put her palms to her forehead. "That sounds more like spring break."

"It's a party, for sure—at least for some people," Marty said. "Do you know what's rising faster than carbon emissions from fossil fuels? Cash emissions from the U.S. Treasury."

Missy fell back in her chair, shaking her head. "Color me stupid," Missy said. "How does any of this make sense?"

Joe put down his pen and folded his hands together. "They would like us to think that if we stop using fossil fuels, renewable sources will magically appear. But there aren't enough places where people will allow windmills and solar farms in their backyards. And there's not enough money to make it happen anyway. If you told them the government would spend fifty trillion dollars on renewable energy, they still couldn't tell you how that would affect the temperature of the planet."

"Why not?" Missy asked.

"Because they don't know," Joe said.

Missy wearily rose from the table and paced, waggling the printout of the speech in her hand. "So if I deliver this speech, I'll sound like a complete idiot." She tossed the script back on the table.

"Not to this crowd," Marty said.

Missy and Joe stared at Marty.

"Think of the audience," Marty said. "They're not coming for a debate on climate change. That issue, to them, is settled. They're coming for communion. They want to be reassured that there's power in numbers, that if everyone just gets together and enforces their will, they can change the world. I've seen this movie before."

"Me, too," Joe said. "When I was a student at Bartleby, we occupied the administrative building. Some of my colleagues never left. They got jobs deciding what was acceptable thought and what wasn't." He sighed. "You'll notice I'm not there anymore."

He got up from the table, wearing his Café Che barista uniform, modeled after a jungle guerrilla. "Sorry, folks, but I've got to get to work." He handed Missy his notated copy of the speech. "I don't know if this is any help or not. But I must tell you: I completely understand if you want to avoid contradicting these people. They could ruin you. They've already ruined a lot of us. I mean, look at me. In another half-hour, I'll be wiping down a latte machine."

Marty said. "From what I've seen, Joe, you do it very well."

"I was barista of the month in July," Joe said with a smile.

"*Felicidades*," Marty replied. "Did they give you something for it?"

"A fifty-dollar gift card. Good for food and beverages at—where else?—Café Che."

Marty laughed. "That should buy you a few scones."

"Maybe half of one," Joe said. "In the interest of equity, my award was divided among all employees equally, whether they showed up for work or not. My share was three dollars and forty cents. I blew it all on a discount for a cappuccino."

"Sounds fair to me," Marty said.

Missy tugged on Joe's arm as he turned to leave. Holding up his version of the script, she asked, "Why did you circle this line where I say 'people are dying from climate change?'"

Joe shrugged. "Because that's the biggest whopper of them all," he said. "Cold kills far more people than heat. The rate of climate-related deaths is down 98 percent over the past hundred years."

Missy slumped against the wall. "Since the founding of Crowe Power."

Joe nodded. "It's not a coincidence."

Missy blushed. "Why have I not made this connection before?"

Joe shrugged. "Because it's not something that's polite to say or even think about," he said. "*Adios, camaradas.*"

Missy watched Joe leave, then picked up the speech and stared at it. "This thing needs a complete rewrite."

"Is that allowed?" Marty asked.

"I'm getting to the point where I don't care."

Marty looked at her with amusement, and a bit of admiration. "You really are a troublemaker, aren't you?"

She shrugged. "There's nothing wrong with telling the truth."

"There is when it comes to the climate apocalypse. It's taboo," Marty said. "But if you decide to say something that challenges the prevailing narrative, I suspect you'll be giving voice to a lot of people who may not be in the crowd Saturday, but who silently agree with you, and will never have the microphone that you have. They don't have your superpower."

She regarded Marty skeptically. "Which is what?"

"You can't be canceled," Marty said. "You're not looking for tenure. Or looking for a job. They can't bust you down to barista. Some people may not like you. But so what? If that's the worst thing that happens, who cares?"

She sighed. "Wouldn't people just dismiss what I say?"

"Why do you think they would do that? It's your story."

"Because I'm privileged?" Missy said.

Marty nodded. "Yeah. That could certainly happen. And you know what? It's okay. You didn't ask to be born into this family. But privilege has its privileges. You might quit apologizing for it and take advantage of it, instead—for one night, on one stage."

"You think so?" Missy asked, biting a nail.

"It's not up to me," Marty said. "I don't have to live with the consequences either way. It's up to you."

37. STEP RIGHT UP

As Marty joined the herd shuffling into Central Park for the Beat Climatosis Now rally, he noticed the late afternoon sun sparkling on the large number of silver-haired people sprinkled through the youthful crowd.

The old-timers were more likely candidates for liver spots than climatosis, but they were energized just the same. Perhaps the walk on the park's West Drive was a reinvigorating trip down memory lane. As a college student, Marty had driven into Manhattan to attend a no-nukes protest here, more in the interest of meeting newly liberated young women than the cause of world peace. He struck out, but the rally was a victory for activists.

This movement was different, and not just in terms of the latest fashions in clothing and haircuts. During the Cold War arms race, the issue had been clear. People faced an imminent threat that could end millions of lives in an instant. Climate anxiety was more of an amorphous enemy whose causes were not well understood, whose timing was impossible to predict, and whose results might not amount to much.

Still, the menace loomed large in the public imagination, since it was relentlessly pushed by an alliance of like-minded people in politics, media, education, and entertainment. No severe weather event was reported without the ominous intonation that this was *even more* evidence of the damage humans had inflicted on their planet. A beaten-down populace looking for answers was assured there were several ways to beat this monster: Give us your money, your vote, your admiration, your gas stove, the controls to your thermostat, and the keys to your car. Then await further instruction.

As a longtime practitioner of public relations and advertising, Marty was impressed by the doom-mongers' skill at mass manipulation. Solutions to the dubious crisis were sold to the public in the same way Madison Avenue once told people that smoking was good for their nerves, morphine was great for teething babies, vitamin donuts were the delicious way to better nutrition, and that "DDT is good for me!" Yet the climatarians took the sloganeering several steps further by indoctrinating children in their worldview starting in kindergarten, embedding the messages into every point of information kids would receive, from textbooks to TV, then infiltrating industry and government agencies to force compliance with their agenda. Those who stepped out of line were blacklisted, shunned, and denied opportunities. Seeing a PhD like Joe relegated to menial labor was a page from the old Soviet Union playbook. How could people not be afraid of pushing back?

Marty broke off from the stampede to find Lindsey standing next to a fenced-off area near the iconic Belvedere Castle, where the federal government measured temperature, wind, and rainfall—the mystical elements formerly known as weather. Lindsey had swapped her conservative Upper East Side look for one favoring the liberal Upper West Side, with faded jeans, a baseball cap, and a pink t-shirt that read, "Fusion is Electrifying."

Marty nodded toward her shirt. "I'm feeling a jolt right now."

"That's the idea," she replied with a smile. "You think anyone will recognize me?"

"You better hope not."

Lindsey reached into her bag and pulled out the laminated VIP badges that Missy had dropped off for her. "Duck," she said, before pulling his lanyard over his head, laying the badge on his chest, and turning it around like hers so that his name didn't show. They joined the throng of twitchy people pouring into the park and followed them through the Big Green Deals marketplace, where entrepreneurs hawked the climate crisis with hats, posters, and key rings dangling windmill tchotchkes. There were lines to sign petitions to ban climate change "misinformation," establish climatosis clinics in underserved communities, and demand taxpayer subsidies for "climate-friendly" appliances.

Reflecting the quasi-religious appeal of the cause, merchants sold caps that urged people to "Repent Your Carbon Sins," and t-shirts declaring, "Climatosis = End of the World," and "Polluters Must Pay. *Do the crime. Do the time.*" The booth garnering the most attention was staffed by the Planetistas activist group, which peddled "WANTED" posters featuring mug shots of energy executives.

"Good lord," Lindsey muttered as she pulled the brim of her cap lower over her eyes.

Marty followed her gaze to the poster on display. Under Lindsey's photo, it read:

WANTED
For Hate Crimes Against the Planet
Assault with Deadly Fossil Fuels
Lindsey Harper Crowe

Marty grimaced. "If I buy one, will you sign it for me?"

She shook her head. "Why do I get the feeling you'd sell it on eBay?"

Marty feigned indignation. "Come on. I'd tape it to the ceiling over my bed."

At the end of the path, they were funneled through a series of chutes where security checked peoples' bags and rally personnel awarded green ribbons to all attendees. A loudspeaker ran a message in a continuous loop: "*You must wear the ribbon for entry... You must wear the ribbon for entry ...*" An event staffer walked along the line, yelling into a bullhorn, warning people not to hit each other with a twitch. "Please be respectful of the people around you and keep a safe distance."

At the checkpoint to the VIP area adjacent to the stage, Marty and Lindsey flashed their badges to allow them past the metal barricades. There, Secret Service agents scoped out the surging crowd as they awaited the arrival of President Fenwick. Marty told Lindsey he'd read that the president and his bagman, Scooter, were coming directly from a fundraiser thrown by a Russian oligarch who had magically escaped a rash of U.S. sanctions.

Marty and Lindsey made their way to the side of the stage, where the activities were in full swing. A man with rainbow-colored dreadlocks and rust-colored robes blessed the proceedings by walking the stage chanting as he swung a cannister with billowing plumes of jasmine incense. Meanwhile, down below, klieg lights from television news crews followed the grand entrance of the famed climate eminence, Rainwater Jones, direct from her treehouse near Seattle. The teenaged soothsayer arrived riding her trademark donkey, this one rented locally from Party Animals, and paused to offer reporters her latest dreary sooth.

In the meantime, newly arrived celebrities, including Jiminy Cratchit, were greeting one another with affirming smiles, hugs, and air kisses. The expressions on their faces confirmed the vibe: *We are the best people on Earth!* Congresswoman Evita Manolo, the socialist celebutante, made her usual dramatic fashion statement, this time by wearing a tailored burlap dress from Mulch Gulch, along with platform combat boots, an homage to her working-class roots in upper-crust Scarsdale. She was meeting and greeting members of the Federal Climatosis Commission, who clearly admired the cut of her jute.

"Do you see Missy anywhere?" Lindsey asked.

"Not yet," Marty said.

On stage, grizzled eighty-two-year-old Canadian rocker Harley Oats warbled a sad little dirge about melting ice. Harley hadn't had a hit song since Woodstock, which Marty thought might explain why he still seemed so angry. As Harley wrapped up his short set and was helped offstage, he encountered Jessica Holtgren, who had clambered up the stairs to embrace one of her father's music idols. Harley roughly shoved her out of the way, lest she bang into his creaky knees, causing Jessica to stumble.

As nimble in physical fitness as she was in ethics, Jessica executed a perfect three-point landing, popped up, grabbed a microphone, and stepped to the center of the stage. Dressed entirely in white, adorned with golden baubles, bangles, and beads, she appeared to emulate a Las Vegas version of Bia, the Greek goddess of power and energy. She shouted into the microphone, "Let's give it up for the great Harley Oats!"

A half-hearted cheer went up from the crowd, most of whom had never heard of Harley Oats, or his pathetic song.

She cried, "How many of you remember Harley from his guest appearance on *One Tree Hill?*"

The cheers grew louder. *Oh, yeah. That guy…*

"That's more like it!" Jessica continued. "Alright. Welcome, fellow climatosians! I'm Jessica Holtgren, Secretary of Energy for the United States of America, and I have a question for you." She paused and the assembly quieted. "Are we going to beat climatosis?"

Yeaaaaah! The crowd roared. *Woo-hoo!*

"That's what I want to hear!" she cheered, clapping her hands. "No matter how steep the odds, no matter how badly we're feeling, we're going to defeat this bugger. And do you know how? *We're going to change the world!*" She waited for the applause to crescendo, then die down. "Now, I'm going to ask you a few questions. And if you agree with me, I want you to shout out with everything you've got, '*I believe!*' Alright?" As the crowd applauded, she bellowed, "Do you believe in climate change?"

The crowd came back in unison, a vast chorus of agreement. "I believe!"

Jessica continued. "Do you believe humans are at fault?"

The people roared louder, "I believe!"

"And do you believe we can fix it if we work collectively for the sake of our planet?"

The response was thunderous. "I believe!"

"Do I hear an 'amen?'"

"I believe!"

Dumbasses, Jessica thought. *You were supposed to say, "Amen."* Oh well… She went on to thank them for being "so, so, *sooo* great!" before announcing the lineup of speakers and performers. The star-studded program featured movie stars taking a break from making family entertainment involving firebombs, car races, and mushroom clouds to declare their allegiance to the low-carbon cause. The crowd would hear from activists demanding a government-ordered phase-out of gas, oil, and basketballs made with petroleum. And the nation's omniscient scientist, Dr. Spanky MacFarlane, would offer his latest estimate on when the world would meet a sad demise—all interspersed with toe-tapping musical ditties such as "Depopulate," by Eugene and the Eugenics and Wretched Excess's high-voltage smash hit, "We're So Screwed."

"It's going to take every one of us to win this fight against the naysayers, the do-nothings, and the terminally greedy who won't sacrifice for the common good," Jessica proclaimed. "Those of us who believe in climate change know that life as usual is unacceptable. We have to listen to The Science. And so, I want to introduce the esteemed director of the President's Council on Climatology, the *Daily Reaper*'s Person of the Year, and winner of the Crystal Award in Davos, Switzerland," she spaced out her words as though announcing a wrestling match, "*Doctor George Spanky MacFarlane!*" She turned to see him striding her way in his suit and tie, waving to the adoring crowd.

Spanky took the microphone and gravely shook his head. "I'll be brief, Jessica, because we don't have much time." He theatrically looked at his watch. "By my calculation, we have just five years, two months, one week, twenty-three minutes and fifty-five seconds before we reach the precipice of a climate catastrophe." A huge groan went up from the crowd. "Sorry to be the bearer of bad tidings, folks, but we're heading for a slippery slope. One false step and, boom! Our reckless disregard for the planet sends us sliding into the dark abyss of climate devastation, an oblivion from which we can never return. So, the way I see it, we have two options: we can fix this planet we live on, or we find another one. But we better choose now. And we better move fast!"

Spanky was pleased to see his patented shtick hit home. The crowd gyrated into a twitchy apoplexy, with arms and legs flailing about, and people ducking this way and that to avoid getting whacked. Oh yeah! He still had the *kavorka*! He'd be booked on talk shows for the next two weeks, easily!

As Marty and Lindsey continued their search for Missy, Jessica turned the stage over to Peach's mother, the famed actress Lilith Anne Buckingham, to lighten the mood. Lilith obliged by reminding people there was something they could do for the cause this very night: they could reduce their energy usage by buying her line of paraffin candles scented like body parts, which would be available at her tractor trailer double-parked on 79th Street, right after the show.

38. SCRIPT SCRAPPED

In a dark corner behind the stage, Blair found Missy preparing for her speech in an unexpected way: by throwing up in the bushes. Blair approached quietly from behind and offered her a tissue. "Are you okay?"

After one last retch, Missy stood up, took the tissue, dabbed her mouth, and shook her head. "No," she said, gasping for breath. "I can't go on. There's no way."

Blair studied Missy a moment, then took Missy by the shoulders and looked deep into her eyes. "Listen, Missy. I've known you a long time. And I can say, without any hesitation whatsoever: you've got this. You hear me?"

"No," Missy replied.

"Yes, you do," Blair persisted, gently shaking her. "You're a strong, brave, independent woman."

"I'm not strong," Missy protested.

Blair withdrew one hand. "Brave?"

"I don't think so."

Blair pulled back the other hand. "Well, you're certainly independent," she said weakly.

"Anything but," Missy replied. "I'm a fucking prop."

Blair gave up and dismissed the whole concept. "Yeah, well," she said with a shrug. "Forget I mentioned it."

"What should I do?" Missy asked.

Blair shrugged. What options were left? "I don't know," she said. "You want to barf again?"

As Missy turned back to the bushes for another heave-ho, Lindsey and Marty approached with alarm. Lindsey asked, "What's going on? Is she sick?"

Blair replied, "She's just clearing her throat."

Missy stood up, flushed red, and wiped her mouth again.

Lindsey asked, "Are you okay, darling?"

"Not really," Missy said. She looked down at her clothing. "Did I get any on me?"

Lindsey, Blair, and Marty all surveyed her distressed jeans and fitted t-shirt. "I think you're clear," Lindsey said.

Over the loudspeakers, they heard Jessica Holtgren telling the crowd about the president's intention to eradicate fossil fuels, a plan she said was supported by their next speaker, Missy Mayburn Crowe.

Lindsey said, "She's introducing you. Do you want me to tell them you're ill?"

"No, Mother," Missy said, wearily. "I'll do it."

Missy took a deep breath, then led Lindsey, Marty, and Blair toward the steps to the stage, where they watched Jessica's introduction.

"I'm sure you've all heard the sad story of Missy Mayburn Crowe," Jessica told the crowd. "A lovely young woman, struck down in her prime by the dreaded contagion, climatosis. She was laid low by a twitch that rendered her—like so many of you—unable to function normally. But she has turned her tragedy into triumph through her brave stand against her own family for their crimes against our planet."

Missy gathered herself and climbed the stairs as if she were making her way to the gallows. At the top of the stairs, she was met by Jessica, who assessed Missy from head to toe through the bottom of her reading glasses. Meanwhile, a stagehand affixed a pair of lavaliere microphones to her top.

"Are we ready for prime time?" Jessica asked curtly.

Missy, starting to sweat, opened her mouth to answer but nothing came out.

"Well, we're moving ahead anyway. The president's on after you and he can't wait," Jessica said. "Any problems with the script?"

Missy sighed, as she found her tongue. "A lot of them."

"Well, it's a little too late to bring that up now, isn't it?" Jessica said. "Your remarks are all loaded on the teleprompter. I suggest you go slowly. Everyone on the commission has had a hand in this. You don't want to leave anything out that they have approved." Jessica arched an eyebrow, then clutched Missy by the upper arm and frog-walked her to the front of the stage as if she were escorting her to the back seat of a police car.

Jessica exited stage left as Missy took her place behind the lectern, located the teleprompters, and looked out at the sea of people, TV cameras, and phones facing her way. Down in front, she could see her mother, Marty, and Blair watching anxiously. Members of the Climatosis Commission were on hand, as were Peach, Gina, and Britney. Her father, Robbie, was hanging out, predictably, with Dover

Soul and the Sluts. Off to the side, she could see the President's squadron of black SUVs arriving with blue lights flashing. *Deep breaths…*

"Good evening," she said. She paused a moment, adjusting to the echo of her voice through the park. "My name is Missy and I have climatosis." Sympathetic, supportive applause rippled through the crowd. Missy smiled uneasily, before saying, "Thank you." She cleared her throat and plunged ahead with the script displayed on the screens in front of her. "I want to talk to you tonight about my experience in the hope that it helps you through your own struggles. We're all in this climate anxiety fight together, and we need to find solutions so that future generations don't have to suffer. Fortunately, we have the best and brightest people in government, science, industry, academia, and technology working together to help us through this crisis. Thanks to their efforts, I know there are essential steps we can and must take."

God, this sounds like political bullshit. Missy thought ahead to the rest of the text, which ticked through the horrors of climate change and offered the Fenwick administration's poll-tested solutions. "The most important thing we can do is, oh… blah, blah, blah." She sighed and looked back down at the puzzled eyes of her friends and family.

"You know what? I'm just gonna skip this speech," she said. "I didn't write it and it kinda sucks. It's just something they, like, handed me and said, 'Here, you. Read this.' But I'm thinking they can tell their own story. They've got, like, a gazillion spokespeople. I'd rather tell my story the way I see it." A murmur rumbled through the crowd at this unexpected twist. "And maybe if we just talk about what happened to me and what happened to you, we can find a way to prevent climatosis from taking away our jobs, our dignity, our sanity, and our future." As she stepped around the lectern, she noticed a frantic Jessica on the sideline shaking her head waving her arms frantically. Missy chose to ignore her and walked to the front of the stage, where she paced slowly as she spoke.

"I know a lot of you are familiar with climatosis. It's this overwhelming feeling that you're destroying the planet. You hear every day that the climate is changing, that the changes are being driven by you and other humans, and that doing things like eating a cheeseburger or using a plastic bag could send us into some climate hell. Any deviation in weather patterns is a 'warning to us all,' a 'red flag', a 'wake-up call' to do something right now, urgently, before it's too late. Then you might stand a chance." As she scanned the uneasy faces in the crowd, she sensed they weren't quite with her, but they were curious.

She continued, "I was so rattled by the constant bombardment of horrible news that I developed a twitch. So did my friends, and so did a lot of you. Maybe it hit me first because I come from a family whose business has been largely based on fossil fuels." She waited for a cascade of booing to stop.

"When I was growing up, I was proud of my family, and the company they built, and their contribution to the world's standard of living. But as I got older, and I heard how angry it made people, my association with Crowe Power became a source of pain—as well as a staggering sense of guilt." She shook her head at the memory. "I felt personally responsible for every broken palm tree in Puerto Rico, every roof that blew off a building in Oklahoma, every wildfire in California, and every breach of a levee in Louisiana. And I know a lot of you feel the same way because we're filling up climate therapists' couches all over the country."

The stage lights flickered, and Missy looked to the side of the stage, where Jessica was running her index finger across her neck and yelling, "Cut!" Missy looked her in the eye and shook her head. Then she turned back to the audience and pointed her thumb toward the wings.

"The Secretary of Energy is over there telling me to stop. But I'm through being her sock puppet. I know she's not going to cut me off, because that would only make all of you more curious about what I'm about to say. So she may as well leave the lights on."

The flickering stopped and the crowd applauded a bit, with a few scattered shouts of encouragement. Missy stepped to the center of the stage and stopped, and looked down at Blair, who gave her two thumbs up. Missy folded her hands in front of her.

"I'm sure you've heard of the Federal Climate Commission. I don't know why they even let me into their meetings, but they did. I suspect they thought I was this compliant, damaged little girl, that I would do anything they told me to because they were all—quote, unquote—experts. So I've heard them talk about their plans around climatosis, and you know what they want more than anything? They want to keep this shit going! Yeah! That's right!" A round of boos rang out from the crowd. "They freaking love climatosis! It's like the greatest thing ever—the perfect excuse to do whatever the hell they want, as fast as possible and at any cost, and to sign everyone up for their program. Their products. Their mandates. Their bill, which you'll pay, whether you'll even realize it or not. So don't expect wisdom from these people. Expect them to use your pain and your anguish to do what's best for themselves."

The lights flickered again, causing Missy to raise her index finger in the direction of Jessica Holtgren, who was fuming at the side of the stage. "Don't even think about it!" Missy said. "If I leave, I'm taking at least a few of these TV cameras with me, not to mention a whole lot of smart phones."

The crowd roared and the lights stopped flickering, Missy continued. "When deciding whether we should take their advice, I think it's important to think about what we can change, and what we can't. A lot of us—" she raised her right hand, as if swearing an oath, "tend to think we're in charge of these massive forces of nature. But there's a hell of a lot more going on besides tailpipes and cow burps. The climate's been changing for four-and-a-half billion years and that will probably continue for another four-and-a-half billion years."

Jessica came striding across the stage, holding a microphone. "This is disinformation, people! Do not listen to her!"

The crowd booed lustily, and Missy turned to Jessica, hunched her shoulders, and stomped her foot, as if to scare her. Jessica scurried back to the side of the stage, then down the stairs to consult with other members of the commission.

Missy continued, "Have you ever heard of one of these apocalyptic predictions that proved right? Probably not since we're still here. Take this one: the Great Horse Manure Crisis of 1894. That's when they predicted that all the horse-drawn carriages and wagons in London and New York would produce piles of poop on the street that were nine-feet-high. That prediction turned out to be horseshit, just like a lot of climate prophecies over the past fifty years."

Another rumbling undercurrent went through the crowd, signaling unease with where this speech might be going. Still, she continued. "That's not to say we shouldn't change the things that we can if it makes things better and doesn't bankrupt us in the process. It took people demanding change to get us cleaner water and cleaner air, to target nasty pollution like nitrogen oxides, volatile organic compounds, and particulate matter. Those are a lot different from the 'pollutant' that's causing so much concern now: carbon dioxide. It's the primary carbon source for life on earth, not to mention the bubbles in your Coke.

"So here are some questions I have." She pulled out her phone, tapped a button, and walked across the stage. "Sorry for the F-bomb, but I'm kinda pissed: why the fuck did they do this to us? Huh? Why did they feel it so necessary to indoctrinate us from the time we were babies? What possible good could come from scaring the crap out of this country's young people about climate change when they'd had virtually nothing to do with it?

"Why did they insist on telling us—in our classes in school, on the news that we see or hear, from our political and business leaders—that we were destroying the world? Look around you. The world is not destroyed. Far from it. Over the past fifty years, as our temperature has risen slightly, our air is cleaner, and so is our water, and so is this park. And far, far fewer people are dying from climate-related issues than ever before.

"If you press them, they'll insist that the reason we should panic is because this is what the computer models say. That's when you have to ask, 'What made the models say it? Your inputs?' You know the saying, 'if you torture the data long enough, it will confess to anything?' That's where we are, folks. They're beating the hell out of the data, or ignoring it altogether, to get their desired outcome: a splashy headline, another government grant, a mandate to impose their will."

Missy looked out at the crowd, which had become unusually quiet. "Here's what I finally figured out. They scare us for the same reason *The Music Man* told the people of River City Iowa that the threat in their community came from the presence of a pool table: to sell us a bill of goods. And they have to do it fast, before you figure out you really don't need it. So please, Jessica—and all your friends—stop telling us to buy your damn band uniforms, alright?"

A murmur grew louder, including a smattering of boos. Missy waved it off. "I hear you. And I get it. A few weeks ago, I would have booed me, too. But climatosis has forced me to think about things. And look, I'm okay that these so-called experts don't have all the answers. I'm okay with the fact that more research is required. And I'm okay with taking efforts to reduce the growth of greenhouse gasses. But don't tell me we don't have time. We do. When I finally realized that, this incredible thing happened to me. I relaxed. I slept through the night. And, last but not least, I lost my twitch." She shrugged her shoulders, then stretched her right arm up to the sky before dropping it. Then she swung her other arm around in a circle. "See that? No strings on me.

"So my message to you tonight is this: stay vigilant. Pay attention. But take everything they tell you with a grain of salt. Be skeptical. Ask questions. Demand answers before they start applying ridiculous solutions, which may be worse than the problem. Explore fusion, and modular nuclear power, and carbon capture—but don't get rid of our other forms of energy until you develop the new stuff. Accept tradeoffs because no solution is perfect. You know how the Great Horse Manure Crisis of 1894 was solved? Henry Ford created a car that could be cheaply produced for the masses. That provided mobility, convenience, and higher wages for the middle class. The tradeoff was fossil fuels. Now, as we look for new answers, I would just ask you, please: don't freak out. As someone once told me, get a grip, honey. That's what we all need to do."

A few cheers sounded from the audience, which were quickly drowned out by boos, hoots, and hisses. As Missy left the stage, passing a seething Jessica, an egg sailed out from the crowd and hit Missy in the head. It dazed her and she wobbled down the stairs, holding her head.

"What the hell was that?"

"The yolk of oppression, I think," Marty said, as he handed her a tissue.

Missy wiped the egg out of her hair and took more tissues from Lindsey and Blair as the booing continued. "I don't think they were ready for a message like that," Missy said. "And that's okay. Maybe I gave them something to think about."

"Are you okay?" Lindsey asked.

"Fine," Missy said with a smile. "Actually… I've never felt better in my life."

Behind her, the president was helped up onto the stage, where he waved to the crowd and received polite applause. As he stood behind a lectern with the presidential seal, a crack of thunder could be heard above. The president looked up in time to see a bolt of lightning and the first fat drops of a cloudburst. As people ran for cover, President Fenwick announced: "It's like I've been saying, folks. The sky is falling!"

39. JERSEY BOUNCE

Blair pulled her raincoat over her head as she dashed from the lobby of her office building on 32nd Street to Missy's black car just as it pulled up. The driver, Harvey, shut the rear door behind Blair as she jumped into the back seat, where Missy was looking at her phone, reading reactions to her speech in Central Park.

"I have a present for you," Blair said.

Missy looked up in surprise. "What is it?"

"See for yourself," Blair said. She handed over a picture frame wrapped in brown paper. Missy excitedly slid a finger under a taped fold on the back and opened it. She pulled the frame out of its wrapping and turned it around to see it was a poster from the Beat Climatosis Now rally with her photo as one of the featured speakers. Across her face in a crudely painted scrawl, it said CLIMATE CRIMINAL.

Missy laughed. "Where do I hang something like this? The Post Office?"

"Like mother, like daughter," Blair said. "You're both on the Wanted list. Maybe you can share a cell."

Missy laid the frame carefully on the floor. "I might need some place to hide," she said. "I've been canceled, shunned, disowned, and excommunicated. The *Daily Reaper* is doing a five-part expose on me and why I should not be believed. They're looking at papers I wrote in the seventh grade, reviewing messages I wrote in classmates' yearbooks, and interviewing everyone I ever knew, or even met in passing. Apparently, their top source is Peach."

Blair shook her head in dismay. "I saw that DingDong put a warning label on your speech and called it disinformation."

Missy shook her head, more amused than disturbed. "I hear I'm even being written into the movie, *Climate Avenger, Wrath of Sheba,* as someone who ultimately gets destroyed. It's strangely empowering to think I'm so threatening to some people. They're really pissed off that I told people we have time to figure this out."

Blair chuckled. "That's way, way, *way* off message."

Missy nodded. "I know. What's kinda cool, though, is all the people sending me thank you notes. I've got hundreds of them. Maybe thousands. They say they appreciate my honesty and my courage and say that I've helped them through their own battles with climatosis. They're feeling better about life, which is so good to hear. There's just one thing that's kind of sad."

"What's that?" Blair asked.

"Very few of them give their last names," Missy said.

"Not surprised," Blair said.

"Right?" Missy said. "They know what can happen if word gets out."

"You're one of the few people who doesn't have to worry about that," Blair said. "They can't get you."

"Oh, yes they can," Missy said. "I just have to figure out how before they do."

The car headed north on Eighth Avenue and made its way to the Lincoln Tunnel, crossed into New Jersey, and wound its way down to the CroFusion lab in Jersey City. When Harvey opened the door for Missy to step out of the car, she felt as if she'd journeyed to a whole new world. This was not just the company's future, it was hers. And with Blair's contributions, Missy needn't be a passive participant in meetings, praying that nobody called on her for an opinion, or worse, a decision. True, she had a lot to learn. But today, she also had something to add.

"I want to introduce you all to my friend, Blair, from Energy Concepts," Missy said to a gathering in the conference room that included PC, Mac, and Andrea. "I think she may have a component that could help us get where we want to go."

Blair nodded and smiled. "Thank you, Missy." She went on to describe the ribbon superconductors developed in her company's laboratory in Manhattan. Lightweight and thin, yet strong and durable, they would help CroFusion create the super-strong magnetic fields they needed to contain the swirling plasma in a tokamak at temperatures of more than a hundred million degrees.

As Blair passed around a sample of her product, PC swooned. "This would allow us to build a much smaller tokamak, and do it faster, too," he said. "If I'm not mistaken, this is rare earth barium copper oxide, right?"

Blair smiled, impressed. "Exactly."

PC was so excited, he struggled to catch his breath. Licking his lips, he beheld the ribbon and uttered, "It feels like I've been looking for you all my life." He turned back to Blair. "Which rare earth mineral do you use? Yttrium? Lanthanum?"

"Yttrium," Blair said.

"Oh, my," PC said, shuddering with excitement. "That's my favorite transition metal."

"Your favorite... *what?"* Blair batted her eyes, processing. She looked to Missy, who merely smiled, and then turned back to PC. "You have a favorite transition metal?"

"Oh yes," PC replied. "For me, it's right up there with gadolinium. Which of course would not be appropriate in this application."

"Oh no. Of course not," Blair said. "Ridiculous to even think of it."

Missy leaned close to Blair. "Please," she said quietly. "Don't get him started."

Blair said, "I think it's too late."

"Well. Whatever you do," Missy said, "don't ask him about isotopes."

PC picked up on the conversation and blushed. "I'm sorry," he said. "It's just that... well. As Missy knows, this is my great passion in life."

"To the exclusion of all else," Missy noted.

PC looked to Mac and Andrea, who were examining the tape. "It looks like an excellent possibility to me," Mac said. Andrea agreed.

PC appeared to be very pleased. "I think this fits the bill beautifully," he said. "We'd love to test it out."

Missy got a chill up her back. She'd actually made a contribution! This was positively exhilarating! After a brief discussion on next steps, Missy escorted Blair to the door, and out to the street, where Harvey waited to take her back to the city.

"You're a magician, Blair. You made me almost look like I knew what I was doing." Missy offered a hug. "Thank you."

Blair broke off and opened the car door. "Want to grab a drink later to celebrate?"

"I'd love to, but..." Missy glanced over her shoulder, then back to Blair. "I've got to work." She giggled at the thought of it.

Blair smiled. "See? It's not so bad."

"I could get used to this," Missy said. "Possibly."

"Do it slowly," Blair said. "You don't want to strain yourself."

"Of course not."

Blair gave Missy one last hug before getting into the car. "I'm proud of you," she said through the window.

Missy smiled. "You know what? For the first time in a long time, I am, too."

40. STATUE OF LIMITATIONS

Harry stood at the window of Robbie's conference room sadly watching a crew in the marina untie the ropes to *My Float Option II*. He heard the muffled roar of the engine, saw a puff of blue-gray smoke from the dual exhausts under the stern, and watched the boat pull away slowly, turning right through an opening in the seawall and sounding its horn before heading out to the Hudson River.

Robbie joined Harry at the window and saw *My Float Option II* picking up speed as it turned toward the sea. "Where are you moving your boat?"

Harry shook his head. "I'm not," he said with a clenched jaw. "The bank is."

"What?"

"Yeah," Harry said. "I gotta scale back a bit. My fund is down 27 percent on the year." He sighed. "It cost me more than a couple of boats. I lost all my clients."

"Save one," Robbie said, patting Harry on the back.

Harry bit his lip. "Uh, yeah. Right," he said as he turned from the window. "We need to talk about that."

Robbie blanched. "Why? What's going on?"

"You may want to sit down," Harry advised. Robbie's heart raced as he took his customary seat at the head of the table. Harry took a chair along the side and leaned over, his elbows on his knees. "We've had a few reversals on our project."

"Like what?" Robbie asked.

"Todd's money never arrived," Harry said.

"No, no. That can't be," Robbie said, furiously shaking his head. "He promised to wire it to us."

"Didn't happen," Harry said. "At first, we thought it was a technical snafu. It took about ten tries before we finally figured out he didn't have the money. Word is that a grand jury is handing down an indictment today against Todd for fraud. They'll arraign him tomorrow."

"Seriously?"

"If they can find him."

"Where is he?" Robbie asked.

"Nobody knows. That includes the U.S. marshals," Harry said. "If you get any intel, call 'em. The reward is a million bucks."

"That makes Todd… what? On the lam?"

"He's not officially a fugitive until they bring the charges in court, but yeah," Harry said. "Sayonara to Todd, and, sad to say, the L. Robertson Crowe III Center for Fusion Excellence."

"It's not going to happen?"

"Kaput."

"What about the money I invested in Todd's company?" Robbie asked.

"I imagine it's in Todd's suitcase."

"Jesus H!" Robbie wailed. He fell forward in his chair, putting an elbow on the table and his hand to his forehead. "What about our other partners?"

"The Chinese are out," Harry said. "They're disappointed that climatosis isn't freaking out our country anymore. They were very happy to see us on a path to shut down our heavy industries in the name of climate change. They've decided to put their money back into coal power."

Robbie contemplated the alternatives. "What about the feds? I thought they committed to putting in a billion dollars."

"You can forget about that, too," Harry said. "Scooter's back in rehab, so I won't have contact with him for three months. And Jessica Holtgren isn't returning my calls."

"She's probably pissed off about Missy's speech," Robbie said.

"They're already over it," he said. "From what I can deduce, they'd rather invest in CroFusion, if they could figure out how. Apparently, Lindsey keeps turning them down. She's got the hottest property in fusion right now."

Robbie covered his eyes with both hands. "Could this get any worse?"

"A bit," Harry said. "Remember Bruno, the union chief we met out at the Fenwick fundraiser in the Hamptons?"

Robbie looked up, his jaw slack. "Of course. The knuckle-dragging 'how's it hangin' guy. Tell me he's still putting in pension funds."

"Nah. He's out, too," Harry replied. "Ten thousand mobile phones meant for his members apparently fell off the truck on their way to the union hall. Cops found them at bodegas all over town, with Bruno's fingerprints all over them. He was arrested this morning."

Robbie slapped the conference table with both hands. "I can't believe this," he said. He stood up, walked to the window, and looked south toward Governor's Island. His grand vision—dashed. "What about my statue? The Father of Fusion?"

Harry shrugged. "I don't know, Robbie. Where would you put it?"

Robbie pointed to the island. "Same spot."

Harry shook his head. "Government gave the land to BlowCo on a one-dollar lease for fifty years," Harry said. "They're putting up a giant wind turbine. Six-hundred feet tall. Dwarfing the Statue of Liberty. The administration has decided that the liberty concept is passe, and it's time to move on. They want this wind turbine to be the shiny new beacon to the rest of the world. 'Give us your tired, your poor, your overheated masses, yearning to breathe free.'"

Robbie sadly shook his head. "I can't believe this," he grumbled, before throwing up his hands. "Another turn in fortune."

41. A LEAK AT THE WHITE HOUSE

The briefing room was packed with journalists as President Fenwick hobbled stiffly to the lectern and cleared his throat. He opened a folder and looked out on the sea of friendly faces and offered them his crooked smile. Despite the messy finish to the public rally in Central Park, it gave the president a warm glow to be back home among his fans. Maybe they didn't love him for who he was. But they surely loved him for who he wasn't—his predecessor.

"I would like to announce today that, thanks to the efforts of my administration, climatosis is on the run," the president declared. "The number of cases has declined rapidly. The number of calls to our crisis centers has fallen dramatically. The CDC estimates the number of people afflicted with that god-awful twitch is down 90 percent. 90 percent! On my watch!"

"So, if you ask whether America is better off than it was not so long ago, I'd say the answer is, 'You're damn right it is."

Hands shot up all over the room, along with the usual calls for "Mr. President! Mr. President!"

The commander-in-chief pointed to Bob Bobson from *YBS News*. "You there. Robson."

Bob stood. "Thank you, sir. Does this mean the climatosis pandemic is over?"

"It's damn close. I've got Spanky on the case, and I expect him to give the final word once he's cooked the numbers. I'd look for an announcement in the coming days," he said. "In the meantime, people should still wear masks." He looked offstage at Jessica Holtgren and Ben Bixby, standing in the wings, who were furiously shaking their heads. "What? Oh." He chuckled. "Wrong pandemic. Forget the mask thing. Just... take precautions. Do something that shows you still care about the planet. Like, wear the ribbon. Everyone should still wear the ribbon." He held out his lapel where a green ribbon was pinned right over the American flag. "See? Like this one right here. And I wear it proudly, even to bed."

Bob held his ground as others clamored for the president's attention. "A follow-up, sir," Bob said. "Does it concern you that the end of the climatosis pandemic means people will drop their guard against climate change?"

"That's a concern," the president acknowledged. "But we're pretty sure another climate crisis will come along any day to show we're still hurtling at breakneck speed toward the end of the world. Thanks to the work a lot of you are doing in the media, all it takes is one strong storm for people to wet their pants."

Nancy Shiffer from the *Daily Reaper* jumped to her feet and shouted, "Mr. President!"

The president nodded. "Yes, Nan... Nanny. You there."

Her tone was urgent. "Are you saying climate incontinence is something we should worry about?"

The president shrugged. He had just made that one up off the top of his head. And it worked! "We don't know a hell of a lot about it just yet. But I would certainly say the early signs are troubling. Climate incontinence is something that should concern us all." He looked off to the side. "Alright. Gotta go."

Bob asked, "Where do you have to go, sir?"

The president scowled at Bob. "To the bathroom. Where do you think?"

42. SKY LARK

Marty nursed a beer and watched the news on the TV over the bar at Sky 55 as he awaited Lindsey's arrival. He found that, despite all the hubbub about climate change over the past few weeks, the world was still spinning in the same direction as it had before.

The Fenwick administration had declared more federal land off limits to oil and gas drillers, even as the president prepared for an overseas trip to beg OPEC nations to pump up the volume on their oil shipments to the U.S. The Planetistas, meanwhile, were demanding a ban on more products made with oil, including balloons, crayons, and petroleum jelly. And a live report from Central Park's Sheep Meadow showed a rally to fight the growing pandemic of climate incontinence.

"As you can see, Merle," the reporter said, "the demonstrators are showing solidarity with the victims by wearing diapers *over* their pants."

"Whoa!" the anchor said. "What a powerful statement."

"Indeed, Merle," the reporter said. "The people here tell me climate incontinence is a problem the grown-ups in the world need to solve. The diapers are a dramatic symbol of just how seriously they're taking this issue. As we are here at Action News."

Merle turned to his co-anchor, Letitia, as he stacked his papers. "So great to see people actually doing something about a big problem," he said.

Letitia nodded solemnly at Merle. "You have to give them credit: they're making a real difference for our planet." She turned to the camera. "Coming up next, a story that would make George Washington proud: the move back to wooden dentures, since traditional dentures use oil. Stay with us."

Marty felt a hand on his back and a kiss on his cheek. He looked up to see Lindsey smiling and taking the seat next to him. She was as relaxed as he'd ever seen her.

"You look happy," he noted.

"I've got my daughter back," she said. "And I have you to thank for it."

"It wasn't me," Marty said. "It was Missy. She would have gotten there eventually."

"Maybe so," Lindsey said. "But I think you got her there faster. You seem to have remarkable powers of persuasion. What in the world did you say to Dr. Iz?"

Marty shrugged and blinked a few times, thinking back. "I just gave her the kind of tough love advice she used to dish out herself."

Lindsey chuckled. "It must have worked. Missy tells me Dr. Iz now offers slapping therapy, and business couldn't be better. Apparently, there are lots of people in Manhattan who think they deserve a good whap in the face."

Marty nodded. "They should just ride the subway. It's cheaper."

Lindsey looked around the restaurant, which was largely empty after the lunch rush. "You up for another assignment?"

He regarded her warily. "Depends," he said.

"Can you get us a bottle of champagne?" she asked. "It's a lovely day. We can enjoy it outside." She slid an envelope across the bar.

He noted the envelope and arched an eyebrow. "In that case, I'll pick up the tab."

They took a table on the patio partly shaded by trees and nearby office buildings. A waiter poured champagne into a pair of flutes and put the bottle on ice next to their table.

Lindsey picked up her glass by the stem and held it up until a ray of sunlight illuminated the bubbles. "There's something so lovely and uplifting about a glass of champagne," she said, clinking glasses with Marty. "Let's hope the climate mopes never notice it releases CO_2 into the atmosphere." She took a sip and cocked her head. "So tell me. What's next for you, Marty?"

He shrugged. "I'm thinking I'll go back to full time goofing off. I was really in a groove there."

"More like a rut," Lindsey scoffed.

"Rut's not to like?" he said.

"You can do more. Better. Something appropriate for your skills."

"Like what?"

She looked around to see if any eavesdroppers lurked nearby. Sensing no one was paying attention, she leaned across the table. "Can you come by the house tonight?"

Marty nodded. "As luck would have it, my calendar's clear."

"Wonderful." She rested her chin on her hand. "I've got an idea I'd like you to explore."

ABOUT THE AUTHOR

JON PEPPER is an author and consultant based in New York City. His company, Indelable, advises leaders on how to define, promote, and defend their businesses. He and his wife, Diane, who designed this book cover, reside in Manhattan.

Jon's *Fossil Feuds* series is comprised of four books, which may be read in any order:

Missy's Twitch (2023)
Green Goddess (2022)
Heirs on Fire (2020)
A Turn in Fortune (2018)

More about Jon and his novels is available at www.jonpepperbooks.com

You can learn about Jon's consulting firm at www.indelable.com

Printed in the USA
CPSIA information can be obtained
at www.ICGtesting.com
LVHW040611130923
757996LV00004B/25